MICROSOFT® OFFICE ACCESS™ 2010
QuickSteps

MICROSOFT® OFFICE ACCESS™ 2010
QuickSteps

JOHN CRONAN

New York Chicago San Francisco
Lisbon London Madrid Mexico City
Milan New Delhi San Juan
Seoul Singapore Sydney Toronto

The McGraw·Hill Companies

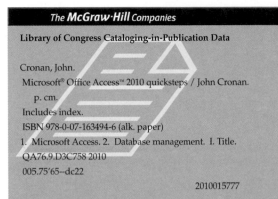

Library of Congress Cataloging-in-Publication Data

Cronan, John.
Microsoft® Office Access™ 2010 quicksteps / John Cronan.
   p. cm.
Includes index.
ISBN 978-0-07-163494-6 (alk. paper)
1. Microsoft Access. 2. Database management. I. Title.
QA76.9.D3C758 2010
005.75′65--dc22

                                    2010015777

MICROSOFT® OFFICE ACCESS™ 2010 QUICKSTEPS

1234567890   WDQ WDQ   109876543210

ISBN   978-0-07-163494-6
MHID   0-07-163494-0

SPONSORING EDITOR / Roger Stewart

EDITORIAL SUPERVISOR / Patty Mon

PROJECT MANAGER / Madhu Bhardwaj, Glyph International

ACQUISITIONS COORDINATOR / Joya Anthony

TECHNICAL EDITOR / Greg Kettell

COPY EDITOR / Lisa McCoy

PROOFREADER / Claire Splan

INDEXER / Ted Laux

PRODUCTION SUPERVISOR / Jim Kussow

COMPOSITION / Glyph International

ILLUSTRATION / Glyph International

ART DIRECTOR, COVER / Jeff Weeks

COVER DESIGNER / Pattie Lee

SERIES CREATORS / Marty and Carole Matthews

SERIES DESIGN / Bailey Cunningham

Para mis profesoras de español, Edith y Carolina:

Gracias a ellas, "Cada vez el camino es menos largo."

About the Author

John Cronan has over 30 years of computer experience and has been writing and editing computer-related books for over 18 years. His recent books include *eBay QuickSteps, Second Edition, Microsoft Office Excel 2010 QuickSteps, Microsoft Office Access 2007 QuickSteps*, and *Dynamic Programming*: *A Beginner's Guide*. John and his wife Faye (and cat Little Buddy) reside in Everett, Washington.

About the Technical Editor

Greg Kettell is a professional software engineer with a diverse career that has covered everything from game programming to enterprise business applications. He has written and contributed to several books about software applications, Web design, and programming. Greg, his wife Jennifer, and their two children currently reside in upstate New York.

Contents at a Glance

Contents

1

2

3 Chapter 3 — Modifying Tables and Fields 59

4 Chapter 4 — Working in the Table 85

5

6

10

Acknowledgments

Greg Kettell, technical editor, who helped me resolve several issues and whose attention to detail caught several errors and omissions.

Lisa McCoy, copy editor, who ensures that the little things, like the correct use of the English language, are attended to.

Ted Laux, indexer, for creating a thorough index to better help those trying to find what they seek.

Joya Anthony, acquisitions coordinator, who keeps track of all the comings and goings of files, art, revisions, schedules, and so on, and on…

Patty Mon, editorial supervisor, and **Madhu Bhardwaj**, project manager, who under a very compressed production process did what it took to bring this book to the shelf on time.

Roger Stewart, sponsoring editor, for his several suggestions to make this a more efficient and complete book.

Introduction

QuickSteps books are recipe books for computer users. They answer the question "How do I...?" by providing quick sets of steps to accomplish the most common tasks in a particular program. The sets of steps are the central focus of the book. QuickSteps sidebars show you how to quickly do many small functions or tasks that support the primary functions. Notes, Tips, and Cautions augment the steps, yet they are presented in such a manner as to not interrupt the flow of the steps. The brief introductions are minimal rather than narrative, and numerous illustrations and figures, many with callouts, support the steps.

QuickSteps books are organized by function and the tasks needed to perform that function. Each function is a chapter. Each task, or "How To," contains the steps needed for accomplishing the function along with relevant Notes, Tips, Cautions, and screenshots. Tasks will be easy to find through:

- The table of contents, which lists the functional areas (chapters) and tasks in the order they are presented

- A How-To list of tasks on the opening page of each chapter

- The index with its alphabetical list of terms used in describing the functions and tasks

- Color-coded tabs for each chapter or functional area with an index to the tabs just before the table of contents

Conventions Used in This Book

Microsoft Office Access 2010 QuickSteps uses several conventions designed to make the book easier for you to follow:

- A 🌐 or a ✐ in the table of contents or the How-To list in each chapter references a QuickSteps or a QuickFacts sidebar in a chapter.

- **Bold type** is used for words on the screen that you are to do something with, such as click **Save As** or open **File**.

- *Italic type* is used for a word or phrase that is being defined or otherwise deserves special emphasis.

- <u>Underlined type</u> is used for text that you are to type from the keyboard.

- When you see the command, CTRL, you are to press the CTRL key; ALT, press the ALT key.

- SMALL CAPITAL LETTERS are used for keys on the keyboard, such as ENTER and SHIFT.

- When you are expected to enter a command, you are told to press the key(s). If you are to enter text or numbers, you are told to type them. Specific letters or numbers to be entered will be underlined.

- Tools are identified on the ribbon by: (1) the tab they fall under, (2) if applicable, the contextual tool family from which they come, (3) the group of tools in which they are located, and (4) the tool's name. For example: "In the Design tab (Report Layout Tools) Grouping & Totals group, click **Hide Details**."

2

3

4

5

6

7

8

9

10

How to...

Chapter 1
Stepping into Access

For many users of Microsoft Office, Microsoft Access is a mysterious and intimidating addition to the suite of Office products. For one, they don't know what Access does. As its name implies, Access provides data collection, organization, and retrieval within a database structure. For example, you can organize your household effects for insurance purposes, including all the pertinent data related to each item along with pictures and links to ancillary information. While maintaining the core features and functionality of Access from years past, this version continues a Microsoft tradition that adds features that support everyone—from the casual user who simply wants to organize and track household assets, as in the example above, to the designer who wants easier ways to create custom forms and reports for his company's finance and marketing departments. Access 2010 adds several features to make working in a database easier for the novice,

2

3

4

5

6

7

8

9

10

UNDERSTANDING AN ACCESS DATABASE

The container for data and the Access objects that manage it is called a Microsoft Office Access database file. It uses an .accdb file extension, for example, MyDatabase.accdb (versions prior to Access 2007 used an .mdb file extension, which you can convert to the newer file format). A *database*, in its simplest form, is just a collection, or list, of data on a related subject—for example, the pertinent information on a publisher's books, such as the title, author, ISBN number, selling price, and the number of books sold and on order.

A database can contain a single collection of data, or it can be divided among subcollections that are related by common categories. A database can also be utilized in different roles. You can be a database *user*, who adds and/or retrieves data, such as account information in a large corporate system. Or you can be a database *designer*, who creates the structure of the database for others to use. In most cases, you're a bit of both: for example, you create your own design for keeping track of your music collection, including its structure, its input forms, and colorful reports of titles and album covers; as well as enter the information yourself.

This book assumes that you have Access 2010 installed on the Microsoft Windows 7 operating system. Procedures and illustrations used throughout the book reflect this assumption. If you have Windows XP or Vista as your operating system, be aware that there might be procedural differences in performing certain tasks and some illustrations might not exactly reflect what you see on your screen.

such as a more robust inventory of database templates to get you going with minimal effort, the ability to reuse prebuilt tables and forms as application parts to minimize redundant effort, and the use of Quick Start fields to help you rapidly construct your data table. Once your project is framed, Access 2010 provides several new features to better display your output by integrating the professionally designed Office-wide themes in its forms and reports, as well as to better analyze your data with improved visual keys to spot trends. And when it's time to share your information, Access 2010 affords you several tools to provide Web access.

In this chapter, I cover the more rudimentary aspects of Access so you can hit the following chapters running. This chapter explains some of the key components of Access, how to open Access and a database file, how to use the ribbon and other aspects of the user interface, and then how to personalize settings to meet your needs. You also will learn how to get help—online and offline—and see how to end an Access session.

Start Access

You can start Access as you would any other program—using the Start menu, using the keyboard, and using shortcuts you have created. Existing Access databases can be opened in similar ways, and recently used databases can be opened quickly from within Access.

Many programs, such as Microsoft Office Excel and Word, open with a new, blank file ready for you to start entering text or data. Access does this in a limited sense, as you are more likely to use a template to assist you in setting up a new database. You will see how to open existing databases in this chapter and how to create new databases in Chapter 2.

Open Access

You can open Access using standard features that were set up by Windows when you installed the program, or you can use other shortcuts more to your own way of computing.

OPEN ACCESS FROM THE START MENU

Normally, the surest way to start Access is to use the Start menu.

1. Start your computer if it is not running, and log on to Windows if necessary.

2. Click **Start**. The Start menu opens. If listed, click **Microsoft Office Access 2010** in the lower portion of the Start menu. Programs you've opened recently will be listed here.

   –Or–

   Click **All Programs**, click **Microsoft Office**, and click **Microsoft Office Access 2010**.

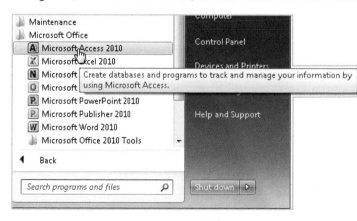

In either case, the Access window opens with the File menu displaying a view of the options for creating a new database, as shown in Figure 1-1.

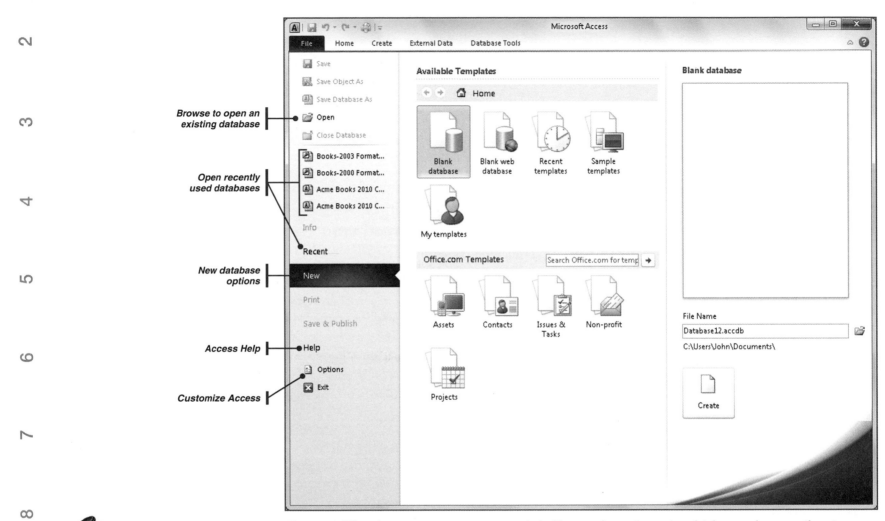

Figure 1-1: When Access opens, you are presented with several ways to create a database and menu options to open existing databases, access Help, and set options.

NOTE

When Access is started without opening an existing database (shown in Figure 1-1), several options on the File menu are not available since they pertain to actions affecting an opened database. These options are explained later in the chapter.

OPEN ACCESS FROM THE KEYBOARD

1. Press the Windows flag key or press **CTRL+ESC**.

2. Type **A** in the Search Programs And Files search box (Microsoft Windows 7).

QUICKFACTS

UNDERSTANDING THE RIBBON

The original menu and toolbar structure used in Office products from the late '80s and early '90s (File, Edit, Format, Window, Help, and other menus) was designed in an era of fewer tasks and features that has simply outgrown its usefulness. Microsoft's solution to the increased number of feature enhancements is the *ribbon*, introduced in the Office 2007 suite. The ribbon is the container at the top of Office program windows for the tools and features you are most likely to use to accomplish the task at hand (see Figure 1-2). The ribbon collects tools you are likely to use into *groups*. For example, the Font group provides the tools to work with text. Groups are organized into tabs, which bring together the tools to work on broader tasks. For example, the Create tab contains groups that allow you to add objects such as tables, forms, and reports.

Each Office program has a default set of tabs and additional tabs that become available as the context of your work changes. For example, when working on a table, a Table Tools (Datasheet) tab displays. The ribbon provides more screen real estate so that each of the tools (or commands) in the groups has a labeled button you can click. Depending on the tool, you are then presented with additional options in the form of a list of commands, a dialog box or task pane, or galleries of choices that reflect what you'll see in your work. Groups that contain more detailed tools than there is room for in the ribbon include a *Dialog Box Launcher* icon 🔲 that takes you directly to these other choices, such as a dialog box or task pane.

Two Office 2010 features that are co-located with the ribbon include the File tab and the Quick Access toolbar. The File menu (similar to the old File menu) lets you work *with* your database (such as saving it), as opposed to the ribbon, which centers on working *in* your document

Continued . . .

3. If necessary, press **DOWN ARROW** until Microsoft Office Access 2010 is selected; press **ENTER** to open it.

> **Programs (18)**
> 🅰 Microsoft Access 2010
> 🔧 Windows Remote Assistance
> 📄 Adobe Acrobat 9 Pro Extended
>
> **Control Panel (262)**
> 🚩 Action Center

CREATE A SHORTCUT TO START ACCESS

1. Click **Start**, click **All Programs**, and click **Microsoft Office**.

2. Right-click **Microsoft Access 2010** to display a context menu and perform one of the following actions:

   - Click **Pin To Taskbar** to add a shortcut to the taskbar. (Similar to adding a shortcut to the Quick Launch toolbar in earlier versions of Windows.

     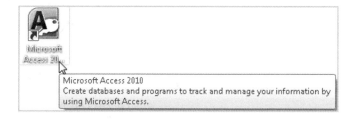

   - Click **Pin To Start Menu** to add a shortcut to the upper-left "permanent" area of the Start menu.

   - Click **Send To** and click **Desktop (Create Shortcut)** to place an icon on your desktop.

> Microsoft Access 2010
> Create databases and programs to track and manage your information by using Microsoft Access.

Work with File View

Access 2010 shares with the other Office 2010 programs an improved way that you can easily access the tasks that affect a document, such as opening, closing, printing, and saving from one screen, avoiding the need to open several dialog boxes.

UNDERSTANDING THE RIBBON

(Continued)

(such as entering and editing data). The Quick Access toolbar is similar to the Windows taskbar, providing an always-available location for shortcuts (in this case, the shortcuts are to Access tools instead of programs pinned to the taskbar). It starts out with a default set of tools, but you can add to it. See the accompanying sections and figures for more information on the ribbon and the other elements of the Access window (see "Customize the Ribbon" later in the chapter for ways to create your own tabs and groups).

This all-encompassing screen is called the File view (see Figure 1-1), which makes sense seeing as it handles background tasks not directly related to working in the database.

To display the File view:

1. Open Access using one of the methods described in the section "Open Access" to create a new database.

   –Or–

   If opening an existing database in Access, click the **File** tab.

2. The File menu is displayed along the left side of the Access window.

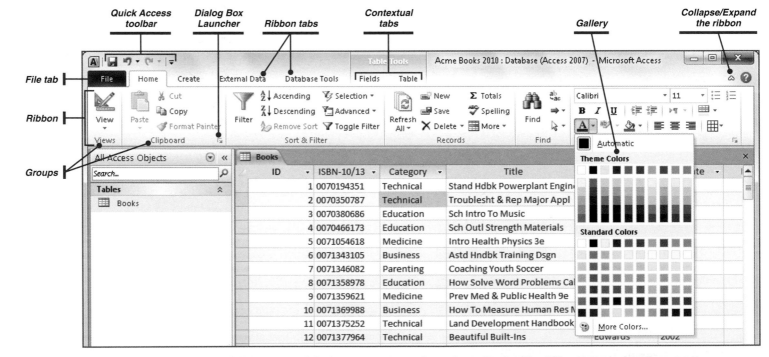

Figure 1-2: The ribbon, containing groups of the most common tools, replaces the familiar Office menu and toolbar structure.

The ribbon adapts to the size of your Access window and your screen resolution, changing the size and shape of buttons and labels. See for yourself by opening a database, maximizing the Access window, and noticing how the ribbon appears. Drag the right border of the Access window toward the left, and see how the ribbon changes to reflect its decreasing real estate.

3. When creating a new database, the New view is displayed (see Figure 1-1). Otherwise, click one of the areas of interest on the menu (many options are unavailable unless a database is open). For example, clicking the **Save & Publish** option displays the view shown in Figure 1-3 and provides several ways to distribute your work.

4. When finished, click the **File** tab to return to the Access window, similar to Figure 1-2.

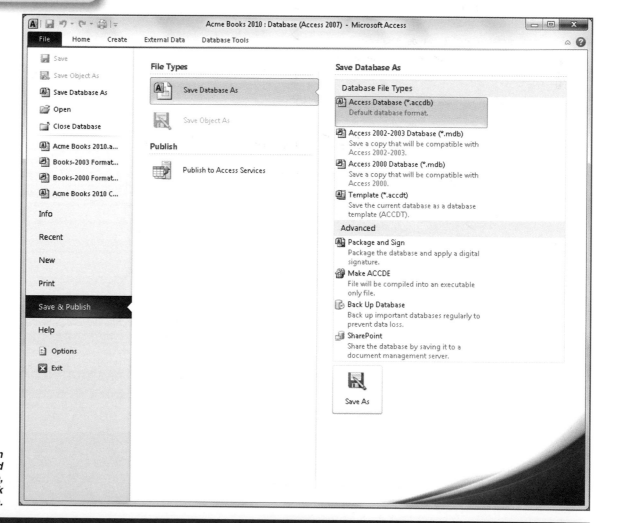

Figure 1-3: The options available from the File menu provide features and tasks related to the overall database, while the ribbon allows you to work with the data in the database.

NOTE

Databases can contain code that could cause serious harm to your computer. To alert you to this potential problem, a Security Warning will appear on a message bar under the ribbon, alerting you that Access has disabled content it cannot determine is from a trusted source. If you trust the source, click **Enable Content**. You will be asked if you want to make it a Trusted Document (shown in Figure 1-4), that is, allow any active content such as macros to execute. Click **Yes** to open the database with executable code enabled, or click **No** to open the database with active content disabled. See Chapter 9 for more information on database security.

Open a Database

You open an Access database by locating the database file. You can manually find the database file using a dialog box, clicking a shortcut on the desktop, from one of the recently opened database links on the File menu, or from Windows Explorer. (If you do not know the location of the file, you can do a search on your drives, as described in "Find a Database" later in the chapter.) For files you have previously opened, Windows and Access provide a number of aids you can use to reopen them quickly.

Figure 1-4: Only enable content in databases that you know come from a trusted source.

TIP

A handy feature in the Open dialog box (and other browse-type dialog boxes) is that you can create links to often-used folders where you store databases and add them to the Favorites area in the left pane of the dialog box. Open Windows Explorer and display an often-used folder in the right pane. Right-click **Favorites** in the left pane, and click **Add Current Location To Favorites**. The next time you use the Open dialog box, you can open the folder with one click from the Favorites area.

BROWSE TO AN EXISTING DATABASE

1. Open Access (see "Open Access" earlier in the chapter).
2. Click **Open** on the File menu along the left side of the Access window.

   –Or–

   Press **CTRL+O**.

In either case, the Open dialog box appears, shown in Figure 1-5.

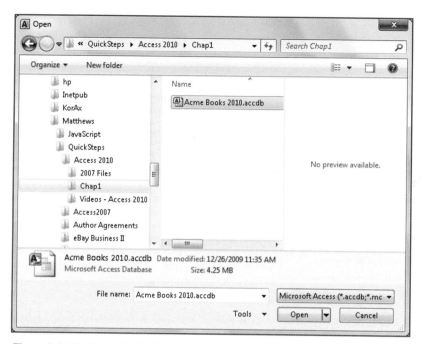

Figure 1-5: The Open dialog box provides several ways to browse for a database file.

NOTE

Access 2010 can open data from other database file formats, such as dBASE, and files that organize data in a database structure, such as an Excel worksheet or text file. In most cases, a wizard will lead you through the steps to accurately organize the data into an Access format. Chapters 5 and 10 describe how to work with external data.

3. Use the address bar or the left pane containing your favorite links and folders to browse to the folder that contains the database you want.

4. To narrow the list of files displayed, click the file types button to the right of the File Name box, and click a file type if different from the type displayed on the button (the default is the Access database file type). Click the file type you want from the list (see the accompanying Note).

5. When you have located the database you want, double-click it.

   –Or–

   Click the database to select it, and click **Open**.

   In either case, the database opens in Access, similar to that shown in Figure 1-6.

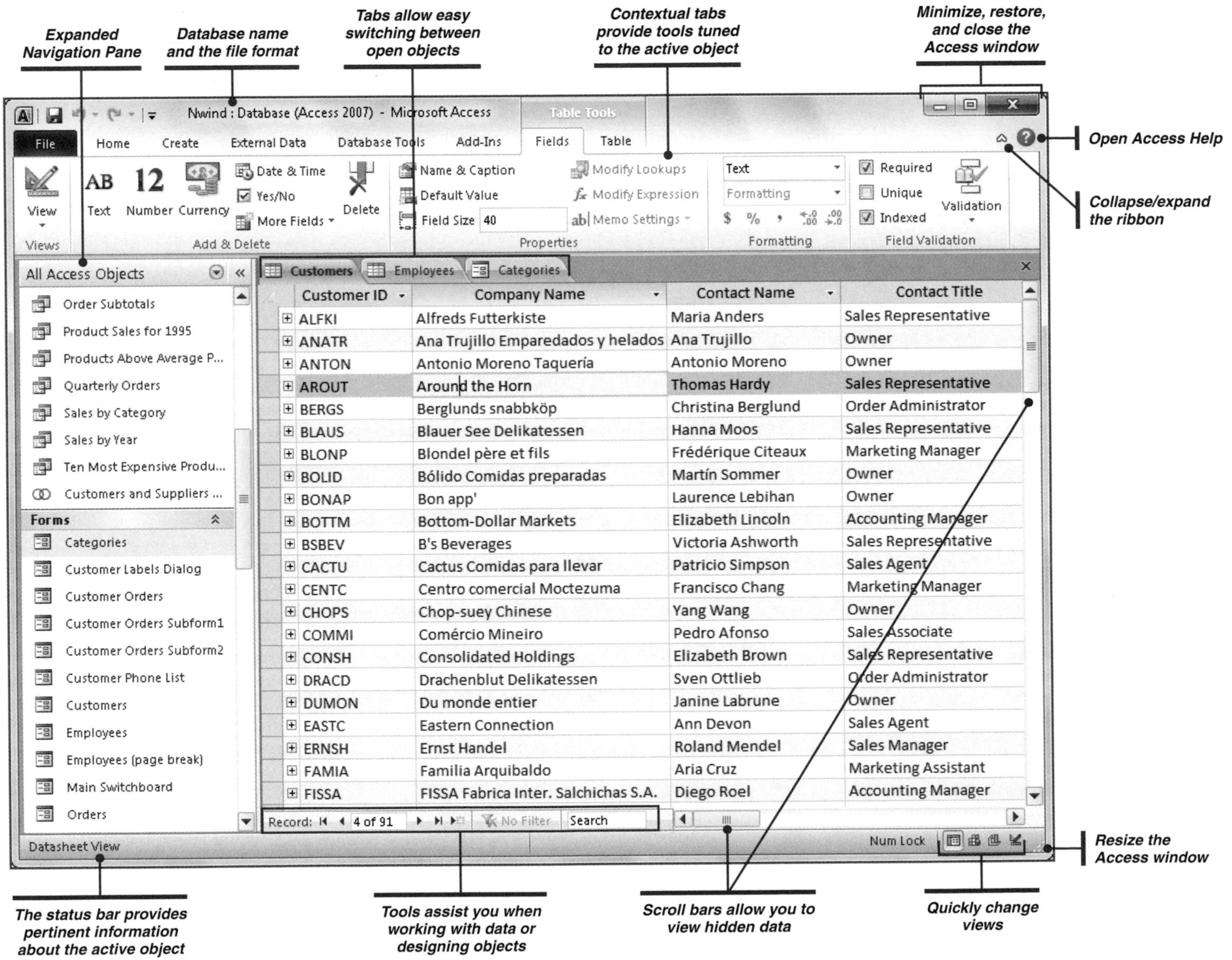

Expanded Navigation Pane

Database name and the file format

Tabs allow easy switching between open objects

Contextual tabs provide tools tuned to the active object

Minimize, restore, and close the Access window

Nwind : Database (Access 2007) - Microsoft Access

Table Tools

File   Home   Create   External Data   Database Tools   Add-Ins   Fields   Table

Open Access Help

AB   12

View   Text   Number   Currency   More Fields ▾   Delete

Date & Time   Name & Caption   Modify Lookups   Text   Required

Yes/No   Default Value   Modify Expression   Formatting   Unique   Validation

Field Size   40   ab Memo Settings $ %   ,   Indexed

Views   Add & Delete   Properties   Formatting   Field Validation

Collapse/expand the ribbon

All Access Objects   «

Customers   Employees   Categories

Customer ID	Company Name	Contact Name	Contact Title
Order Subtotals	ALFKI	Alfreds Futterkiste	Maria Anders	Sales Representative

All Access Objects:
- Order Subtotals
- Product Sales for 1995
- Products Above Average P...
- Quarterly Orders
- Sales by Category
- Sales by Year
- Ten Most Expensive Produ...
- Customers and Suppliers ...

Forms
- Categories
- Customer Labels Dialog
- Customer Orders
- Customer Orders Subform1
- Customer Orders Subform2
- Customer Phone List
- Customers
- Employees
- Employees (page break)
- Main Switchboard
- Orders

Customer ID	Company Name	Contact Name	Contact Title
⊞ ALFKI	Alfreds Futterkiste	Maria Anders	Sales Representative
⊞ ANATR	Ana Trujillo Emparedados y helados	Ana Trujillo	Owner
⊞ ANTON	Antonio Moreno Taquería	Antonio Moreno	Owner
⊞ AROUT	Around the Horn	Thomas Hardy	Sales Representative
⊞ BERGS	Berglunds snabbköp	Christina Berglund	Order Administrator
⊞ BLAUS	Blauer See Delikatessen	Hanna Moos	Sales Representative
⊞ BLONP	Blondel père et fils	Frédérique Citeaux	Marketing Manager
⊞ BOLID	Bólido Comidas preparadas	Martín Sommer	Owner
⊞ BONAP	Bon app'	Laurence Lebihan	Owner
⊞ BOTTM	Bottom-Dollar Markets	Elizabeth Lincoln	Accounting Manager
⊞ BSBEV	B's Beverages	Victoria Ashworth	Sales Representative
⊞ CACTU	Cactus Comidas para llevar	Patricio Simpson	Sales Agent
⊞ CENTC	Centro comercial Moctezuma	Francisco Chang	Marketing Manager
⊞ CHOPS	Chop-suey Chinese	Yang Wang	Owner
⊞ COMMI	Comércio Mineiro	Pedro Afonso	Sales Associate
⊞ CONSH	Consolidated Holdings	Elizabeth Brown	Sales Representative
⊞ DRACD	Drachenblut Delikatessen	Sven Ottlieb	Order Administrator
⊞ DUMON	Du monde entier	Janine Labrune	Owner
⊞ EASTC	Eastern Connection	Ann Devon	Sales Agent
⊞ ERNSH	Ernst Handel	Roland Mendel	Sales Manager
⊞ FAMIA	Familia Arquibaldo	Aria Cruz	Marketing Assistant
⊞ FISSA	FISSA Fabrica Inter. Salchichas S.A.	Diego Roel	Accounting Manager

Record: 4 of 91   No Filter   Search

Datasheet View   Num Lock

Resize the Access window

The status bar provides pertinent information about the active object

Tools assist you when working with data or designing objects

Scroll bars allow you to view hidden data

Quickly change views

Figure 1-6: An Access database is surrounded by a framework of tools to work on its constituent objects.

TIP

In Windows 7, you can open recently opened databases directly from the Start menu. Click **Start**, point to the right arrow next to Microsoft Access 2010, and click the database you want from the Recent list. If you want to retain/pin the database on the Start menu Recent list, click its push pin to the right of its name.

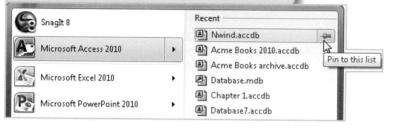

TIP

You can change the number of recently opened databases that are displayed on both the File menu and the Recent Databases list. To change the number that appears directly on the File menu, click the **File** tab, click **Recent**, and at the bottom of the Recent Databases list, click the **Quickly Access This Number Of Recent Databases** spinner to increase or decrease the number.

☑ Quickly access this number of Recent Databases: 4 ⬍

To change the number of databases that appear on the Recent Databases list, click the **File** tab, click **Options** near the bottom of the menu, and click **Client Settings**. Under Display, click the **Show This Number Of Recent Documents** spinner to change the number of recent databases displayed (50 is the maximum).

OPEN RECENTLY USED DATABASES

There are several opportunities to open databases that you have created or have opened in previous Access sessions.

1. Start Access (see "Open Access" earlier in the chapter).

2. From the File menu, click the database you want to open from those that appear on the menu. The four most recently opened database file names are displayed.

–Or–

Click **Recent** on the File menu. The Recent Databases list shows the 17 most recent databases that have been opened. Click the one you want to open.

Recent Databases

	Nwind.accdb
	\\Main\c\Matthews\QuickSteps\Access2007
	Acme Books 2010.accdb
	\\Main\c\Matthews\QuickSteps\Access 2010\Chap1
	Acme Books archive.accdb
	\\Main\c\Matthews\QuickSteps\Access 2010\Chap1
	Database.mdb
	\\Main\c\Matthews\QuickSteps\Access2007\Chap1
	Chapter 1.accdb
	\\Main\c\Matthews\QuickSteps\Access2007\Chap1

–Or–

Display the Open dialog box (see "Browse to an Existing Database" earlier in this chapter), and click **Recent Places** in the Favorites area in the left (Navigation) pane of the dialog box. Click the database you want to open from the list in the right pane.

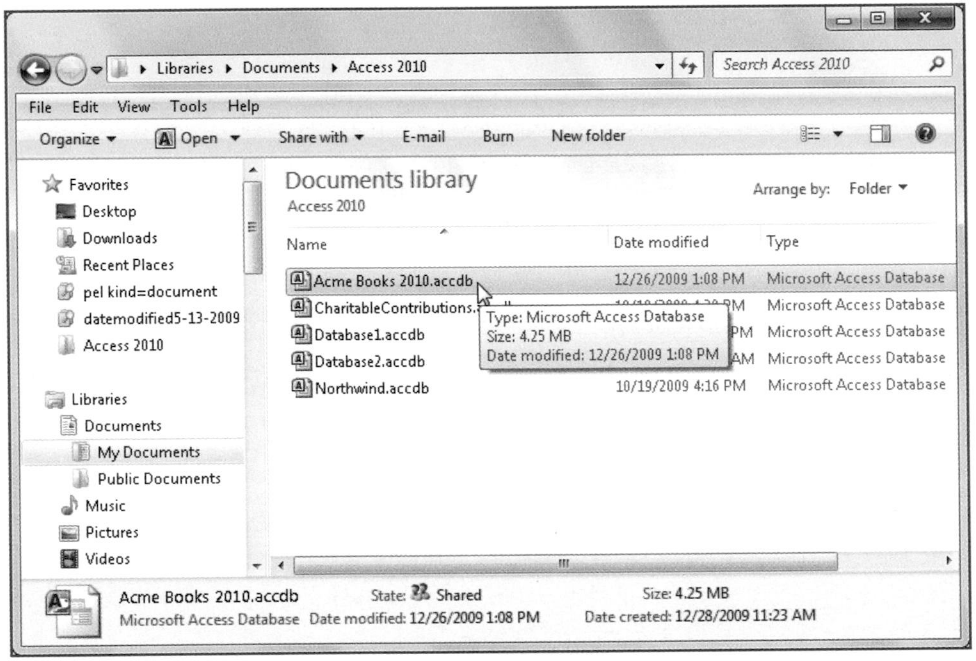

Figure 1-7: The Windows Explorer window in Windows 7 provides the best means to navigate to seldom used databases, stored locally or on your network.

USE WINDOWS EXPLORER TO OPEN A DATABASE

1. Click **Start** and click **Computer**. (If necessary, under Organize, click **Layout**, and then click **Navigation Pane** to display a list of folders and links in the left pane).

2. In Windows Explorer (the name of the window that opens when you click Computer), open the link, or drive and folder(s) that contains the database you want to open. When you open the folder that contains the database in the left pane, the database file will be displayed in the right pane.

3. Double-click the file name to open the database in Access, as shown in Figure 1-7.

CREATE A DESKTOP SHORTCUT TO OPEN A DATABASE

Just as you can create a shortcut to start Access, you can create a shortcut to a database file. Opening the file will open the database in Access, starting Access if it isn't already open.

1. Locate the database file, as described in the previous section, "Use Windows Explorer to Open a Database."

2. Click the file using the right mouse button, and holding the button down, drag it to the desktop.

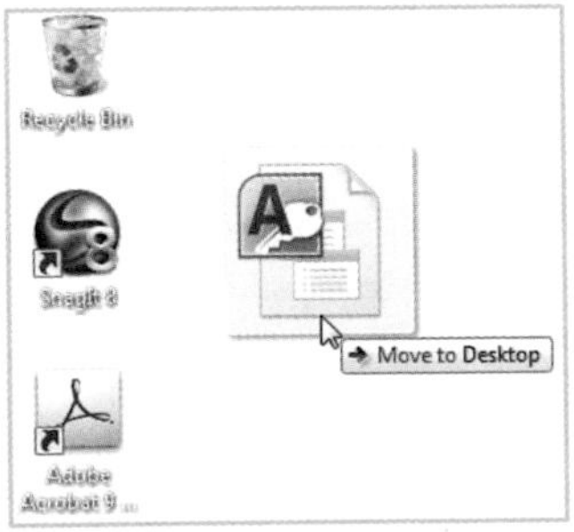

3. Release the mouse button, and click **Create Shortcuts Here** from the context menu.

TIP

If you are familiar with versions of Access prior to Access 2007, you are probably wondering what happened to the Database window, the "Grand Central Station" for working with database objects, when you opened a database. The window was recast into the Navigation Pane in Access 2007 and is used in Access 2010.

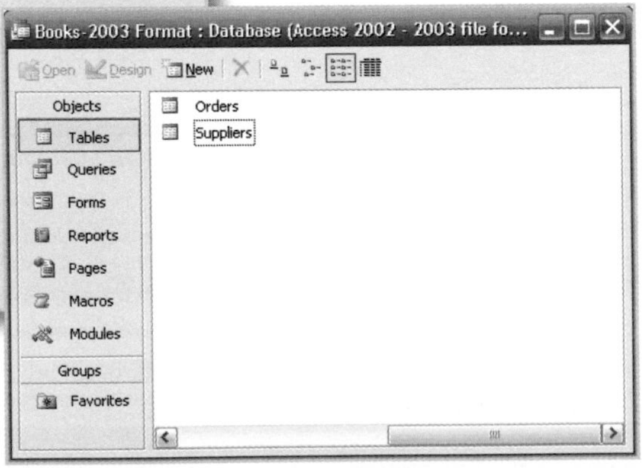

UNDERSTANDING ACCESS OBJECTS

Objects comprise a database. Objects let you store, find, enter, present, and manipulate your data:

- **Tables** contain data, organized by categories called *fields*, into unique sets of data called *records*.

- **Queries** are requests you make of your data to extract just the information you want or to perform maintenance actions, such as inserting or deleting records.

- **Forms** provide a user-friendly interface for entering or displaying data.

- **Reports** allow you to take mundane collections of data, organize them in a creative package, and print the result.

- **Macros** provide a means to automate actions in Access without in-depth programming skills.

- **Modules** package Visual Basic code into a single container, providing a convenient interface for coupling Access to the possibilities offered by a programming language.

The remaining chapters in this book describe the first four objects in more detail. Macros and modules involve advanced techniques and are not covered in this book.

Use the Navigation Pane

From the Navigation Pane (see Figure 1-8), you can open, design, organize, import and export data, and delete the objects that comprise a database (see the "Understanding Access Objects" QuickFacts).

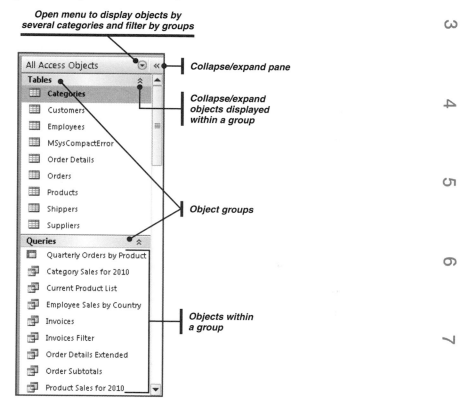

Figure 1-8: The Navigation Pane lists your Access objects in multiple categories.

EXPAND AND COLLAPSE THE NAVIGATION PANE

When a database is first opened, you may see the Navigation Pane displayed as a *shutter* bar on the left side of the Access window, shown in Figure 1-9:

- To view the objects contained within the database and access the Navigation Pane's many features, click the bar or the right-pointing Shutter Bar Open button on top of the bar to expand the pane.

Figure 1-9: The Navigation Pane stands by innocuously until you are ready to use it.

- To collapse the Navigation Pane to its *docked* location on the left side of the Access window, click the left-pointing Shutter Bar Open/Close button on the right side of its title bar.

DISPLAY ONLY THE OBJECTS YOU WANT

Expand the Navigation Pane, and click its title bar to display its menu. There are two sections on the menu that let you display the objects in your database as you want to see them:

- Under **Navigate To Category**, click the category that most closely matches how you want to view the objects.

Navigate To Category
Custom
✓ Object Type
Tables and Related Views
Created Date
Modified Date

- Under **Filter By Group**, click the group whose objects you want displayed; other groups and their objects will be hidden (the grouping options that are available to you will change according to the category you selected at the top of the menu).

Filter By Group
Tables
Queries
Forms
Reports
Macros
Modules
✓ All Access Objects

COLLAPSE AND EXPAND GROUPS

Click the upward- and downward-pointing arrows on the right end of a group's name.

Tables	≫
Queries	≪
Quarterly Orders by Product	Queries
Category Sales for 1995	

TIP

You can combine your database's objects into any collection, or *group*, you want, and access them on the Navigation Pane. Create a group by clicking **Custom** on the Navigation Pane menu. Right-click the new group, click **Rename**, type a meaningful name, and press **ENTER**. To add an object to the new group (an object can be listed in multiple groups), right-click the object, click **Add To Group**, and then click the group name.

TIP

The Access window title bar displays the file format version of the open database.

QUICK**FACTS**

UNDERSTANDING ACCESS FILE COMPATIBILITY

The Access database file format changes somewhat in each newly released version to accommodate new features and provide better security. However, Access is not generally *forward-compatible*, meaning that older versions of Access cannot recognize newer file formats without converting them to the older file format (if that's even possible). Access 2010 can open database files created in versions since Access 95; however, Access 2010

Continued ...

PERFORM ACTIONS ON OBJECTS

Right-click the object you want to work with, and select the action you want to perform from its context menu (the context menu for a table is shown here).

Open Older Databases

You can open earlier versions of Access databases, though what you can do with them and whether Access offers to convert them to a more recent version depends on how old they are. (Though Access 2007 is an earlier version, it shares the same file format as Access 2010; therefore, its files open similarly to files created in Access 2010.)

OPEN ACCESS 95 AND ACCESS 97 DATABASES

If you try to open a database created in Access 95 or Access 97 in Access 2010, you will be presented with the option of *converting* (updating) the database to the default file format you currently have chosen or opening it using its native format (see the "Understanding Access File Compatibility" QuickFacts for more information on Access file formats).

1. Open the database using the techniques described in "Open a Database." The Database Enhancement dialog box appears, shown in Figure 1-10.

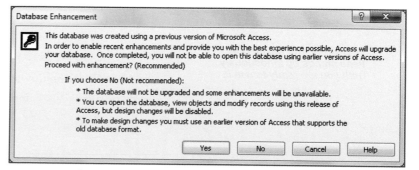

Figure 1-10: You can choose to convert an earlier Access database to a recent version or open it without conversion but with very limited capabilities.

UNDERSTANDING ACCESS FILE COMPATIBILITY *(Continued)*

can only provide the same level of functionality as the original Access program with database files saved in Access 2000 and later file formats.

By default, Access 2010 uses the 2007 file format (using the .accdb file extension). You can change that to either of two earlier formats (using the .mdb file extension common to earlier versions), ensuring that your database files can be opened by users who have Access 2000 and later.

When deciding which database format to use, you will have to weigh the features offered by Access 2010 against the ability to share your work with users of earlier versions of Access.

NOTE

Many databases encounter errors during the conversion process. The errors are listed in a Conversion Errors table that's added to the database. See Chapters 2–4 for information on working with tables.

Microsoft Access

Microsoft Access encountered one or more errors during conversion. To view a summary of these errors, open the 'Conversion Errors1' table.

OK   Help

2. Click **Yes** if you want to convert the file to your default Access file format. Doing so will prevent the database from being opened by earlier Access versions. (See the section, "Change the Default File Format in Access" for information on changing the default format from the Access 2007 file format to an earlier format.)

3. The Save As dialog box appears. Locate the folder where you want the database stored, change the file name if needed, and click **Save**. After the conversion, you are notified that the database has been upgraded and are advised of any errors or limitation on opening the database by earlier versions.

Microsoft Access

This Database has been upgraded to the Access 2007 File Format. The new database cannot be shared with users of Access 2003 or earlier versions.

For more information about conversion, click Help.

OK   Help

4. Click **No** if you want to open the database in its original file format. Doing so limits your ability to use many newer Access features. Most notably, you won't be able to change the structure (design) of the database.

OPEN ACCESS 2000 THROUGH ACCESS 2003 DATABASES

Open the database using the techniques described in "Open a Database." The database opens without needing to convert it to a more recent database format. You can work on the database as you did in earlier versions of Access, but features provided by the Access 2007 file format will not be available to you.

Convert an Older Database After Opening It

If you open an older Access database in its native file format without converting and later decide to convert it to the default file format, you can do so within Access 2010 without having to reopen the database.

A | 🔒 ⋆ ⋆ | ⋆   Books-97 Format : Database (Access 97 file format) - Microsoft Access

File   Home   Create   External Data   Database Tools

1. Click the **File** tab, and click **Save Database As**. The Save As dialog box appears.

2. Locate the folder where you want the database stored, change the file name if needed, and click **Save**. After the conversion, you are notified that the database has been upgraded and are advised of limitations on opening the database by earlier versions.

Change the Default File Format in Access

New databases and converted databases can be created in the three latest Access file formats. (See the "Understanding Access File Compatibility" QuickFacts for information on the pros and cons of using older file formats.) Unless changed, Access uses the 2007 (.accdb) file format. To change to an earlier file format:

1. Open Access (see "Open Access" earlier in the chapter).
2. Click the **File** tab, click **Options**, and click the **General** option.
3. Under Creating Databases, click the **Default File Format For Blank Database** down arrow, and click **Access 2000** or **Access 2002-2003**.
4. Click **OK** when finished.

Find a Database

To find a database whose name and location you have forgotten, you can search in and out of Access.

SEARCH FOR A DATABASE IN WINDOWS 7

Click **Start** and type the file name, or any part of the file name, in the Search Programs And Files search box, as shown in Figure 1-11. As you type, a list of possible choices appears. The more you type, the more focused the list becomes. Click the name of your database when it appears.

SEARCH FOR A DATABASE IN ACCESS

1. Click the **File** tab, and click **Open**. The Open dialog box appears (see Figure 1-5).
2. Use the Navigation pane or the address bar to narrow your search to the drive and/or folder where you think the database is located.
3. In the **Search** box, type words you know are contained in the database or keywords (words or phrases associated with the database). As you start typing, possible matches are found and displayed in the dialog box. (See Chapter 2 for ways to add identifying information to a database file.)
4. To open the database you've found, select the file and click **Open**.

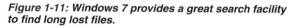

Documents (3)
- Acme Books 2010.accdb
- ✗ Acme Books Suppliers.odc
- ✗ Acme Books Books.odc

Files (9)
- Acme Books 2010.accdb
- Acme Books archive.accdb
- Acme Books.accdb
- Vista_Win7_R226.zip
- 3344-05a - Copy (7).doc
- 3344-05a - Copy (7).doc
- Listing 5-xx Drop Down.html
- Listing 5-xx Drop Down.html
- license.html

🔎 See more results

| acm | ✗ | Shut down ▸ |

Figure 1-11: Windows 7 provides a great search facility to find long lost files.

Personalize Access

You can personalize how you work with Access by choosing to display task panes; customizing the ribbon, toolbars, and menus; and rearranging windows.

Customize the Ribbon

The default ribbon consists of four standard tabs (and the special File tab), each standard tab containing several groups and subgroups that combine related tasks. While Access strives to provide a logical hierarchy to all the tasks available to you, it also recognizes that not everyone finds their way of thinking to be the most convenient and offers you the ability to change how things are organized. You can remove groups from the existing standard tabs, create new tabs and groups, and populate your new groups from a plethora of available commands and tasks.

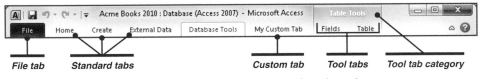

File tab   Standard tabs   Custom tab   Tool tabs   Tool tab category

Figure 1-12: The ribbon allows you to add custom tabs to its other tab types.

> **NOTE**
>
> You'll see four types of tabs on the ribbon, shown in Figure 1-12. The standard tabs appear when you open a database and contain a generalized set of tools. Tool tabs appear when you are working with certain Access features such as tables, print preview, and add-ins (optional Access components) and contain specific tools for working with these features. Custom tabs allow you to assemble your own groups and tools. And, there is the special File tab.

To customize the ribbon:

Click the **File** tab, and in the left pane, click **Options**. In the Access Options dialog box, also in the left pane, click **Customize Ribbon**.

–Or–

Right-click any tool on the ribbon, and click **Customize The Ribbon**.

In either case, the Customize The Ribbon view, shown in Figure 1-13, displays the list of available commands, tasks, and tools on the left and a hierarchy of tabs and groups on the right.

REARRANGE TABS AND GROUPS

You can easily change the order in which your tabs and groups appear on the ribbon.

1. On the Customize The Ribbon view, click the **Customize The Ribbon** down arrow, and select the type of tabs that contain the groups you want to work with.

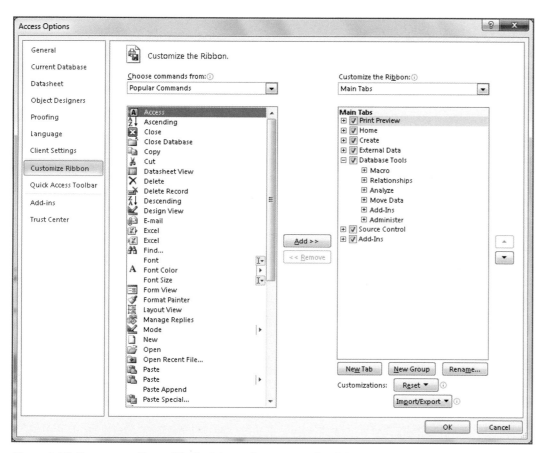

Figure 1-13: You can easily modify the tabs and groups on the ribbon and assign tools where you want them.

2. To rearrange tabs, select the tab whose position on the ribbon you want to change, and click the **Move Up** and **Move Down** arrows on the right side of the tabs list to reposition the tab. (The topmost items in the list appear as the leftmost on the ribbon.)

3. To rearrange groups, click the plus sign next to the tab name to display its groups, and then click the **Move Up** and **Move Down** arrows to the side of the tabs list to reposition the group.

4. If finished, click **OK** to close the Access Options dialog box.

CREATE NEW TABS AND GROUPS

You can create new tabs and groups to collocate your most often used tools.

To add a new tab:

1. Click **New Tab** at the bottom of the tabs list. A new custom tab and group is added to the list.

2. Move the tab where you want it (see the previous section "Rearrange Tabs and Groups").

3. Rename the new tab and new group by selecting the item and clicking **Rename** at the bottom of the tabs list.

–Or–

Right-click the tab or group, and click **Rename**.

In either case, type a new name and click **OK**.

TIP

Don't be afraid to experiment with your ribbon by adding tabs and groups. You can always revert back to the default Access ribbon layout by clicking **Reset** under the tabs list and then choosing to either restore a selected tab or all tabs.

New Tab	New Group	Rename...

Customizations: Reset ▾ ⓘ

Reset only selected Ribbon tab
Reset all customizations

OK   Cancel

TIP

You can create a file that captures your customizations to the ribbon and the Quick Access toolbar so that you can use it on other computers running Access 2010. In the Access Options dialog box, click either **Customize The Ribbon** or **Quick Access Toolbar**, click **Import/Export** in either view, and then click **Export All Customizations**. To use a customization file previously created, click **Import/Export** and then click **Import Customization File**. Depending on whether you're creating or importing a customization file, a File Save or File Open dialog box appears that allows you to store a new file or find an existing one.

To add a new group:

1. Select the tab where you want to add a new group, and then click **New Group** at the bottom of the tabs list. The list of all groups in that tab appears with a new custom group at its bottom.

2. Rename and rearrange the group within the tab as previously described.

3. If finished, click **OK** to close the Access Options dialog box.

ADD OR REMOVE COMMANDS AND TOOLS

Once you have the tabs and groups created, named, and organized, you can add the tools you want to your custom groups.

1. On the Customize The Ribbon view, click the **Choose Commands From** down arrow, and choose to view available Access tools from several categories (or just choose **All Commands** to see the full list). Select (highlight the tool by clicking it) the first tool you want to add to a custom group.

2. In the tabs list, select the custom group to which you want to add the tool.

3. Click **Add** between the lists of commands and tabs. The command or tool is added under your group.

4. Repeat steps 1 through 3 to populate your groups with all the tools you want.

5. If you make a mistake, remove a tool from a custom group by selecting the tool and clicking **Remove**.

6. Use the **Move Up** and **Move Down** arrows to the right of the tabs list to organize the added tools within your groups, and click **OK** when finished.

Customize the Quick Access Toolbar

You can provide one-click access to your favorite Access tools by adding them to the Quick Access toolbar, which, by default, is above the File tab. The starter kit of tools includes Save, Undo, and Redo.

ADD OR REMOVE TOOLS FROM A LIST

1. Click the **Customize Quick Access Toolbar** down arrow, and click **More Commands**.

   –Or–

   Click the **File** tab, click **Options**, and click **Quick Access Toolbar**.

   –Or–

TIP

Several popular tools can be quickly added to the Quick Access toolbar by clicking the down arrow to the right of the Quick Access toolbar and clicking the tool you want.

Acme Books 2010 : Database (Access 2007)

Customize Quick Access Toolbar

	New
	Open
✓	Save
	E-mail
	Quick Print
	Print Preview
	Spelling
✓	Undo
✓	Redo
	Mode
	Refresh All
	Sync All
	More Commands...
	Show Below the Ribbon

Add to Quick Access Toolbar

Right-click a tool and click **Customize Quick Access Toolbar**

In any case, the Access Options dialog box appears with the Customize The Quick Access Toolbar options displayed, as shown in Figure 1-14.

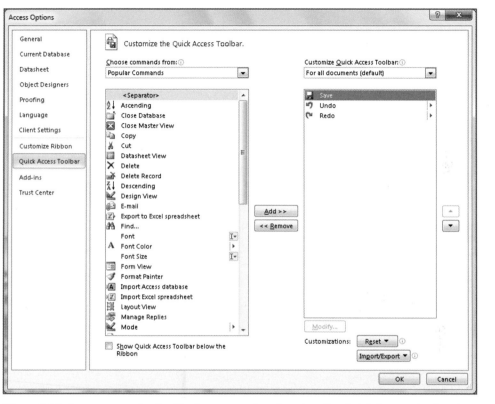

Figure 1-14: Any command or tool in Access can be placed on the Quick Access toolbar for one-click access.

2. Click the **Choose Commands From** down arrow, and click the tab or other option from the drop-down list to find the tool you are looking for.

3. In the list box below, click the tool to select it, and click **Add** between the panes. The tool appears in the list of current toolbar tools to the right.

4. To remove a tool from the toolbar, select it from the list on the right, and click **Remove**.

5. To reset to the default tools, click **Reset**, and click **Reset Only Quick Access Toolbar** (clicking **Reset All Customizations** will remove any changes to the ribbon as well).

6. Click **OK** when finished.

TIP

Though not specifically designed as a site map for all the tools and commands in Access, the list of tools and commands in the Customize pane in the Access Options dialog box for the ribbon and Quick Access toolbar performs as a substitute. You can select each Access tab and see what tools and/or commands are contained therein. See how in the section "Customize the Quick Access Toolbar."

TIP

You can hide the tools on the ribbon and show only the list of tabs, thereby providing more "real estate" within the Access window for the object you are working with. Right-click a tool on the Quick Access toolbar or on the ribbon, and click **Minimize The Ribbon**. Click the command a second time to restore the ribbon to its full height. Alternatively, double-click a tab name to minimize the ribbon, double-click a second time to restore it; or click the **Minimize The Ribbon/Expand The Ribbon** arrow ⌃.

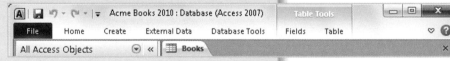

ADD OR REMOVE TOOLS DIRECTLY ON THE TOOLBAR

- To add a tool to the Quick Access toolbar, right-click a tool on the ribbon, and click **Add To Quick Access Toolbar**.

- To remove a tool from the Quick Access toolbar, right-click the tool and click **Remove From Quick Access Toolbar**.

RELOCATE THE QUICK ACCESS TOOLBAR

You can display the Quick Access toolbar at its default position (above the ribbon) or directly below the ribbon using one of the following methods:

- Right-click a tool on the Quick Access toolbar or on the ribbon, and click **Show Quick Access Toolbar Below The Ribbon** (once located below the ribbon, you can move it above the ribbon in the same manner).

  –Or–

- In the Customize The Quick Access Toolbar view (click the **File** tab, click **Options**, and click **Quick Access Toolbar**), click the **Show Quick Access Toolbar Below The Ribbon** check box, and click **OK** (to return the toolbar above the ribbon, open the pane and clear the check box).

CUSTOMIZE THE QUICK ACCESS TOOLBAR FOR A DATABASE

By default, changes made to the Quick Access toolbar are applicable to all databases. You can create a toolbar that only applies to the database you currently have open.

1. In the Customize The Quick Access Toolbar view (click the **File** tab, click **Options**, and click **Quick Access Toolbar**), click the **Customize Quick Access Toolbar** down arrow (see Figure 1-14).

2. Click the option that identifies the database to which the toolbar will apply.

3. Click **OK** when finished.

QUICKSTEPS

USING THE KEYBOARD IN ACCESS

Though most of us live and die by our mouse while using our computers, there isn't much in Access that can't also be done from the keyboard.

USE THE START MENU

1. Press the Windows flag key ⊞ on the bottom row of your keyboard, or press **CTRL+ESC**.
2. Use the arrow keys to move to the item you want.
3. Press **ENTER**.

OPEN A DATABASE

1. Press **CTRL+O**.
2. Press **TAB** to move between the various controls in the window, and use the arrow keys to select drives and folders.
3. Press **ENTER** to open folders, and use the arrow keys to select the database file.
4. Press **ENTER** to open the database in Access.

CLOSE AN OBJECT

Select the object's window or tab (see "Change How You View Objects"), and press **CTRL+F4**. Hold down **CTRL** and continue pressing **F4** to close any other open objects.

CLOSE ACCESS

Press **ALT+F4**.

REARRANGE TOOLS ON THE QUICK ACCESS TOOLBAR

You can change the order in which tools appear on the Quick Access toolbar.

1. In the Customize The Quick Access Toolbar view (see Figure 1-14), select the tool in the list on the right whose position you want to change.
2. Click the up or down arrows to the right of the list to move the tool. Moving the tool up moves it to the left in the on-screen toolbar; moving it down the list moves it to the right in the on-screen toolbar.
3. Click **OK** when finished.

Display and Use Ribbon Shortcut Keys

Though ScreenTips display many shortcut keys (for example, **CTRL+C** is shown when you point to the Copy icon in the Home tab Clipboard group), you can view shortcut keys for commands on the ribbon, the File tab, and Quick Access toolbar commands more readily.

1. Press **ALT**, and shortcut icons displaying shortcut letters and numbers will appear on top-level screen elements (the File tab, Quick Access toolbar, and ribbon tabs).

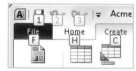

2. Press the corresponding key(s) to open the next level of detail and display those shortcut icons (see Figure 1-15). Continue working through groups and lists until you reach the tool or command to perform the action you want.
3. Press **ALT** a second time to remove the shortcut icons from the window.

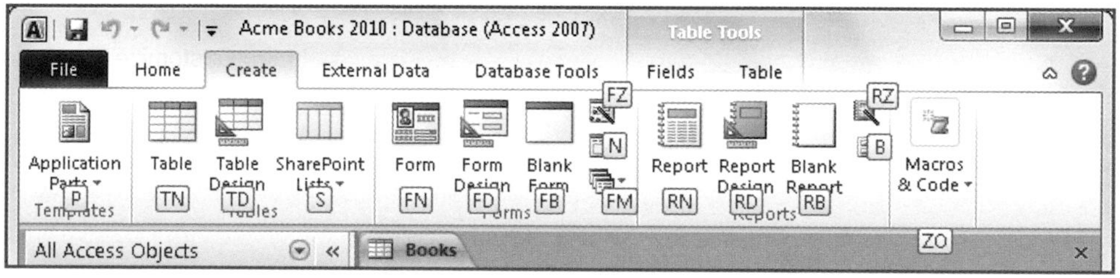

Figure 1-15: Shortcut key icons provide access to tools for keyboard users.

NOTE

By default, databases created using the Access 2007 file format use tabbed documents, and databases created in earlier versions use overlapping windows. You can switch to either format after the database is opened.

Change How You View Objects

Although you can only work with one database at a time, you can have several Access objects open as tabbed documents or as overlapping windows. Each style provides unique features for working with multiple open objects. Figures 1-16 and 1-17 show some of the features of each.

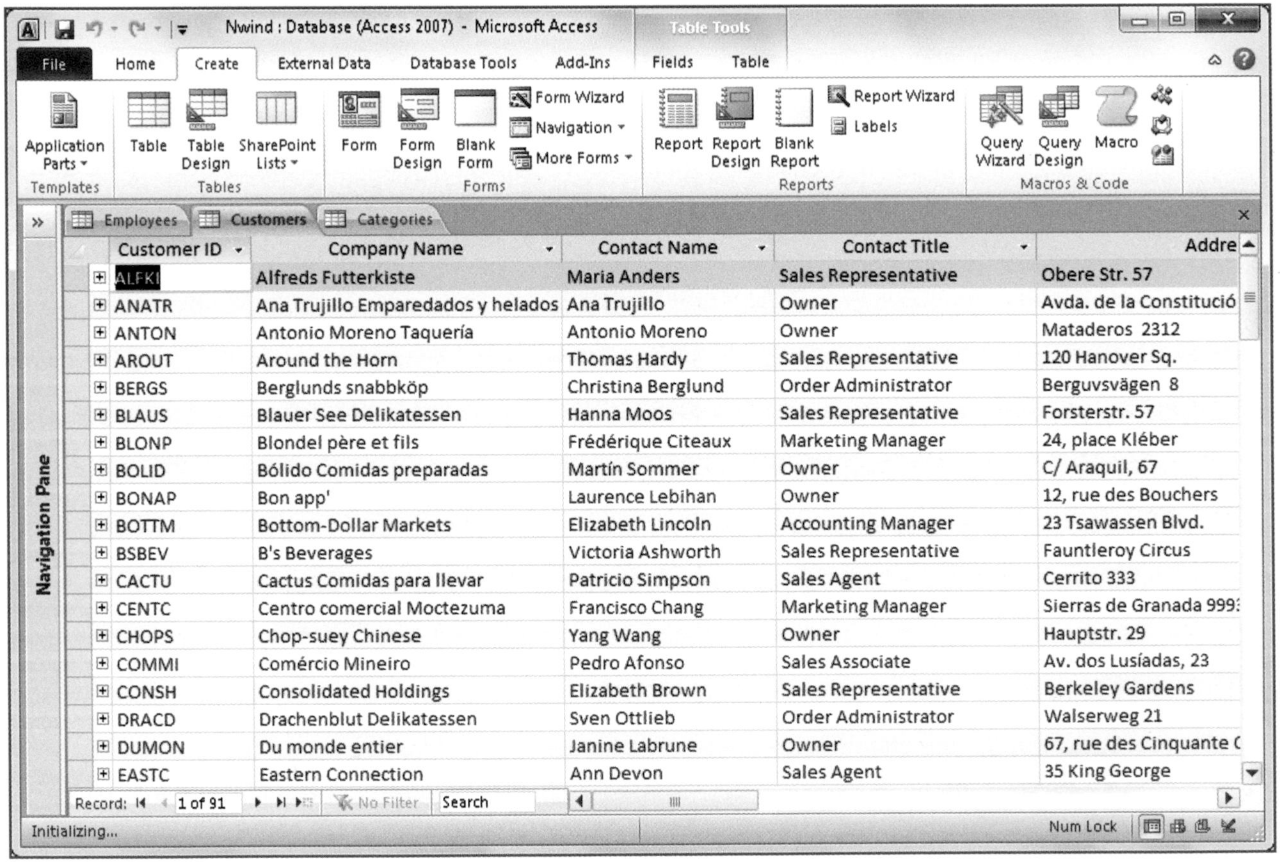

	Customer ID	Company Name	Contact Name	Contact Title	Addre
⊞	ALFKI	Alfreds Futterkiste	Maria Anders	Sales Representative	Obere Str. 57
⊞	ANATR	Ana Trujillo Emparedados y helados	Ana Trujillo	Owner	Avda. de la Constitució
⊞	ANTON	Antonio Moreno Taquería	Antonio Moreno	Owner	Mataderos 2312
⊞	AROUT	Around the Horn	Thomas Hardy	Sales Representative	120 Hanover Sq.
⊞	BERGS	Berglunds snabbköp	Christina Berglund	Order Administrator	Berguvsvägen 8
⊞	BLAUS	Blauer See Delikatessen	Hanna Moos	Sales Representative	Forsterstr. 57
⊞	BLONP	Blondel père et fils	Frédérique Citeaux	Marketing Manager	24, place Kléber
⊞	BOLID	Bólido Comidas preparadas	Martín Sommer	Owner	C/ Araquil, 67
⊞	BONAP	Bon app'	Laurence Lebihan	Owner	12, rue des Bouchers
⊞	BOTTM	Bottom-Dollar Markets	Elizabeth Lincoln	Accounting Manager	23 Tsawassen Blvd.
⊞	BSBEV	B's Beverages	Victoria Ashworth	Sales Representative	Fauntleroy Circus
⊞	CACTU	Cactus Comidas para llevar	Patricio Simpson	Sales Agent	Cerrito 333
⊞	CENTC	Centro comercial Moctezuma	Francisco Chang	Marketing Manager	Sierras de Granada 999:
⊞	CHOPS	Chop-suey Chinese	Yang Wang	Owner	Hauptstr. 29
⊞	COMMI	Comércio Mineiro	Pedro Afonso	Sales Associate	Av. dos Lusíadas, 23
⊞	CONSH	Consolidated Holdings	Elizabeth Brown	Sales Representative	Berkeley Gardens
⊞	DRACD	Drachenblut Delikatessen	Sven Ottlieb	Order Administrator	Walserweg 21
⊞	DUMON	Du monde entier	Janine Labrune	Owner	67, rue des Cinquante C
⊞	EASTC	Eastern Connection	Ann Devon	Sales Agent	35 King George

Record: 1 of 91   No Filter   Search

Initializing...   Num Lock

Figure 1-16: Displaying open objects as tabbed documents allows you to quickly view any one with a single click.

SELECT TABBED DOCUMENTS OR OVERLAPPING OBJECT WINDOWS

1. Open the database.

2. Click the **File** tab, click **Options**, and click the **Current Database** option.

Microsoft Access		Table Tools	

File Home Create External Data Database Tools Add-Ins Fields Table

Application Parts ▾ | Table | Table Design | SharePoint Lists ▾ | Form | Form Design | Blank Form | Form Wizard / Navigation ▾ / More Forms ▾ | Report | Report Design | Blank Report | Report Wizard / Labels | Query Wizard | Query Design | Macro

Templates   Tables   Forms   Reports   Macros & Code

Categories ☐ ▣ ☒

Customers ☐ ▣ ☒

Employees ☐ ▣ ☒

Employee I ▾	Last Nam ▾	First Nam ▾	Title ▾	Title Of Courtes ▾	Birth Dat ▾
1	Davolio	Nancy	Sales Representative	Ms.	08-Dec-4
2	Fuller	Andrew	Vice President, Sales	Dr.	19-Feb-5
3	Leverling	Janet	Sales Representative	Ms.	30-Aug-6
4	Peacock	Margaret	Sales Representative	Mrs.	19-Sep-3
5	Buchanan	Steven	Sales Manager	Mr.	04-Mar-5
6	Suyama	Michael	Sales Representative	Mr.	02-Jul-6
7	King	Robert	Sales Representative	Mr.	29-May-6
8	Callahan	Laura	Inside Sales Coordinato	Ms.	09-Jan-5
9	Dodsworth	Anne	Sales Representative	Ms.	27-Jan-6
(New)					

Navigation Pane

Initializing...   Num Lock

Figure 1-17: Overlapping windows offer several configurations to view open objects.

NOTE

The Window group is only available on the Home tab when using overlapping windows to display objects.

Size to Fit Form   Switch Windows ▾

Window

3. Under Application Options, in the Document Window Options area, click **Overlapping Windows** or **Tabbed Documents**.

Document Window Options
- ◉ Overlapping Windows
- ○ Tabbed Documents
- ☑ Display Document Tabs

4. Click **OK** when finished. Click **OK** a second time after reading the message informing you that you must close and reopen the database for the change to take effect.

TIP

You can check for new updates for Office, activate your copy of Office, view your product version details, and contact Microsoft technical support from one handy location (see Figure 1-18). Click the **File** tab, and click **Help**.

ARRANGE MULTIPLE OVERLAPPED WINDOWS

1. Open two or more object windows.

2. In the Home tab Window group, click **Switch Windows**. Select one of these options from the menu that opens:

- Click **Tile Vertically** to align open object windows side by side in vertical panes (four or more open windows are *tiled* to fit the available space).

- Click **Cascade** to align open object windows in an overlapping stack (as shown in Figure 1-17).

- Click **Tile Horizontally** to align open object windows on top of each other in horizontal panes (four or more open windows are tiled to fit the available space).

Figure 1-18: You can get assistance from Microsoft technical support on Access and other Office programs.

Access Help

products   support   images   templates

Getting started with Access 2010

- Getting started with Access 2010
- Introduction to templates
- Build a database to share on the Web
- Create a desktop database

Browse Access 2010 support

- Access basics
- Designing applications
- Expressions
- Forms

- Macros
- Queries
- Tables
- Videos

see all

All Access   Connected to Office.com

Figure 1-19: The Access Help window allows you to search online and offline articles and topics using tools similar to those in a Web browser.

Get Help

Microsoft provides a vast amount of assistance to Access users. If you have an Internet connection, you can automatically take advantage of the wealth of information available at the Microsoft Web site. When offline, information is limited to what is stored on your computer. Also, "super" tooltips provide detailed explanatory information about tools when the mouse pointer is hovered over them.

Open Help

You are never far from help in Access. Click the **Microsoft Access Help** question mark icon above the rightmost end of the ribbon.

–Or–

Press **F1**.

In either case, the Access Help window opens, as shown in Figure 1-19.

Use the Access Help Window

The Access Help window provides a simple, no-nonsense gateway to volumes of topics, demos, and lessons on using Access. The main focus of the window is a Search text box, supported by a collection of handy tools.

SEARCH FOR INFORMATION

1. Open the Access Help window by clicking the **Access Help** icon or pressing **F1**.

2. In the Search text box below the toolbar, type keywords that are relevant to the information you are seeking.

3. Click the **Search** down arrow to view the connection and filtering options for the search:

    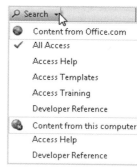

    - **Connection options** allow you to choose between options regarding online (Content From Office.com) or offline (Content From This Computer) information. If you have an active Internet connection, Help automatically assumes that you want online content each time you open the Help window.

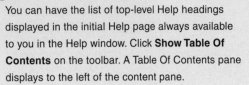

TIP

You can have the list of top-level Help headings displayed in the initial Help page always available to you in the Help window. Click **Show Table Of Contents** on the toolbar. A Table Of Contents pane displays to the left of the content pane.

NOTE

The Keep On Top tool only works in relationship to Office programs. If you are multitasking with non-Office programs, they will move to the forefront (on top) when active.

- **Filtering options** let you limit your search to categories of information. For example, if you only want a template to create a family budget, click **Access Templates**. Your search results will display only templates.

4. Click the **Search** button to have Access search for your keywords.

BROWSE FOR HELP

The initial Help window (see Figure 1-19) displays a list of Help categories similar to a table of contents. Click any of the headings to display a list of available topics and articles and/or subcategories of information. Continue following the links to drill down to the information you seek.

USE HELP TOOLS

Several tools are available to assist you in using Access Help. The first collection of buttons contains standard Web browser tools. Table 1-1 describes these and other Access Help tools.

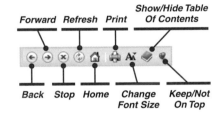

TOOL	DESCRIPTION
Back and Forward	Allows you to move from the current Help page, one page at a time, in the respective direction
Stop	Halts the current attempt at loading a Help page (useful when loading an online demo if you have a slow connection speed)
Refresh	Reloads the current page to provide the most recent information
Home	Displays the Access Help home page
Print	Opens a Print dialog box from which you can choose common printing options
Change Font Size	Opens a menu that lets you increase or decrease the size of text displayed in Help pages
Show/Hide Table Of Contents	Displays or removes a pane showing the list of highest-level Help categories
Keep/Not On Top	Keeps the Help window on top of the Access (and other Office programs) window or allows it to move to the background when switching to the program

Table 1-1: Tools to Enhance Your Search for Access

End Your Access Session

Changes that require saving are made as you work in the database object level, such as when you change the design of a table. Therefore, you don't need to "save" a database when you exit, as you would a typical file, such as a Word document.

Close a Database

If you want to close a database and keep Access open to work with other databases, use this procedure. Otherwise, to close the database and exit Access in one step, see "Exit Access."

Click the **File** tab, and click **Close Database**.

Exit Access

Click **Close** in the upper-right corner of the Access window.

–Or–

Click the **File** tab, and click the **Exit Access** button.

How to...

- *Use Database Templates*
- *Understanding How to Create an Access Database*
- *Create a Database from a Stored Template*
- *Build a Database on Your Own*
- *Using Datasheet and Design Views*
- *Close a Database After Creating It*
- *Set Up a Table in Datasheet View*
- *Add Fields in Datasheet View*
- *Rename Fields in Datasheet View*
- *Close and Save a New Table in Datasheet View*
- *Construct a Table in Design View*
- *Understanding the Primary Key*
- *Assign a Primary Key*
- *Add Identifying Information to Your Database*
- *Define Relationships*
- *Relate Tables in the Relationships Tab*
- *Understanding Referential Integrity*
- *Enforce Referential Integrity*

Chapter 2

Creating Databases and Tables

Access 2010 provides some great tools to assist in the creation of a turnkey database solution. These tools expedite the building process and help you create a new database with all of its tables, relationships, forms, and reports available at once. While using these templates might rob you of the experience to better understand database structure, if speed is what you want, the database templates will allow you to be up and running quickly. This chapter will show you how to use the featured templates, as well as other templates from Office.com, to quickly create an Access database. If, however, you choose to obtain a more thorough understanding of databases, you will learn how to step through the process, which includes basic database design, table creation, and table connections through relationships.

1 2 3 4 5 6 7 8 9 10

Design a Database

Databases are created to provide quick, easy access to information. When you consider creating a database, think clearly about why you need it, what purpose the database will fulfill, and how it will be used. A few minutes of planning before you start creating your new database can pay off in hours saved in re-creating a poorly designed database.

The data, or information, in your database is stored in *tables* that resemble spreadsheets, as shown in Figure 2-1. They have columns, or *fields*, which span the vertical space of the window; and rows, or *records*, which cover the horizontal area of the window.

After creating the tables, *forms* can be made to ease the task of data entry. You can ask questions, or create *queries*, about the data stored in the database and generate *reports* to attractively display the information from your tables or queries. Forms, queries, and reports are covered in subsequent chapters.

There are several steps you can take to ensure your database efficiently performs the tasks you need, does not contain duplicate information, and that all of the information in the database is complete and correct. To create a successful database:

1. Decide why you are creating the database. What do you want it to accomplish?
2. Determine if your database will be desktop-based or Web-based. Web databases are designed to be published to Access Services running on a Microsoft SharePoint server. These databases have some limitations compared to standard databases run on desktop Access. Chapters 9 and 10 discuss sharing and security databases, including Web databases.
3. Think about who will be using the database. Consider not only the reports and forms the database will incorporate, but also the expertise of the people who will be entering the data.
4. Organize the information that you want in your database, and separate it into major areas. For example, a database used by a manufacturing firm might need information about their customers, their raw materials, the products they manufacture, and so on.

TIP

Sketching out the tables, forms, reports, and other objects on paper may help to clarify the requirements for your new database.

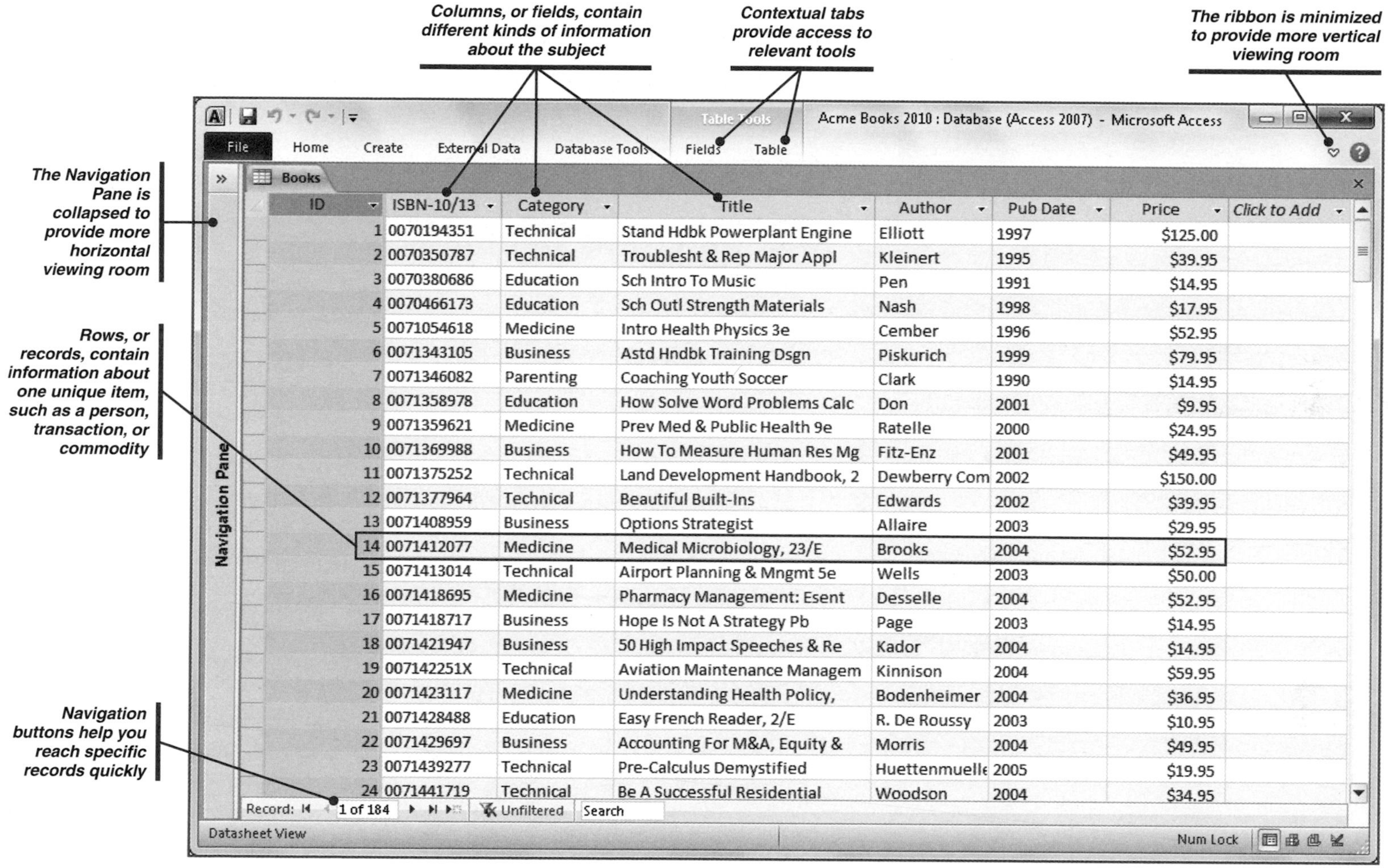

Columns, or fields, contain different kinds of information about the subject

Contextual tabs provide access to relevant tools

The ribbon is minimized to provide more vertical viewing room

The Navigation Pane is collapsed to provide more horizontal viewing room

Rows, or records, contain information about one unique item, such as a person, transaction, or commodity

Navigation buttons help you reach specific records quickly

ID	ISBN-10/13	Category	Title	Author	Pub Date	Price	Click to Add
1	0070194351	Technical	Stand Hdbk Powerplant Engine	Elliott	1997	$125.00	
2	0070350787	Technical	Troublesht & Rep Major Appl	Kleinert	1995	$39.95	
3	0070380686	Education	Sch Intro To Music	Pen	1991	$14.95	
4	0070466173	Education	Sch Outl Strength Materials	Nash	1998	$17.95	
5	0071054618	Medicine	Intro Health Physics 3e	Cember	1996	$52.95	
6	0071343105	Business	Astd Hndbk Training Dsgn	Piskurich	1999	$79.95	
7	0071346082	Parenting	Coaching Youth Soccer	Clark	1990	$14.95	
8	0071358978	Education	How Solve Word Problems Calc	Don	2001	$9.95	
9	0071359621	Medicine	Prev Med & Public Health 9e	Ratelle	2000	$24.95	
10	0071369988	Business	How To Measure Human Res Mg	Fitz-Enz	2001	$49.95	
11	0071375252	Technical	Land Development Handbook, 2	Dewberry Com	2002	$150.00	
12	0071377964	Technical	Beautiful Built-Ins	Edwards	2002	$39.95	
13	0071408959	Business	Options Strategist	Allaire	2003	$29.95	
14	0071412077	Medicine	Medical Microbiology, 23/E	Brooks	2004	$52.95	
15	0071413014	Technical	Airport Planning & Mngmt 5e	Wells	2003	$50.00	
16	0071418695	Medicine	Pharmacy Management: Esent	Desselle	2004	$52.95	
17	0071418717	Business	Hope Is Not A Strategy Pb	Page	2003	$14.95	
18	0071421947	Business	50 High Impact Speeches & Re	Kador	2004	$14.95	
19	007142251X	Technical	Aviation Maintenance Managem	Kinnison	2004	$59.95	
20	0071423117	Medicine	Understanding Health Policy,	Bodenheimer	2004	$36.95	
21	0071428488	Education	Easy French Reader, 2/E	R. De Roussy	2003	$10.95	
22	0071429697	Business	Accounting For M&A, Equity &	Morris	2004	$49.95	
23	0071439277	Technical	Pre-Calculus Demystified	Huettenmuelle	2005	$19.95	
24	0071441719	Technical	Be A Successful Residential	Woodson	2004	$34.95	

Record: 1 of 184   Unfiltered   Search

Datasheet View   Num Lock

Figure 2-1: Access tables resemble spreadsheets and are the core containers of information for your database.

5. Define the information you want included in each major area. These definitions will become fields in your tables.

6. Consider who will see the information produced from the data in the database. Think about how the reports can be designed to best communicate the information.

7. Take into account the underlying table data that will be necessary to produce the reports.

8. Reflect on how the tables will interrelate. What primary keys will be used in each table? (See the "Understanding the Primary Key" QuickFacts later in this chapter.) For example, if you want your database to generate purchase orders for a company, you will need tables for product information, purchase order information, vendor information, and so forth.

9. After you have thoroughly planned your database, you can start actually building it.

Use Database Templates

The New view, available from the File tab, provides several ways to obtain templates in order to make the process of creating a database easier. There are samplings of prestructured templates provided by Access, those that you can use from Office.com (to search Office.com requires an Internet connection), and the means to locate templates on your network. To find and use a template:

1. Open Access 2010 using one of the procedures described in Chapter 1.

2. If a database is open, click the **File** tab, and click **Close Database**. The current database closes and the Access window displays the New view, as shown in Figure 2-2. You can choose from several categories of templates: Those available from your computer are displayed on the top of the page and those available from Office.com are in the lower part of the page.

3. Click any of the categories of templates displayed. Depending on your choice, you may be presented with folders organizing the templates within a category. Continue navigating through the choices until you see a template that approximates your needs.

4. Click the icon for the template you want to use. Tools to name, store, and create the database from the template are displayed in the pane on the right of the page, as shown in Figure 2-3.

5. Type a name for your database, or use the default name already in the File Name text box.

6. If you want to designate a location for your database other than the default folder, click the folder icon 📁 to display the File New Database dialog box, as seen in Figure 2-4. If you do not want to store your database in the default folder, browse to locate the folder in which you want your new database stored.

7. Type a name for your database in the File Name text box if you want to make a change.

8. Click **OK**, and you are returned to the New view.

CAUTION

Be careful when creating a new database from either a template or a blank database. In both cases you have an opportunity to choose a standard Access database or a Web database. Though the two share the same Access file format (.accdb), Web databases do not provide some features of standard Access databases. They are designed to be published to and run on a Microsoft SharePoint server and viewed in a Web browser. The majority of the procedures and examples in this book assume a standard Access database is being used. Chapters 9 and 10 describe topics related to sharing databases.

Blank database   Blank web database

File Name

Annual Neighborhood Garage Sale.accdb

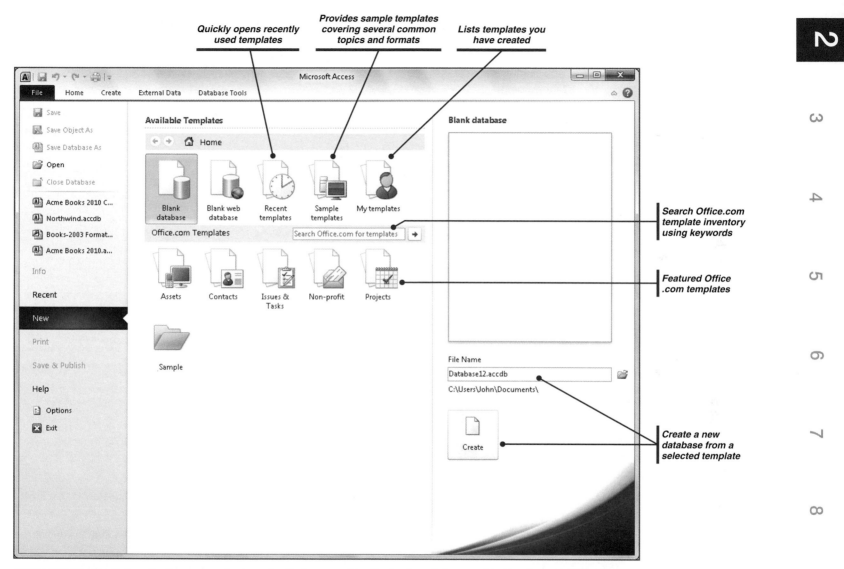

Quickly opens recently used templates

Provides sample templates covering several common topics and formats

Lists templates you have created

Search Office.com template inventory using keywords

Featured Office .com templates

Create a new database from a selected template

Figure 2-2: The New view displays several categories that are used to display templates provided by Access, Office.com, or those you created.

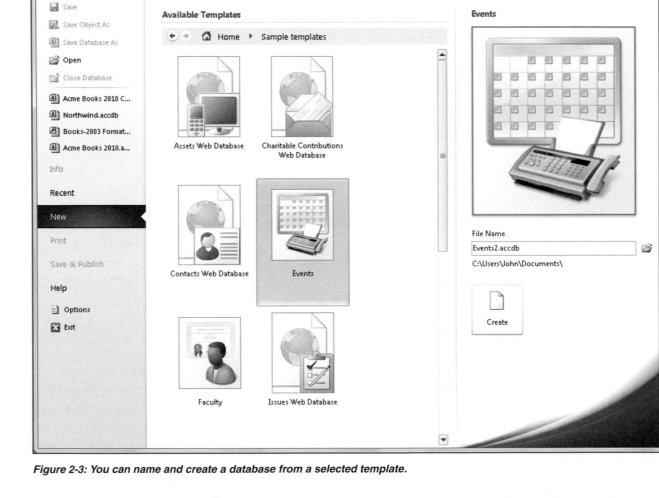

Figure 2-3: You can name and create a database from a selected template.

9. Depending on where the template is located, click the **Create** or **Download** button below the preview in order to open the template in Access as a new database. Access will prepare the new database for you to use. Your new database opens in Form view so that you may start entering data at once. First, click **Enable Content** in the Security Warning toolbar to allow any active content to operate. (Who can you trust if you can't

QUICKFACTS

UNDERSTANDING HOW TO CREATE AN ACCESS DATABASE

There are many ways to create an Access database. As in several Office-wide features, such as applying formatting to Excel workbooks and PowerPoint presentations, there is a quick and easy way to get you close to where you want to be, and then there is a more hands-on approach that allows you full flexibility. Many times, a combination of both techniques provides the best results. In Access 2010, you can choose from:

- **Fully contained templates** provided by Microsoft (both included with Access and available online) that provide sample tables, forms, reports, and more. If your needs are similar to the template, just add data and you're on your way. Some even contain a few sample records to help you understand how to use the database.

- **Application parts**, which are new to Access 2010, allow you to integrate prebuilt subsections of a database to an existing database. For example, if you wanted to add a table identifying contacts to your database, the Contacts application part would not only add a table with contacts-related fields, but also would include other relevant objects, such as queries, forms, and reports that are connected to contacts—all fully meshed (or *related*) with your existing data.

- **Going your own way**, which means you can create and build your individual objects, starting with tables. Of course, there are also varying degrees of how much under the hood you want to get here as well. You can set up your tables field by field, or you can use Quick Start field collections to, for example, set up a table with all the typical fields used to

Continued . . .

Figure 2-4: A standard Windows Save-type dialog box lets you store the database anywhere on your computer or network.

trust Microsoft?) To begin entering data, click in the first empty field, and type your first record (see Chapter 6 for more information on working with forms). Later sections in this chapter, and Chapters 2 and 3 describe how to modify and work with a table.

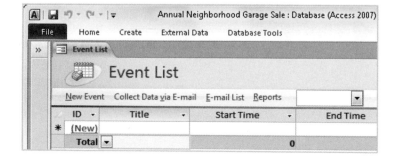

QUICK**FACTS**

UNDERSTANDING HOW TO CREATE AN ACCESS DATABASE *(Continued)*

handle payments or provide addressing information for clients, employees, or other contacts—all with a single click.

As you can see, Access tries to offer all things to all levels of needs and all levels of involvement that you might want. This chapter, as well as subsequent chapters, will help guide you through the options.

TIP

You can change the location of the default folder used to store databases and templates (by default, it's c:\Users\ *user name*\Documents). Click the **File** tab, click **Options**, and click **General**. In the Creating Databases area, click **Browse** next to Default Database Folder to open the Default Database Path window, and navigate to a folder to use as the default folder. Click **OK** twice to close both open windows.

Creating databases

Default file format for Blank Database: Access 2007

Default database folder: C:\Users\John\Documents\   Browse...

New database sort order: General - Legacy

10. If you don't initially find a template that meets your needs, click the tools on the toolbar to navigate back through your choices.

← → 🏠 Home ▸ Sample templates

–Or–

Type search keywords in the Search Office.com For Templates search box, and click the **Start Searching** arrow ➡ to do a more exhaustive search in Microsoft's online inventory.

Create a Database from a Stored Template

You can easily create a database from a template that is available on your network, though it might not appear under My Templates in the New view unless you created it. These templates may be located on a network server or stored in folders on your computer not commonly used exclusively for templates.

CREATE A DATABASE FROM YOUR OWN TEMPLATES

Databases you create in Access 2010 are saved in a templates folder based on your user name and are displayed by default under My Templates in the New view.

1. Click the **File** tab, and click **New**. In New view, click **My Templates** (see Figure 2-2) to view any templates you have created (see the accompanying Tip). Click the template from which you want to create a database.

2. In the right pane, accept the file name and location.

–Or–

Retype a file name and click the folder icon to navigate to a new folder location.

3. Click **Create** when finished.

CREATE A DATABASE FROM TEMPLATES ON YOUR NETWORK

For templates stored elsewhere on your network:

1. Click the **File** tab, and click **Open**. In the Open dialog box, click the file type down arrow to the right of the File Name box, and select **Microsoft Access Database Templates**.

TIP

You can create your own template from an existing Access database, complete with an icon and preview image, as those shown in Figure 2-3 for Access templates. See Chapter 9 for information on how to do this and other ways to share Access databases.

2. Browse to the folder that contains the template you want, select it, and click **Open**.

3. In the File New Database window (see Figure 2-4), navigate to where you want to store the database, name it, and click **OK**.

4. Alternatively, you can use Windows Explorer to locate the template you want, right-click it, and click **Open**. The File New Database window opens as described in the previous step.

5. In both cases, the database is created and opened in Access.

Build a Database on Your Own

Although the ease of using templates when creating databases is undeniable, there is something to be said for working from your own blueprint. Sometimes, templates don't have the solution you are looking for. Sometimes, you want to create a more simplistic database to better understand the inner workings of Access. Either way, it is at this point that you will start with a blank database.

1. Click the **File** tab, and click **New**. In New view, click **Blank Database** (see Figure 2-2).

2. The Blank Database pane appears at the right side of the Access window. Click the **File Name** text box, and type a file name for your database or use the default name.

3. If you want to designate a location for your database other than the default folder, click the folder icon 📂 to display the File New Database dialog box (Figure 2-4). If you do not want to store your database in the default folder, browse to locate the folder in which you want your new database stored.

4. Type a name for your database in the File Name text box if you want to make a change.

5. Click **OK**, and you are returned to the Blank Database pane.

6. Click **Create** to create your new database in the default folder. Access creates the new database and opens an empty table, shown here. A column headed Click To Add is highlighted and is ready to accept text and be assigned a data type. To start entering information into this new table and assign data types to fields, see "Add Fields in Datasheet View" later in this chapter.

Close a Database After Creating It

When you have finished creating your new database, you may start working with it, as described later in this chapter, or you may close it.

When finished, close the database by clicking the **File** tab and clicking **Close Database**.

- If you only added data, the database will save your changes in the default table and close.

- If you made any changes to the design of the table, such as adding a field, Access will ask you to accept those changes to the table and then close. If you neither added data nor changed the table design, the database will close and you will need to create a new table the next time you open the database (see the next several sections for ways to do this).

Build the Framework with Tables

Although Access is composed of many objects, the basic database framework revolves around tables. Each table usually holds information about a single topic and is connected or related to other tables through similar pieces of information (or fields). Each row of a table contains information about a specific item. For example, in a table that contains information about your friends, you might have fields such as first name, last name, address, and so on. Each row is called a *record*, and in this example, would pertain to one friend. You can create a new table by several different methods, using two different ways to view the table. This chapter describes how to create a new table in a new database. In subsequent chapters, you will see how to create tables from imported or linked information and from online sources, such as a SharePoint site or a Web service.

Set Up a Table in Datasheet View

Whether you open a table that was created as part of a blank database, or you create a new table, you will have to organize it by creating fields so you can categorize your information into columns of similar information. Otherwise, as you start adding data, as shown in Figure 2-5, your new table will soon be gathering data without a clear roadmap as to which data goes where.

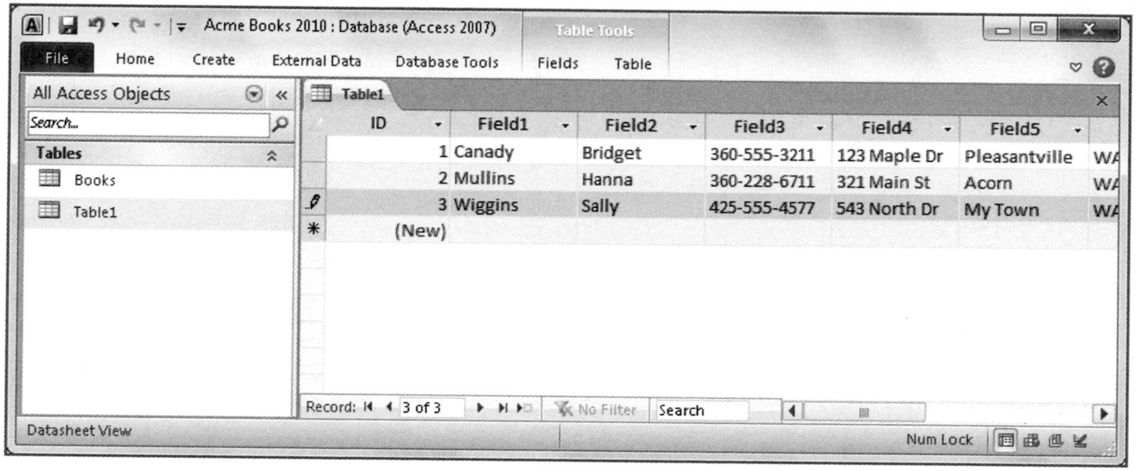

Figure 2-5: An unstructured table may contain data but it lacks discernible organization.

You can display a new table by either opening one previously created or creating a new one.

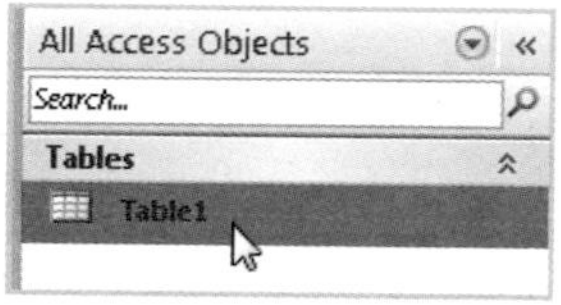

1. To open a table previously created, open the database it's contained in, expand the Navigation Pane, and double-click the table name, typically Table1. (If you see only groups, click the downward-pointing arrows in the group title to display all the objects in each group.)

   –Or–

   Right-click the table name, and click **Open**.

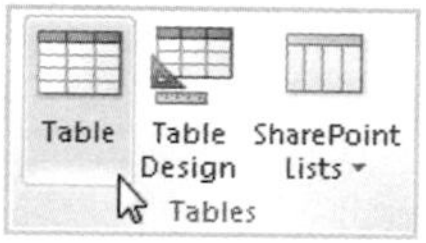

2. To create a new table, open the database the table will be contained in, and on the Tables group on the Create tab, click **Table**.

In either case, the table opens in Datasheet View with one column already containing a field name (the first column, ID, contains the primary key, described later in the chapter) and a second column ready to accept data and be assigned a *data type*, which sets properties for a given set of similar data.

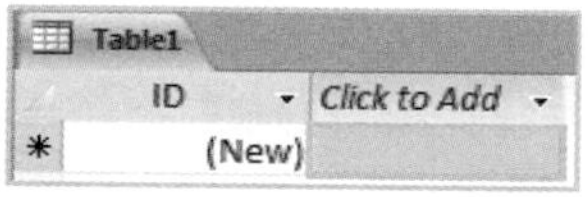

Add Fields in Datasheet View

There are several methods you can use to set up a new table with fields, which organize your data into columns.

TIP

Don't be concerned about the number of fields your data might be organized into. You can have up to 255 of them per table!

NOTE

In database parlance, the intersection of a column/field and record/row is commonly referred to as a "field." In spreadsheet usage, such as in Microsoft Excel, that same location would be called a "cell." As Microsoft continues to blur the distinction between tables in its Office suite, the terminology used within each program will eventually have to be reconciled. In the meantime, this book will use both terms interchangeably.

ADD FIELDS BY ADDING DATA

If you are an active spreadsheet user, it may be more comfortable for you to create a table simply by entering data into the datasheet when you open Access (at some point you will have to assign field names and data types). When you open or create a blank database, the database opens in Datasheet View with a new, blank table named Table1.

Press either **TAB** or **ENTER** to move from one field to the next. As shown in Figure 2-5, the column headings become Field1, Field2, Field3, and so forth. As you move down from one row to the next, Access saves that row, or record.

ADD FIELDS BY ASSIGNING A DATA TYPE

When setting up a new table, each column or field of information must be assigned a data type, which sets the parameters and properties for the data it contains. See Table 2-1 for the different data types and their usage. Text is the default data type, as it provides the most flexibility with data entry. Data types are discussed in more detail in Chapter 3.

To add a field and assign a data type:

1. At the rightmost end of the field name header row, click **Click To Add**.

2. On the drop-down menu, click the data type you want for the new field. The field is given a default name, such as Field1. See how to rename the field name in "Rename Fields in Datasheet View" later in the chapter.

INSERT FIELDS

Besides building a field structure by continually adding fields in sequence to the right end of the table, as previously described, you can also insert a new field anywhere in the field header row. You both insert the new field and assign its data type in one action.

1. Click anywhere in the field to the right of where you want to add a new field.

2. In the Add & Delete group of the Fields tab (Table Tools), click an icon for one of the more common data types and apply standard formatting.

–Or–

Click **More Fields** to choose from other data types.

–Or–

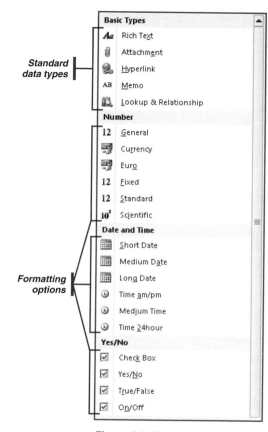

Standard data types

Formatting options

Figure 2-6: You can apply formatting to fields as you assign them a data type.

DATA TYPE	DESCRIPTION	COMMENTS
Text	Numbers or letters	Stores up to 255 characters
Memo	Text that is too long to be stored in text fields	Up to 65,535 characters if you enter them manually. Up to 2GB if you enter them from the program.
Number	Digits only	You set the field size, up to 16 bytes of information
Date/Time	A valid date or time	
Currency	Same as number, but with decimal places and currency symbol added	Can be up to four decimal places. Used to store financial data.
AutoNumber	A unique sequential number	
Yes/No	Accepts yes/no; true/false; on/off	
OLE Object	Any object that can be linked or embedded in a table	Limited to 2GB and can make your program run slowly. Using an attachment field is a better option in most cases.
Hyperlink	A path to an object, file, or Web site	
Attachment	Any supported type of file, including pictures, charts, text files, and so on	Works only with the .accdb file format. It is more flexible than the OLE Object data type.
Calculated	Is based on the calculation from data in other fields in the same table	
Lookup Wizard	Creates a drop-down list from existing data or data you enter	A special usage of the Text data type

Table 2-1: Data Types That Can Be Assigned to Table Fields

If using the Number, Date And Time, or Yes/No data type, select one of several formatting options, as shown in Figure 2-6.

INSERT PREDEFINED FIELDS

Some field names are commonly used over and over again when creating tables. Instead of creating the structure each time, you can have Access insert the fields and make whatever changes you might need. (In some cases, only one field is inserted, but its properties have been set up to perform a specific purpose.)

1. Click anywhere in the field to the right of where you want to add the new fields.

2. In the Add & Delete group of the Fields tab (Table Tools), click the **More Fields** button.

TIP

When naming or renaming a field in Datasheet View, select a name that is both meaningful and succinct. This is the name Access first uses when referencing the field. You can change the display name in Datasheet View to something more compatible with other programs using Design View; that is, you can have essentially a display name (in Datasheet View) and a computer name (Design View) for each field. Depending on which programs your data might interact with in the future, consider conforming to their conventions by eliminating spaces, or use an underline character to separate words—for example, LastName or Last_Name instead of Last Name.

3. In the Quick Start area at the bottom of the menu, click the field or collection of fields you want. The fields are inserted with suggested field names and appropriate data type.

Rename Fields in Datasheet View

The default field names Access assigns new fields are not very descriptive of the data within the field (Field 1, Field2, etc.). You can easily rename the field names to something that makes more sense to you.

1. Right-click the column header that contains the field name you want to change.

2. On the context menu, click **Rename Field**. The current field name is highlighted for editing.

3. Type a new field name, using up to 64 characters, including spaces. Press **ENTER**. (The field name you provide in Datasheet View acts as both a display name and a functional name used by Access. In Chapter 3 you will see how you can change the functional name to something more succinct using Design View.)

Close and Save a New Table in Datasheet View

The first time you close a table that you created and added any data to, Access will inform you that you changed its design (by adding at least one field of data, you have created the field the data is in) and then give you the opportunity to change its name. When you are finished working with

NOTE

There is no space between the word "Table" and the number 1 in a new table's name. This convention is used throughout Access; however, you can rename a table with up to 64 characters, including spaces.

TIP

While Access automatically saves your work in Datasheet View when you exit the table, it's not a bad idea to periodically manually save your work as well. Computers don't crash as often as they once did, but occasionally they do. To save your work at any time, right-click the table's tab, and click **Save**.

NOTE

As mentioned in Chapter 1, you can choose to have your database objects opened either as tabbed documents or as overlapping windows. This book assumes you are using the default tabbed display. There are some procedural differences between the two methods used to access housekeeping tasks such as naming, closing, or saving objects. In most cases, it's just a matter of right-clicking a tab instead of a window's title bar to access the options.

a table in Datasheet View, Access automatically saves your work when you close the table or close Access.

1. Click **Close** ⊠ at the right of the tabs bar, under the Access Help icon.

 —Or—

 Right-click the **Name** tab of any table. From the context menu, click **Close**.

2. Click **Yes** that you want to save changes to the design of the table.

3. In the Save As dialog box, type a meaningful name for the table, and click **OK**.

Construct a Table in Design View

Design View provides an alternative way to structure a table and also contains the full complement of field properties that allow you to format, identify, and otherwise make your data more useful. An example of an existing table in Design View is shown in Figure 2-7.

Change between Datasheet View and Design View here ... or on the status bar

Create new tables using the Field Name, Data Type, and Description fields

A description can help users understand the type of data to be entered in a field

You can set the data type for each field; "Text" is the default

Field properties are specific to each data type and define how data is entered and formatted

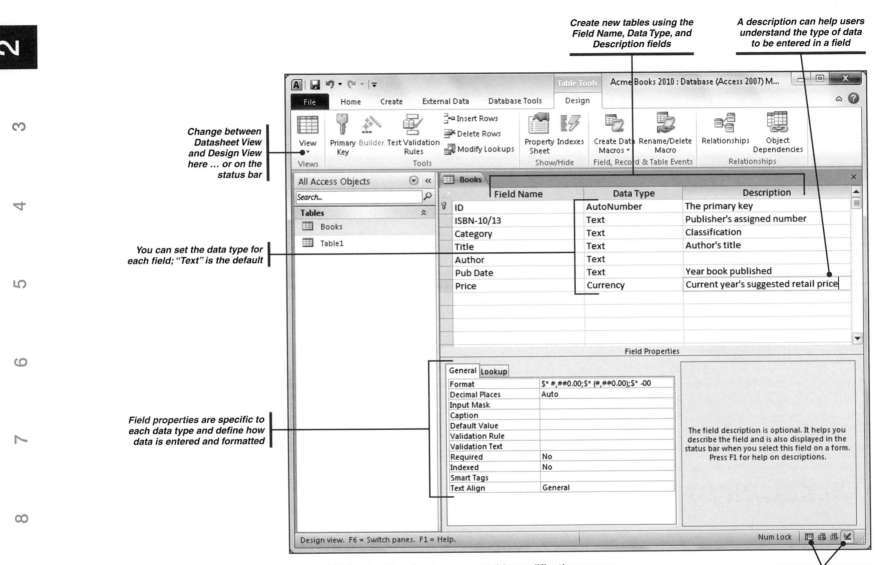

Figure 2-7: Design View is where most table modifications occur.

Click to change views

TIP

When choosing fields, try and break down your information categories into their smallest components. For example, when adding people's names, use two or even three fields to contain a person's first name, middle name, and last name, instead of using a single field to contain all. It's easier to remove a field that proves to be extraneous than to try and separate one comprehensive field into smaller parts.

CREATE A TABLE IN DESIGN VIEW

1. Open a blank or existing Access database. See Chapter 1 for ways to open an existing database, or see "Build a Database on Your Own" earlier in this chapter to see how to create a new database.

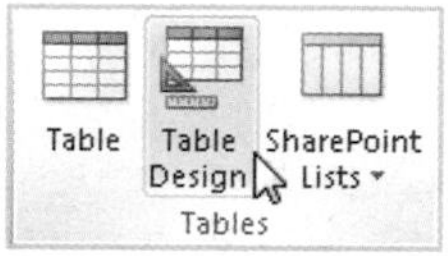

2. In the Create tab Tables group, click **Table Design**. A new blank table opens in Design View, shown in Figure 2-8, with the insertion point blinking in the first Field Name field or cell.

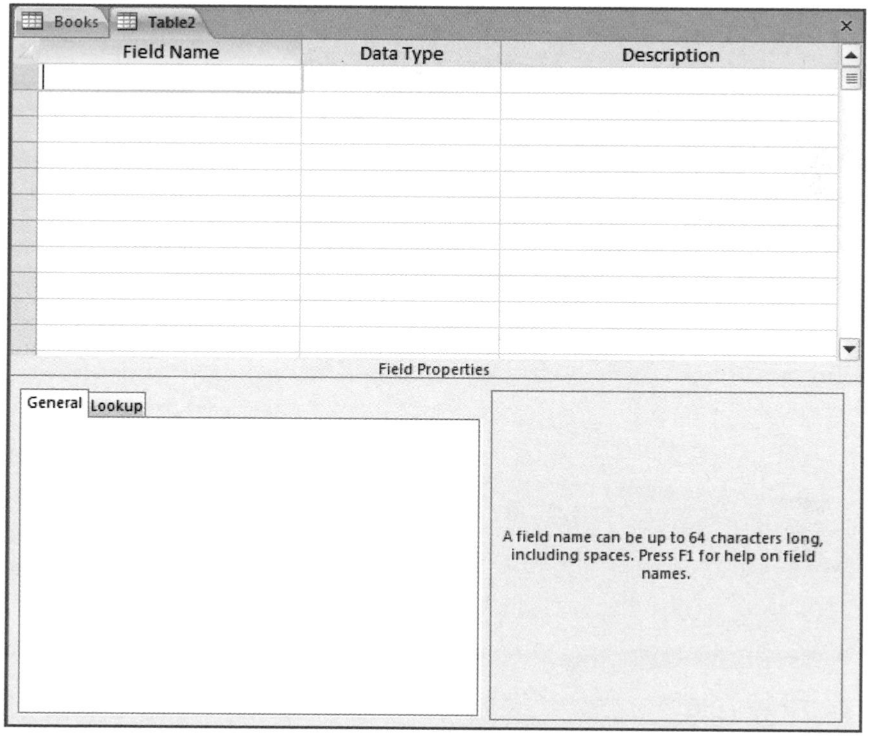

Figure 2-8: You can design a new table by creating its structure in Design View.

CREATE THE FIELD STRUCTURE

The upper section of the table design window has columns that hold the basic definitions for each field included in your table. The field name, data type, and description for each individual field are entered into the rows.

> Pre-Calculus Demystified
>
> Record: 1 of 184
>
> Current year's suggested retail price

There are several data types from which to choose. The lower portion of this window is where you set more specific field properties, which is discussed in more detail in Chapter 3. This section changes as you select different fields. The optional Description field is used to provide other information that may be required, such as the type of information that is expected in this field.

Design View opens with an insertion point in the first field name. To complete your table in Design View:

1. Type a field name. Select a name that is both meaningful and succinct. Remember, this is the name Access uses when referencing the field internally and to other programs.

> Table3
>
> **Field Name**
>
> Last Name

2. Press **ENTER**. This will move your insertion point to the Data Type column and display the default data type, which is Text.

> Microsoft Access
>
> The name you supplied is a reserved word. Reserved words have a specific meaning to Microsoft Access or to the Microsoft Access database engine.
>
> If you use a reserved word, you may receive an error when referring to this field.
>
> OK   Cancel   Help

Figure 2-9: Access identifies reserved words and recommends you avoid using them.

3. Click the **Data Type** down arrow to open the Data Type menu. Data types are listed in Table 2-1 and are discussed in more detail in Chapter 3.

4. Select a data type. Press **TAB** to move to the Description column. Enter a description for your field if you choose.

5. Press **TAB** or **ENTER**, or use your mouse to move to the next field or row.

6. Repeat steps 1–5 until you have entered all of the field names, assigned data types, and provided descriptions for the table.

> Data Type
>
> Text
>
> Text
> Memo
> Number
> Date/Time
> Currency
> AutoNumber
> Yes/No
> OLE Object
> Hyperlink
> Attachment
> Calculated
> Lookup Wizard...

UNDERSTANDING THE PRIMARY KEY

It is important to assign at least one field in each table as a primary key. Primary keys are fields that identify records as unique. They ensure that duplicate records are not entered and expedite locating records in the database. It is also through primary keys that tables are connected, or related.

Once a primary key is established in a table, you can use it to connect tables. For example, in a Vendors table, the primary key might be a vendor identification number. This number might also appear in a Products table so that you can establish a relationship between products that you sell and the vendors that supply them. In the Products table, the vendor key would be known as a *foreign key*, or simply another table's primary key.

There are several attributes for a primary key:

- A primary key is unique and is never repeated in the table.
- A primary key is never empty.
- A primary key never changes.

Access 2010 automatically assigns a primary key when you create a new table in Datasheet View, with ID as its field name and the data type of AutoNumber (tables created in Design View are not automatically provided a primary key). AutoNumber is the best choice for a primary key, since using an automatic number will ensure that no two IDs are the same, no matter how many records are entered into the table.

SAVE THE TABLE

After you have changed or added fields to a table, you should save the new design. While records within your database are saved automatically, new designs are not. To save your table:

1. Click the **File** tab, and click **Save**.

   –Or–

   Right-click the table's **Name** tab, and click **Save** in the context menu.

2. If this is the first time you are saving a table, the Save As dialog box appears. Type a meaningful name, and click **OK**. The new table will appear in the Navigation Pane in whichever manner you have the pane grouped to view the objects in your database.

Assign a Primary Key

It is important to assign at least one field in each table as a primary key to ensure that each record is unique. For information on using primary keys, see the "Understanding the Primary Key" QuickFacts.

ADD A PRIMARY KEY TO A NEW TABLE

1. Open a new or existing database.

2. In the Create tab Tables group, click **Table**. This opens a new table in Datasheet View.

3. The first field is labeled "ID," as shown in Figure 2-10. Type some data in the field labeled "Add New Field."

4. Continue to add new information, as described earlier in this chapter. After you have completed entering data, click **Close**. You are asked if you want to save the changes to the design of this table. Click **Yes**, and the Save As dialog box appears. Type a name for your new table. Click **OK**, and the table closes.

5. In the Navigation Pane, right-click the new table. Click **Design View** in the context menu to open the table. Note that the ID field has been set as the primary key, as seen in Figure 2-11.

Figure 2-10: A new table opens with two fields, one for the "ID" and the second field available for you to add information.

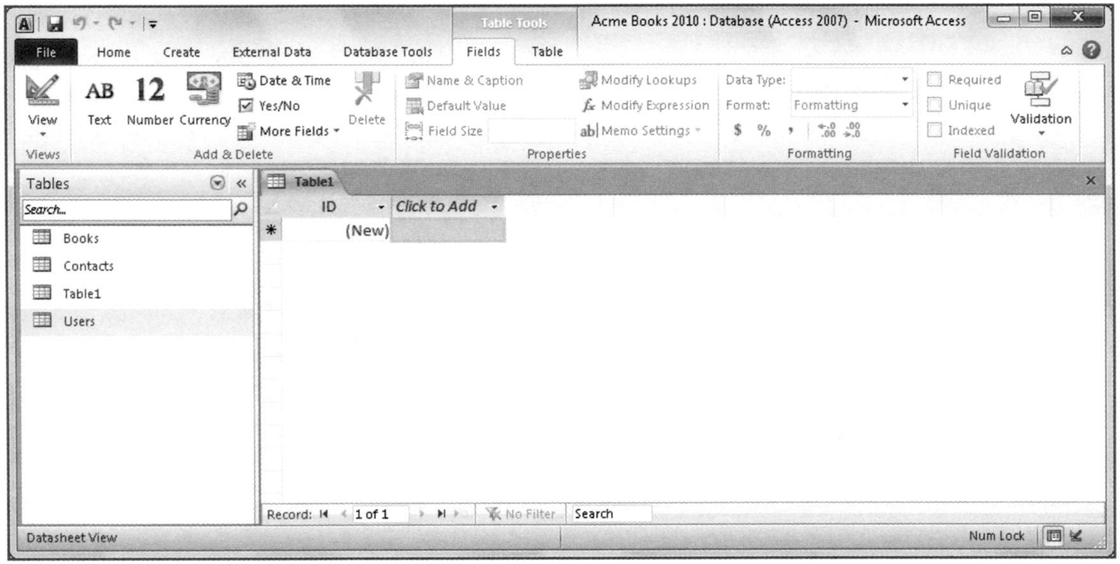

Figure 2-11: A small key indicates which field in Design View is the primary key in your table.

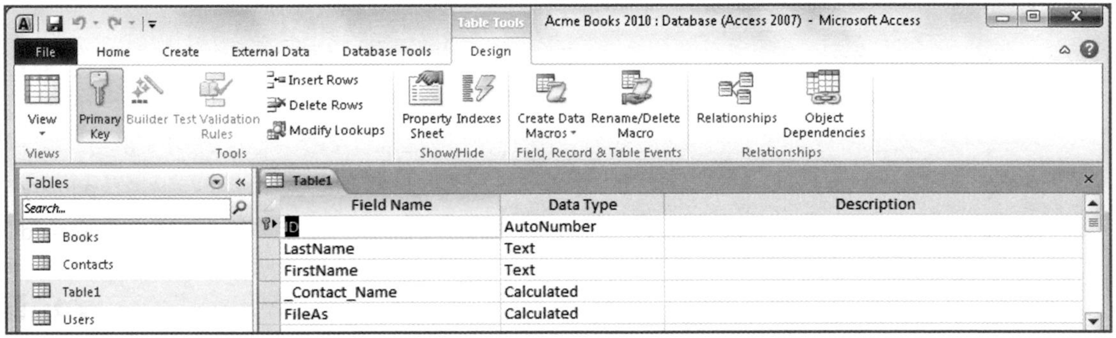

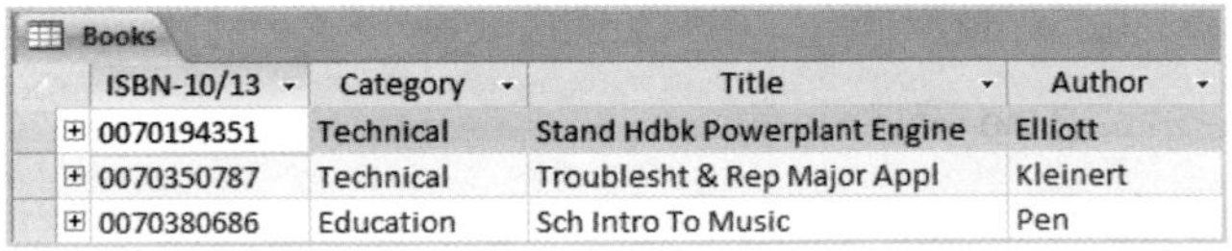

ISBN-10/13	Category	Title	Author
0070194351	Technical	Stand Hdbk Powerplant Engine	Elliott
0070350787	Technical	Troublesht & Rep Major Appl	Kleinert
0070380686	Education	Sch Intro To Music	Pen

USE AN EXISTING FIELD AS THE PRIMARY KEY

In some tables, you may already have a unique identifier. This could be a serial number or some other combination of numbers and letters that is unique to a specific record. Any such symbol makes a good primary key. To use this unique code as a primary key:

1. Open an existing database.
2. In the Navigation Pane, right-click the table in which you want to create the primary key. Click **Design View** in the context menu to open the table.

Books	
Field Name	Data Type
➡ ISBN-10/13	Text

3. Click the row selector for the field row that you want to set as the primary key.

4. In the Design tab Tools group (Table Tools), click **Primary Key**. The key indicator appears in the row selector for each field you have chosen.

REMOVE AND CHANGE A PRIMARY KEY

If you need to change a primary key within a table:

1. Open the database you want to use.

2. In the Navigation Pane, right-click the table in which you want to remove the primary key, and click **Design View**.

   –Or–

   If you are already working in a table in Datasheet View, click the **Design View** icon in the Views group or on the status bar. ☑

3. Click the row selector for the current primary key field.

4. In the Design tab Tools group, click **Primary Key**. The key indicator disappears from the selected field.

5. Set a new primary key by creating a field and assigning it the AutoNumber data type and then assigning it as a primary key.

   –Or–

   Assign an existing field to be the primary key.

   See the two previous sections for procedures on how to assign a primary key.

Add Identifying Information to Your Database

As you start defining your database by adding data and objects, it may be useful to add properties that include identifying information. This can help you (and others) locate your database file easily when using search tools.

1. Open your database using one of the methods discussed in Chapter 1.

2. Click the **File** tab, and click **Info**.

3. In the right pane of Info view, click **View And Edit Database Properties**, as shown in Figure 2-12.

NOTE

If you want to use more than one field as a primary key, hold down the **CTRL** key, and click the row selector for each field you want to use.

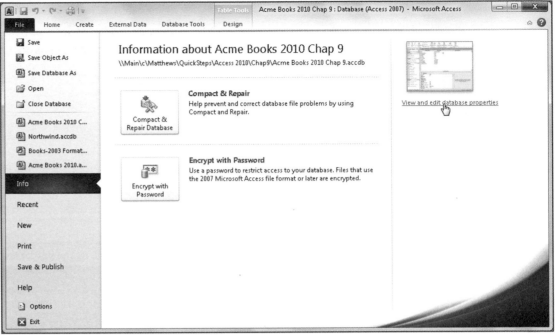

Figure 2-12: Info view provides tools to work on your database, including adding identifying properties.

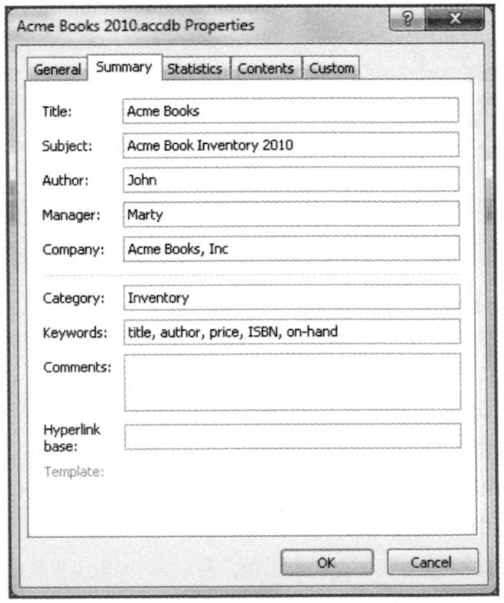

Figure 2-13: The search for a particular database can be eased by entering identifying information.

4. In the database Properties dialog box, click the Summary tab if it is not already open. Enter any identifying information, as shown in Figure 2-13. Good descriptors can include a title, subject, and keywords (words or phrases that are associated with the database).

Identify Relationships

Access is a *relational* database: it uses relationships to establish connections between tables. Each table, or group of data, should have a primary key, and that primary key can also be part of another table but viewed as a *foreign key*. Because this same primary key is in both tables, the two tables can relate and mix in multiple settings—such as queries, forms, and reports. Relationships allow you to record data only one time and use it as many times as needed. For example, you could include the addressing information for your clients in a Customers table. By relating the Customers table to a table of orders, you could avoid reentering a customer's address for every order he or she might make. You keep the size of your database file smaller and also avoid typing errors. Figure 2-14 shows a form whose components are derived from several related tables.

☰ Purchase Order Details			— ◻ X

Purchase Order #146

Status: Submitted   Submit for Approval   Approve Purchase   Cancel Purchase   Close

Supplier	Supplier B ▾	Expected Date	
Created By:	Andrew Cencini ▾	Creation Date	4/26/2006
Submitted By:	Andrew Cencini ▾	Submitted Date	4/26/2006
Approved By:	▾	Approved Date	

Purchase Details | Inventory Receiving | Payment Information

Product ▾	Qty ▾	Unit Cost ▾	Total Price ▾
Northwind Traders Marmalade ▾	40	$60.00	$2,400.00
Northwind Traders Dried Apples	40	$39.00	$1,560.00
*			

Record: ◄ ◄ 1 of 28 ► ►I ►⊠   🕱 No Filter   Search

Figure 2-14: You can use records from several tables to display in a common object such as a form.

Define Relationships

There are three types of table relationships: one-to-many; many-to-many; and, in some cases, one-to-one:

- **One-to-many relationships** are the most common, whereby one table can have many matching records in a second table but the second table has only one matching record in the first. As an example of a one-to-many relationship (see Figure 2-15), a Tasks table can hold many tasks assigned to the same person taken from a Contacts table, but there is only one contact for each task.

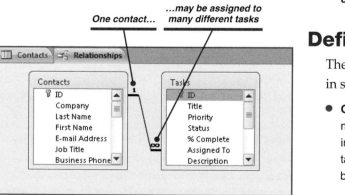

One contact...   *...may be assigned to many different tasks*

Figure 2-15: Different relationships can be created among the tables in your database.

- **Many-to-many relationships** illustrate how each table can have many matching records in one another. For example, each order can have multiple products on it and, reversing the thought, each product can be on multiple orders. The ideal way to relate the latter relationship is to create a third *junction*, or linking table, as shown in Figure 2-16.

The Customer Interests table acts as a junction table between the...

...Interests and Customers tables

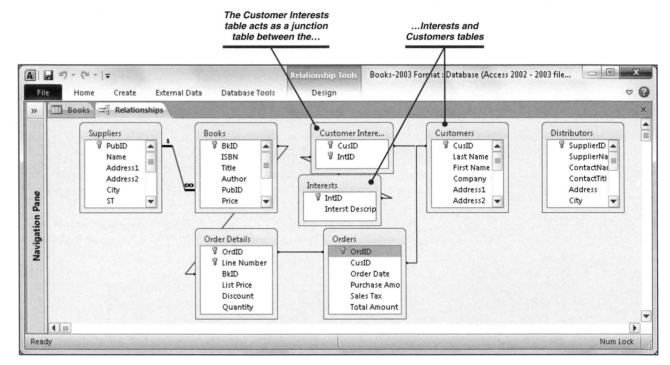

Figure 2-16: Junction tables create the connection between tables having a many-to-many relationship.

- **One-to-one relationships** exists when each record in the first table can have only one matching record in the second table and each record in the second table can have only one matching record in the first table. Usually, this type of information can be stored in only one table; however, you could establish a one-to-one relationship to isolate part of a table for security reasons, for instance, or to archive part of a large table. For example, if a few of your 705 employees are subject to a miscellaneous deduction every third year, you might store that information in a separate table, because storing the information in the Employee table would result in empty spaces for every employee to whom the deduction does not apply.

Relate Tables in the Relationships Tab

Access has an easy way to relate tables once you've defined their primary keys.

1. Open an existing database in Access 2010 using one of the procedures described in Chapter 1.

2. In the Database Tools tab Relationships group, click **Relationships**. The Show Table dialog box will appear if you have not yet established any relationships. (If it does not appear, in the Design tab Relationships group, click **Show Table**.) The Show Table dialog box, shown in Figure 2-17, displays both the tables (and queries) in your database (queries are described in Chapter 5).

3. Select a table and click **Add**. Repeat to add all the tables needed to create relationships.

4. Click **Close**. The Relationships tab will be displayed. The primary key fields are indicated by the small key by the field name within each table list.

NOTE

Earlier versions of Access referred to the container where relationships are diagrammed as the *Relationships* window. You can view relationships in a window if you change how you view open objects from the default for Access 2007— tabbed documents—to overlapping windows. Chapter 1 describes how to change the way you view open objects.

Figure 2-17: You can relate tables and queries in the Relationships tab by first selecting them in the Show Table dialog box.

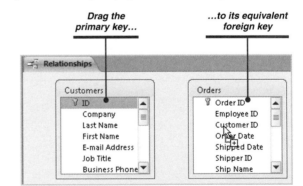

Figure 2-18: *The Edit Relationships dialog box displays relationship options and pairings.*

QUICK**FACTS**

UNDERSTANDING REFERENTIAL INTEGRITY

As you work with tables and relationships, the very nature of data is that it changes. The relationships you so carefully create can be damaged if only one facet is removed. For example, if you have established a one-to-many relationship between your Employee table and your Customer table to identify sales representatives and their clients and an employee leaves your company, the employee ID in the Customer table is no longer valid because the record that particular employee ID references is no longer available. The customer records that contain those references are called "orphans" after the Employee record is deleted.

Access has a method, called *referential integrity*, that prevents these situations and ensures that all references are synchronized. See "Enforce Referential Integrity" for instructions on how to ensure your relationships are not damaged when one part of a relationship is changed.

5. Drag the primary key field from one table to the equivalent foreign key field in another table. Verify the correct fields are shown in the Edit Relationships dialog box, shown in Figure 2-18. Click the Enforce Referential Integrity check box to select it (see the "Understanding Referential Integrity" QuickSteps). Click **Create** to establish the relationship. A relationship displays, as shown in Figure 2-15.

6. Continue dragging the primary key fields to foreign key fields until all chosen tables are related. When finished, click **OK** to close the Edit Relationships dialog box.

7. Click **Close** in the Design tab Relationships group (Relationship Tools) to close the Relationships tab. If prompted, select **Yes** to save changes to the relationships layout.

Enforce Referential Integrity

Referential integrity allows Access to check the validity of relationships between records. It also ensures that changes, such as deleting or altering related data, don't impair the relationships.

1. Open the database whose referential integrity you want to enforce.

2. In the Database Tools tab Relationships group, click **Relationships**.

3. In the Design tab Relationships group, click **All Relationships** to ensure that all relationships are displayed.

4. Double-click the line representing the relationship to which you want to apply referential integrity.

5. At the bottom of the Edit Relationships dialog box (see Figure 2-18), select **Enforce Referential Integrity**.

   ● Click **Cascade Update Related Fields** to ensure that changing a primary key value in the primary table automatically updates the foreign key field.

   ● Click **Cascade Delete Related Records** to ensure that when records are deleted in the primary table, corresponding records in a related table will also be deleted.

6. Click **OK** to return to the Relationships tab.

7. If prompted, select **Yes** to save changes to the relationships layout.

Chapter 3

Modifying Tables and Fields

As with any powerful machine, an Access database requires some fine-tuning to optimize its purpose and performance. The modifications covered in this chapter involve making changes to tables and adjustments to both table and field properties. Properties are those characteristics of an object (tables and fields in this case) that allow you to control how the object behaves. For example, you can use a field property to create an input mask that properly formats a Social Security number into the standard 3-2-4 digit style. Basic table changes can occur within the Navigation Pane, as shown in Figure 3-1. You can make some changes to table and field properties in Datasheet View, though Design View has been the historical location to make these changes, and continues to be where you have the full array of tools at your disposal.

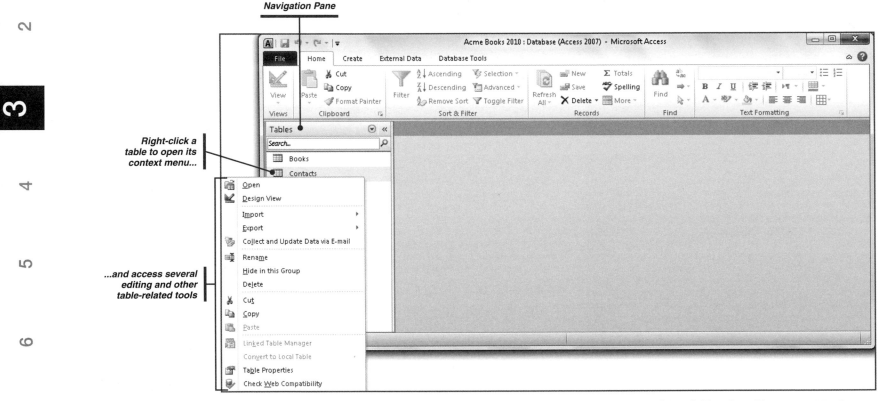

Navigation Pane

Right-click a table to open its context menu...

...and access several editing and other table-related tools

Figure 3-1: Basic edits to tables (and more) can be made from the Navigation Pane by right-clicking the table you want to change.

CAUTION

If the table is open, a dialog box will appear, saying that you cannot rename or delete the database object while it is open. Click **OK** and close the table. Chapters 1 and 2 describe how to work with tabbed and windowed objects.

Modify Tables and Table Properties

You will sometimes need to make basic changes to the objects in your database. For example, you may want to rename, delete, and/or copy tables. These common bookkeeping tasks can be performed from the Navigation Pane. If you want to fine-tune characteristics of the table, there is a collection of table properties that you can change to better fit the particular needs of an individual table.

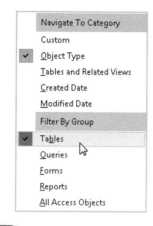

Delete a Table

When a table is no longer necessary, you can easily delete it.

1. Close the table you want to delete.

2. Within the Access window, expand the Navigation Pane. If you do not see the list of tables, click the **Navigation Pane** down arrow, and under Navigate To Category, click **Object Types**, and then click the **Navigation Pane** down arrow a second time. Under Filter By Group, click **Tables**.

3. Right-click the table you want deleted, and click **Delete**. A dialog box will appear, stating that deleting this table will remove it from all groups. Click **Yes** to confirm the deletion. This will bring you back to the Access window. (If you have established relationships between tables, continue to step 3.)

4. If you have established relationships between the table you want deleted and other tables, you will see another alert dialog box. (See Chapter 2 for information regarding table relationships.) The alert informs you of the need to delete the relationships with this table prior to its deletion. It also offers to delete the relationships for you. Click **Yes** if you would like to delete both the relationships and the table. This will bring you back to the Access window.

> **Microsoft Access** ☒
>
> ⚠ **You can't delete the table 'Customers' until its relationships to other tables have been deleted.**
> Do you want Microsoft Access to delete the relationships now?
>
> [Yes]   [No]

Rename a Table

In order to rename a table, you must have the table closed and be in the Access window.

Expand the Navigation Pane, if necessary. Right-click the table whose name you want to change, and click **Rename**. The name field will be highlighted. Type the new name, and press **ENTER**.

TIP

Don't panic if you mistakenly delete a table. Click **Undo** on the Quick Access toolbar, and the table will be restored.

TIP

Unlike versions of Access prior to Access 2007, you do not have to perform a separate procedure to save a table after you have changed its name or the name of a field. Access saves these changes automatically.

RENAMING AN ACCESS DATABASE

While you can rename an Access database from several locations using Windows Explorer, you can also easily do it from within Access. (To learn about file management using Microsoft Windows 7, read *Microsoft Windows 7 QuickSteps*, published by McGraw-Hill/Professional.)

1. Close the database whose name you want to change.

2. In Access, click the **File** tab, and click **Open**.

3. In the Open dialog box, locate the folder in which you store your database, and open the folder so that its files appear in the contents pane.

4. In the contents pane, right-click the database file whose name you want to change, and click **Rename**, as seen in Figure 3-2.

5. Type the new name for the database, and press **ENTER**.

Remember that Microsoft Access is a "relational database." That means all the objects within a table work together. As you learn more about making the individual components work together, renaming could disable some functions.

Figure 3-2: You can quickly rename a database from within Access using the Open dialog box.

–Or–

Click the table name to select it, and press the **F2** key to highlight the name field. Type the new name, and press **ENTER**. The new table name is displayed within the Navigation Pane.

Duplicate a Table by Copying

A quick way to set up a new table that conforms closely with a field structure you have already created is to copy an existing table's structure, with or without its data. To copy a table:

1. Close the table whose field structure you want to copy.

2. Within the Access window, expand the Navigation Pane. If you do not see the list of tables, click the **Navigation Pane** down arrow, and under Navigate To Category, click **Object Types,** and then click the **Navigation Pane** down arrow a second time. Under Filter By Group, click **Tables**.

3. Right-click the table you want to copy, and click **Copy**.

QUICKSTEPS

SWITCHING VIEWS

When editing tables, and the fields within those tables, you will be switching between Datasheet View and Design View frequently. There are several ways to switch views. Find the way that is quickest for you.

USE THE RIBBON

In the Home or Design tab, the Views group is available. Click the **View** button down arrow to display a list of the available views. Click the view that you want to use. (See Chapter 10 for information regarding PivotTable and PivotChart Views.)

–Or–

Click the upper half of the **View** button to switch to the last view that was displayed.

USE THE STATUS BAR

Click the particular **View** button for the view you want at the right end of the status bar.

USE A TABLE'S CONTEXT MENU

Right-click a table in the Navigation Pane.

–Or–

Right-click the tab of an open table.

In either case, click **Design View** or **Datasheet View**.

TIP

The property sheet is "docked" at the right side of the Design View pane. You can move the sheet by dragging its title bar, and then size it by dragging a side or corner.

4. Open the database in which you want the new table. Expand the Navigation Pane, and display the Table group.

5. Right-click in the Table group, and click **Paste**. In the Paste Table As dialog box, type a table name and select where to create the structure, with or without the data from the original table.

6. When finished, click **OK**. The new table appears in the Navigation Pane.

Change a Table's Properties

Unlike fields, whose properties are determined by the data type of a field, table properties are a generic set of properties that are available to all tables, though each table can have its own *attributes* (an attribute is a specific option that determines a property's behavior; for example, the Default View property has two attributes: Design View and Datasheet View). You can set all table properties in Design View, and you can access a subset of the full list in Datasheet View.

SET TABLE PROPERTIES IN DESIGN VIEW

Design View offers a complete list of a table's properties, as shown in Figure 3-3.

1. Switch to Design View (see the "Switching Views" QuickSteps).

2. If the table's property sheet is not displayed on the right of the Access window (see Figure 3-3), in the Design tab Show/Hide group (Table Tools), click **Property Sheet**.

–Or–

Press **ALT+ENTER**.

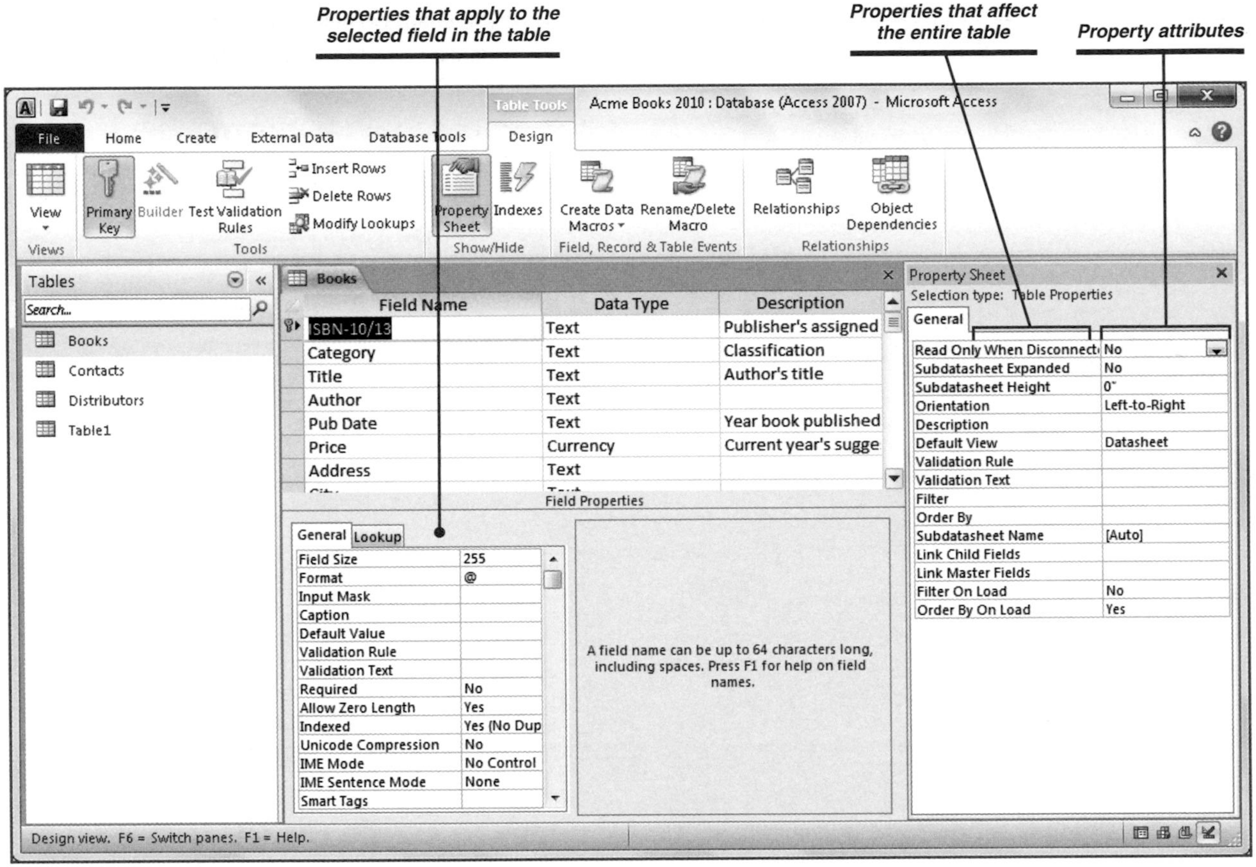

Figure 3-3: Table properties are listed on a property sheet that is initially displayed at the right side of the Design View pane.

3. You change property attributes in two different ways, depending on whether the attribute has a default setting or not.

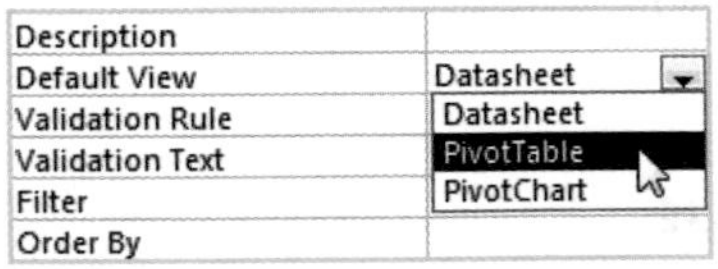

● For properties that have a selection of attributes, the default attribute is shown next to the property name. To change the attribute, click its box to display a down arrow. Click the attribute down arrow, and click another choice.

● For properties that don't have a default attribute, select an attribute by clicking its box and typing what you want. (Some properties show an Expression Builder icon ⋯ in their attributes' box when selected. Clicking the icon opens a dialog box that assists you in setting up the attribute. Building expressions is covered in later chapters.)

Enter Table Properties

Order By

Filter By

Orientation   Left-to-Right ▼

Read Only When Disconnected   No ▼

OK   Cancel

4. When finished, close the table or switch to Datasheet View. You will be prompted to either save the design of the table or save the table, respectively. In either case, click **OK**.

SET SELECTIVE TABLE PROPERTIES IN DATASHEET VIEW

While working with data in Datasheet View, you can set a few selective table properties.

1. Open a table in Datasheet View.

2. In the Table tab Properties group (Table Tools), click **Table Properties**.

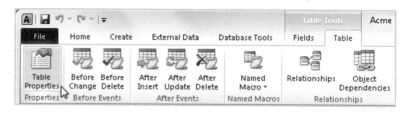

3. In the Enter Table Properties dialog box, enter or change the properties you want (filtering and ordering of data is covered in Chapter 5).

4. Click **OK** when finished.

Fine-Tune the Fields

The fine-tuning that can take place within fields and their properties is quite extensive. The first part of this fine-tuning revolves around the field's data type. As discussed in Chapter 2, there are several data types to choose from when first defining a field. This section takes you a step deeper into not only the data types, but also the properties that further define those data types. You can fine-tune your fields in either Datasheet or Design View, though Access will automatically assign a data type based on the data that's entered in a field.

Change a Data Type in Datasheet View

The mechanics of changing a data type, in either Datasheet View or Design View, is the same as initially establishing a database as discussed in Chapter 2.

TIP

To quickly enter a data type in the data type field in Design View, just type the first letter.

So, while it may be easy to change data types, this doesn't imply that you should do it without considering the ramifications to your database. For example, changing a field from Number or Currency to Text will change the alignment in the field from right-aligned to left-aligned (something you could easily change back), but more importantly, it will eliminate the possibility of performing calculations (you cannot "calculate" text). See the "Understanding Restrictions When Changing Data Types" QuickFacts for more concerns to think about before changing data types.

CHANGE A DATA TYPE IN DATASHEET VIEW

1. From the Navigation Pane, open the table to be customized.

2. Click anywhere in the column corresponding to the field you want to change.

3. In the Fields tab Add & Delete group (Table Tools), click one of the common data type buttons displayed in the group.

   –Or–

   Click the **More Fields** button to display the remaining data types (under Basic Types) and concurrent formatting choices for the Number, Date & Time, and Yes/No data types.

4. Select the data type or data type/formatting combination you want, as shown in Figure 3-4.

CHANGE A DATA TYPE IN DESIGN VIEW

If you are going to make several changes, or want to work with formatting beyond what is available on the Datasheet View Fields group, it is often easier to work in Design View.

1. From the Navigation Pane, right-click the table with which you want to work.

2. Switch to Design View (see the "Switching Views" QuickSteps).

3. Click the Data Type field you want to change. Click the down arrow that appears to display the list of data types.

4. Click the data type you want.

5. Press **CTRL+S** to save the change.

Figure 3-4: Much data type formatting can be done from the Datasheet View Fields tab.

UNDERSTANDING RESTRICTIONS WHEN CHANGING DATA TYPES

When you change a data type, the information you have already entered into your table may be affected. For example, if you change a data type from Memo to Text, since Text allows only 255 characters, all of the other information in that field will be deleted. The following data types cannot be changed:

- Attachment fields
- Number fields when you have chosen a field size setting of *Replication ID*—a special Microsoft setting that creates a randomly generated 16-byte number
- OLE Object fields

Table 3-1 lists some things to consider when changing from Text to several other data types.

ORIGINAL DATA TYPE	NEW DATA TYPE	CONCERNS
Text	Memo	None
	Number	The original text must be numbers. Also acceptable are currency symbols and decimals. The size set for the number of text characters must fit with the new number size.
	Date/Time	The original text must be recognizable as either a date or a time, such as 11-13-2010 or 13:50:27.
	Currency	The original text must be numbers and decimals.
	AutoNumber	Allowed *only* when the field is *not* the primary key.
	Yes/No	The original text must be Yes/No, On/Off, or True/False.
	Hyperlink	Access converts original text to a hyperlink if it is a Web address.

Table 3-1: Effects of Changing the Text Data Type

Change Display of Data Through the Format Property

One of the most used field properties is Format, which can be applied from both Datasheet View and Design View. Formatting options can be selected from a menu or can be applied using special formatting symbols. Which formatting options you have available are dependent on the field's data type (some data types have no selectable formatting options) and their appearance may differ between Datasheet and Design Views, for example.

Currency ▾
General Number
Currency
Euro
Fixed
Standard
Percent
Scientific

Currency formatting options (Datasheet View]

Currency ▾	
General Number	3456.789
Currency	$3,456.79
Euro	€3,456.79
Fixed	3456.79
Standard	3,456.79
Percent	123.00%
Scientific	3.46E+03

Currency formatting options (Design View)

Yes/No ▾
True/False
Yes/No
On/Off

Yes/No formatting options (Datasheet View)

Yes/No ▾	
True/False	True
Yes/No	Yes
On/Off	On

Yes/No formatting options (Design View)

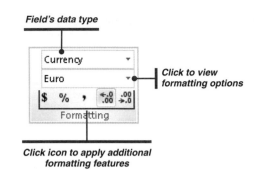

Field's data type

Click to view formatting options

Click icon to apply additional formatting features

SELECT FIELD FORMATTING IN DATASHEET VIEW

To apply formatting in Datasheet View:

1. Click a record within the field whose data type you want to format.

2. In the Fields tab Formatting group (Table Tools), the upper text shows the current data type for the field. Click the lower down arrow to view the field's formatting options, and click the one you want.

   –Or–

   If available, click one of the formatting icons.

SELECT FIELD FORMATTING IN DESIGN VIEW

1. Click the field in the Field Name, Data Type, or Description column at the top of the view whose data type you want to format. The field you chose will display a color (yellow by default) in the record selector field at the left of the row.

2. In the Fields Properties area, click the **General** tab, and then click the **Format** text box to view its down arrow.

3. Click the down arrow, and select the formatting options you want, as shown in Figure 3-5.

4. To view your changes, you need to switch to Datasheet View. Save the table when prompted.

Books

Field Name	Data Type	Description
ISBN-10/13	Text	Publisher's assigned number
Category	Text	Classification
Title	Text	Author's title
Author	Text	
Pub Date	Text	Year book published
Price	Currency	Current year's suggested retail price
Address	Text	
City	Text	

Field Properties

General | Lookup

Format	Euro	
Decimal Places	General Number	3456.789
Input Mask	Currency	$3,456.79
Caption	Euro	€3,456.79
Default Value	Fixed	3456.79
Validation Rule	Standard	3,456.79
Validation Text	Percent	123.00%
Required	Scientific	3.46E+03
Indexed	No	
Smart Tags		
Text Align	General	

The display layout for the field. Select a predefined format or enter a custom format. Press F1 for help on formats.

Figure 3-5: The Field Properties area within the Design View provides several ways to fine-tune the fields.

WORK WITH FORMAT SYMBOLS

You can change the way data is displayed (but not stored) in a database by entering specific symbols into the Format text box of the Field Properties area. Several symbols are used within the Format text box, many unique to one or two data types. The symbols used in the Text data type are listed in Table 3-2. See "Display All Characters in Uppercase" for one example of how to use format symbols.

DISPLAY ALL CHARACTERS IN UPPERCASE

You can format a field to display its contents in uppercase letters. For example, if you have a State field, you could ensure that all two-letter abbreviations, such as WA, are uppercase.

1. Open the table in Design View.

2. Click the field you want formatted. The field you chose will be outlined to confirm the field is active, and a color will appear in the record selector field at the left of the row.

3. Click the **General** tab in the Field Properties area.

4. Click the **Format** text box, and type $\geq$ (or to accomplish another formatting task, choose the appropriate symbol, as shown in Table 3-2). If you have additional objects within the database that use the field name, the Property Update Options Smart Tag will display to the left of the text box.

SYMBOL	DISPLAY PURPOSE
>	Uppercase characters.
<	Lowercase characters.
@	Placeholder for character or space. (Placeholders fill underlying data from right to left.)
&	Placeholder for character or optional space.
!	Left-aligns data and forces placeholders to fill from left to right; must be the first character in format string.
"Text"	Displays the item in quotation marks exactly as typed, in addition to data.
\	Displays a character immediately following data.
*	Fills all blank spaces with character following *.
[color]	Formats data text in black, blue, green, cyan, red, magenta, yellow, or white; must be used with other symbols.

Table 3-2: Formatting Symbols for Text Data Types

General	Lookup	
Field Size	255	
Format	⚡ ▾	>@
Input Mask		
Caption		Update Format everywhere Title is used
Default Value		
Validation Rule		Help on propagating field properties
Validation Text		

5. Click the **Property Update Options** Smart Tag down arrow, and click **Update Format Everywhere** *Fieldname* **Is Used**. By doing so, the format you have chosen will be propagated across all objects with the selected field name. For example, if you formatted the state field to uppercase, all state fields—whether in forms, queries, reports, or other tables—will be changed to uppercase. If no objects contain the same field name as your newly formatted field, a dialog box will display a message stating that no objects needed to be updated. Click **OK**.

> Microsoft Access ☒
>
> No objects needed to be updated.
>
> OK

6. In order to view your changes, you must save the table. If you try to switch views prior to saving, a dialog box will appear asking if you want to save the table now. Click **Yes** to save changes, and the display will switch to Datasheet View.

UNDERSTANDING INPUT MASKS

Input masks provide a pattern for formatting data within a field by using characters or symbols to control how data will be displayed. There are actually three parts to an input mask. The first part includes the mask characters or mask *string* (series of characters) along with embedded literal data—such as parentheses, periods, and hyphens. The second part is optional and refers to the embedded literal characters and their storage within the field. If the second part is set at "0," it will store the characters; "1" means the characters will only be displayed, not stored. The third part of the string indicates the single character used as a placeholder. An example of a telephone number input mask would be: **!\(999")"000\-0000;0;_**:

- Exclamation point (!) indicates the mask should fill data from right to left.

- Backslash (\) causes characters immediately following to be displayed as a literal character. In this case, the parenthesis is the literal character.

- "9" means optional digits can be entered into these spaces.

- Double quotation ("") is like the backslash, in that anything enclosed in this will be taken literally.

- "0" means a single digit is mandatory.

An example of the displayed phone number would be (555)555-1212. Table 3-3 provides more detailed descriptions of mask characters. However, Access provides an easier way to enter input masks than to create one from scratch. See "Create a Pattern for Data Entry with Input Masks" for information on using the Input Mask Wizard.

Create a Pattern for Data Entry with Input Masks

The Input Mask Wizard provides you with a guide to step you through selecting and creating an input mask.

1. Open a table in Design View.

2. Click the field for which you want to have an input mask.

3. In the General tab in the Field Properties area, click the **Input Mask** text box, and then click the **Builder** button at the right side of the text box to display the Input Mask Wizard. [...]

4. In the first Input Mask Wizard dialog box, under Input Mask, click the mask you want to use, as shown in Figure 3-6. (Click **Try It** to enter data and see how it will be displayed.) If no changes are needed, click **Next**. (The "Creating a Custom Input Mask" QuickSteps describes how to create your own input masks by modifying those on the list.)

5. If changes in the input mask are needed, type them in the Input Mask text box (see Table 3-2). Also, you can change the default placeholder character by clicking the **Placeholder Character** down arrow and selecting from the drop-down list. When finished, click **Next**.

Do you want to change the input mask?

| Input Mask Name: | Phone Number |
| Input Mask: | !(999) 000-0000 |

What placeholder character do you want the field to display?
Placeholders are replaced as you enter data into the field.

Placeholder character: _

Input Mask Wizard

Which input mask matches how you want data to look?

To see how a selected mask works, use the Try It box.

To change the Input Mask list, click the Edit List button.

Input Mask:	Data Look:
Phone Number	(206) 555-1212
Social Security Number	831-86-7180
Zip Code	98052-6399
Extension	63215
Password	*******
Long Time	1:12:00 PM

Try It: (555) 555-1234

Edit List   Cancel   < Back   Next >   Finish

Figure 3-6: Input masks assist in formatting common data types.

Continued . . .

QUICKSTEPS

CREATING A CUSTOM INPUT MASK

The Input Mask Wizard provides great sample patterns for some of the most common formatting situations. However, you may want to customize one of the patterns to use a format specific to your circumstances. There are two methods for doing this. The first is within the Input Mask Wizard itself, and the second is directly in the Input Mask text box.

1. Open your database in Design View, and click the field you would like to format with an input mask.

2. Click the **Builder** button (at the right of the Input Mask text box in the General tab of the Field Properties area) to start the Input Mask Wizard.

3. Click **Edit List** at the bottom of the first Input Mask Wizard page (see Figure 3-6). The Customize Input Mask Wizard dialog box will appear, as shown in Figure 3-7.

4. If you want the description to appear differently, type a new description in the Description text box. Press **TAB** to move to the Input Mask text box.

5. Type a new input mask based on the symbols listed in Table 3-3. Press **TAB** and type a placeholder symbol, as displayed in Figure 3-7, in the Placeholder text box. Press **TAB**. In the Sample Text box, type sample data to see how the mask will appear.

6. Press **TAB**, click the **Mask Type** down arrow, and choose a mask type. (More information about bound and unbound types can be found in Chapter 6.)

6. Choose **With The Symbols In The Mask** or **Without The Symbols In The Mask** to establish how to store your data. (Although choosing to store data with symbols allows them to be displayed in all objects, this method makes the size of your database slightly larger.) Click **Next** and then click **Finish** to return to Design View.

How do you want to store the data?
- ○ With the symbols in the mask, like this:
  (976) 472-3491
- ◉ Without the symbols in the mask, like this:
  63121454

Establish a Field's Default Value

In many cases, a field contained in multiple records will include the same data. For example, employees of a small company may all reside in the same state. Rather than entering that state several times, place a default value for the state name in field properties.

1. Open a table in Design View, and click the field you want to have a default value.

2. Click the **General** tab in the Field Properties area, and in the Default Value text box, type a value, and press **ENTER**. The typed value will automatically become enclosed in double quotes.

3. Press **CTRL+S** to save your table, and switch to Datasheet View to see how the default value has affected your table. You will notice that the new record row displays your new default value.

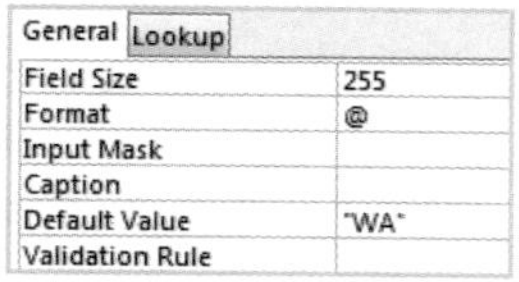

General	Lookup	
Field Size		255
Format		@
Input Mask		
Caption		
Default Value		"WA"
Validation Rule		

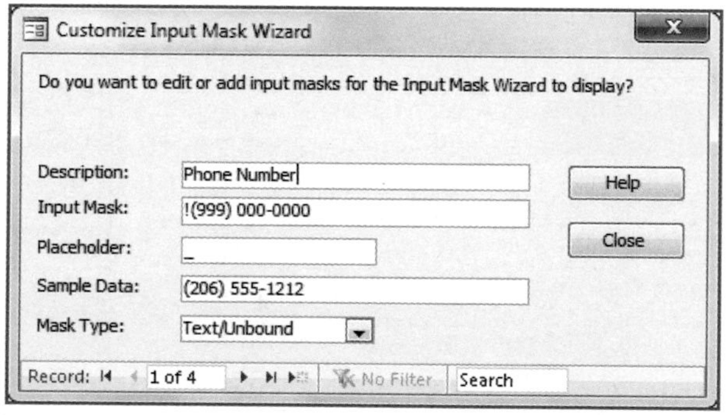

Customize Input Mask Wizard

Do you want to edit or add input masks for the Input Mask Wizard to display?

Description:	Phone Number		Help
Input Mask:	!(999) 000-0000		
Placeholder:	_		Close
Sample Data:	(206) 555-1212		
Mask Type:	Text/Unbound		

Record: 1 of 4 | No Filter | Search

Figure 3-7: You can create your own input mask by modifying an existing one.

QUICKSTEPS

CREATING A CUSTOM INPUT MASK

(Continued)

7. Click **Close**. The Input Mask Wizard dialog box appears, and your new input mask is listed within the sample list.

Input Mask:	Data Look:
Patient Chart Number	45-65666-66
Patient Phone Number	831-86-7180
Zip Code	98052-6399
Extension	63215
Password	*******
Long Time	1:12:00 PM

To manually edit or enter an input mask, simply click the **Input Mask** text box in the Field Properties area. Type your new mask based on the symbols found in Table 3-3.

Format	@
Input Mask	!00\-00000\-00;;-
Caption	

SYMBOL	EXPLANATION
0	Required single digit (0 to 9)
9	Optional digit (0 to 9)
#	A digit, a space, the plus sign, and the minus sign can be entered
L	Required letter
?	Optional letter
>	Converts all letters that follow to uppercase
<	Converts all letters that follow to lowercase
A	Required digit or letter
a	Optional digit or letter
&	Required character or space
C	Optional character or space
!	Mask will fill from right to left
\	Characters immediately following will be displayed literally
""	Characters enclosed in double quotation marks will be displayed literally

Table 3-3: Input Mask Definition Characters

CAUTION

Changing the default value of a field will affect only future entries, not records you have already entered into your database.

TIP

You can also establish a default value in Datasheet View by clicking **Default Value** [Default Value] in the Fields tab Properties group (Table Tools). In the upper Expression Builder text box, type a value and click **OK**. Chapter 5 describes the Expression Builder in more detail.

Expression Builder

Enter an Expression to return the <u>default</u> value of the field:
(Examples of expressions include [field1] + [field2] and [field1] < 5)

=WA

OK
Cancel
Help
<< Less

Limit Field Values with Validation

Validation rules set parameters around the values inputted. Access applies these validity checks during data entry. A validation rule is made up of an *expression* (a group of functions, characters, and field values) that defines the acceptable values. The expression may be entered manually, or you can use a tool called Expression Builder. Not a wizard, Expression Builder is more of an organizational tool that helps you see the fields you can use and the operators or functions that are available. Chapter 5 provides more detail on using Expression Builder. You can, and should, include some validation text with your validation rule. This text will be displayed in a dialog box if the rule is violated. For example, let's say you have an employee table that holds a "gender" field. It is designed to have either "M" for male or "F" for female. If a character other than "M" or "F" is entered into the field, the validation text will pop up in a dialog box to inform the user.

CREATE A VALIDATION RULE

1. Open a table in Datasheet View or Design View, and click the field you want to receive a validation rule and validation text.

2. In Design View, in the General tab of the Field Properties area, type your rule or expression in the Validation Rule text box, as shown in Figure 3-8. (To use the Expression Builder, click the **Builder** button).

   –Or–

   In Datasheet View, in the Fields tab Field Validation group (Table Tools), click **Validation**, and click **Field Validation Rule**. In the upper text box in Expression Builder, type your rule or develop it using expression components in the lower half of the dialog box (see Chapter 5). Click **OK**.

3. Right-click the table's tab, and click **Save**.

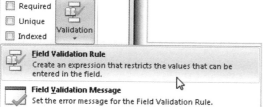

Type a validation rule...   ...or use the Expression Builder

Field Properties

General	Lookup
Field Size	255
Format	
Input Mask	
Caption	
Default Value	
Validation Rule	"M" Or "F"
Validation Text	Please enter M for male or F for female. Thank you!
Required	No
Allow Zero Length	Yes
Indexed	No
Unicode Compression	Yes
IME Mode	No Control
IME Sentence Mode	None
Smart Tags	

An expression that limits the values that can be entered in the field. Press F1 for help on validation rules.

Type text that will appear in an error dialog box

Figure 3-8: Validation rules should include validation text to aid in data entry.

SET UP A VALIDATION ERROR MESSAGE

You use the Validation Text property to provide a message to users that have violated your validation rule.

1. In Design View, in the General tab in the Field Properties area, type the text you want to appear in a dialog box in the Validation Text text box (see Figure 3-8). Press **ENTER**.

   –Or–

   In Datasheet View, in the Fields tab Field Validation group (Table Tools), click **Validation**, and click **Field Validation Message**. Type your validation text in the Enter Validation Message dialog box, and click **OK**.

2. Press **CTRL+S** to save your table, and select **Datasheet View** to experiment with data entry in the field with validation rules and text. If you don't adhere to the rule you established, Access will alert you with a dialog box and prevent you from making the illegal entry.

Require Entry but Allow a Zero-Length String

For certain fields within your database, you may want to require data entry in order to maintain integrity within your database structure. There are situations where an entry is important, but there is no data to place in the field(s). For example, in a customer table, you may choose to require entry of the customers' fax numbers in order to send reservation confirmations. Some customers, however, may not have a fax machine. You would want to require the entry but allow a *zero-length string*. This way, a blank space or double quotation marks (" ") could be entered into the fax number field, confirming the customer has no fax number.

1. Open a table in Datasheet View or Design View, and click the field you would like to make required.

2. In Design View, click the **General** tab in the Field Properties area. In the Required text box, click the down arrow at the right of the text box, and click **Yes** or **No**.

   –Or–

   In Datasheet View, in the Fields tab Field Validation group (Table Tools), click **Required**.

3. To establish the zero-length string, you need to be in Design View. In the Allow Zero Length text box, click its down arrow and click **Yes** or **No**.

4. Right-click the table's tab, and click **Save**. Switch to Datasheet View to experiment with required fields. If you don't type data in the required field, Access will alert you with a dialog box and prevent you from entering the record, as seen here.

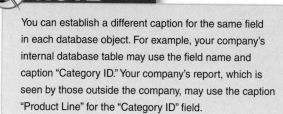

Microsoft Access

⚠ You must enter a value in the 'Books.Title' field.

OK   Help

Use the Caption Field Property

You may have noticed many of the wizard-based data fields have names with no embedded spaces. For example, rather than "Home Phone," the field name is "HomePhone." If you foresee growth in your database and the potential for upsizing it to a SQL-based database, it is a good idea to follow this practice. Chapter 10 describes upsizing to a Microsoft SQL Server. SQL databases, such as Oracle or Microsoft SQL Server, do not support spaces within names. To ensure that "friendly" names are displayed within your database, however, use the Caption Field property. This will display your field names in Datasheet View with embedded spaces.

1. Open a table in Datasheet View or Design View, and click the field name you would like to provide with a "friendly" name.

2. In Design View, click the **General** tab in the Field Properties area, and enter your "friendly" name for the field in the Caption text box, as shown in Figure 3-9.

   –Or–

   In Datasheet View, in the Fields tab Properties group (Table Tools), click **Name & Caption**. In the Enter Field Properties dialog box, type a caption and click **OK**.

3. Save the table when finished.

Enter Field Properties

Name	Pub_Date
Caption	Publication Date
Description	Year book published

OK   Cancel

Index a Data Field

An *index* is an internal table that contains two columns. One holds the value in the field or fields being indexed, and the other holds the physical location of each record in the table containing that value. Access uses an index in a manner

1
2
3
4
5
6
7
8
9
10

Field name acceptable for
use in other databases

User-friendly caption...

...appears as column
header in Datasheet View

Books

Field Name	Data Type	Description
ISBN-10/13	Text	Publisher's assigned number
Category	Text	Classification
Title	Text	Author's title
Author	Text	
Pub_Date	Text	Year book published
Price	Currency	Current year's suggested retail price
Address	Text	

Field Properties

General Lookup

Field Size	255
Format	@
Input Mask	
Caption	Publication Date
Default Value	
Validation Rule	
Validation Text	
Required	No
Allow Zero Length	Yes
Indexed	No
Unicode Compression	No
IME Mode	No Control
IME Sentence Mode	None
Smart Tags	

The label for the field when used on a form. If
you don't enter a caption, the field name is
used as the label. Press F1 for help on
captions.

Books

ISBN-10/13	Category	Title	Author	Publication Date
9780071496827	Computers	Ocp Oracle Dbase 11g New Feat	Alapati Sam	2008
0071408959	Business	Options Strategist	Allaire	2003
0830621369	Technical	Pbs Wells & Septic Systems	Alth	1991
9780072229387	Computers	Ht Do Everything W/Access 2003	Andersen Virgi	2003
9780072947755	Computers	Corporate Information Strategy	Applegate Lyn	2005
9780071486620	Computers	Do It Yourself Home Networking	Aspinwall Jim	2008

Figure 3-9: Use captions to make field names more intuitive for you and your users.

similar to how you use a book index: it finds the value desired and jumps
directly to the page, or place, where that value is held. Each time a record is
added to or updated in the database, Access updates all of its indexes. This may
sometimes slow down the process of data entry, however, so overuse of indexes
is not recommended.

1. Open a table in Design View, and click the field you want to have indexed.

2. In Design View, click the **General** tab in the Field Properties area, and click the
   Indexed down arrow, located to the right of the text box. "No" is the default choice

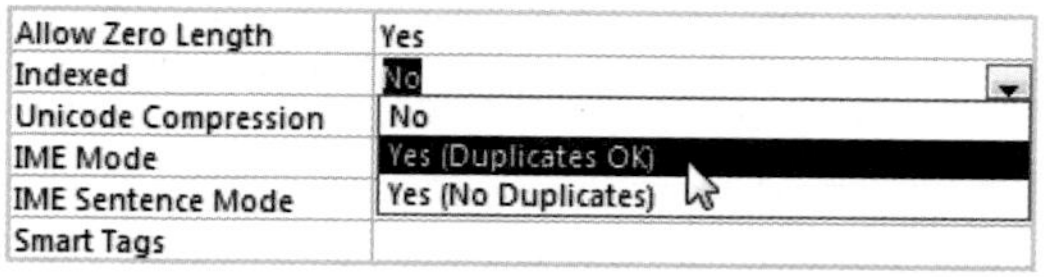

Allow Zero Length	Yes
Indexed	No
Unicode Compression	No
IME Mode	Yes (Duplicates OK)
IME Sentence Mode	Yes (No Duplicates)
Smart Tags	

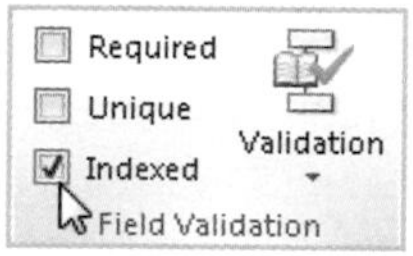

within the Indexed field. Click **Yes (Duplicates OK)** if the field will have multiple entries with the same value, or click **Yes (No Duplicates)** if you do not allow duplicate values in this field.

–Or–

In Datasheet View, in the Fields tab Field Validation group (Table Tools), click **Indexed** (this is the same as selecting **Yes (Duplicates OK)** in Design View).

3. Save your table.

Add Smart Tags

Smart Tags are like hyperlinks on steroids. They are little applications you can hook into fields to recognize items—such as names, addresses, or stock symbols—and provide options, or actions, for those recognized items. Smart Tags are limited in the number available within the standard Access application. There is, however, a button within the Smart Tags dialog box, as shown in Figure 3-10, that can connect you to Microsoft Office.com and let you check out current offerings within the Smart Tag product line. The current Smart Tags included with Access are:

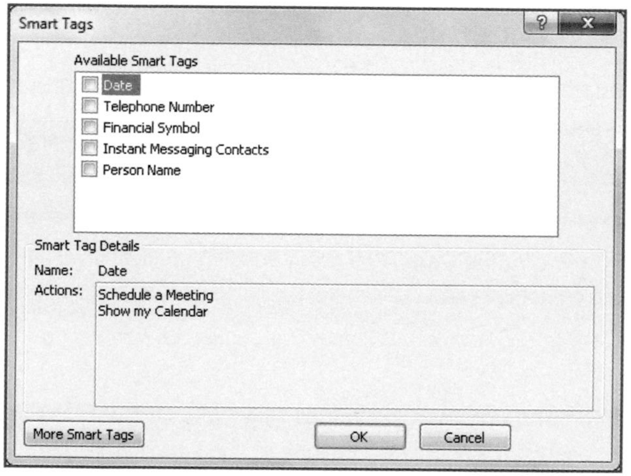

- **Date** is used to schedule a meeting or check your calendar within Microsoft Outlook.
- **Telephone Number** adds a telephone number to your Contacts list in Microsoft Outlook.
- **Financial Symbol** is used to obtain a stock quote, company reports, or news surrounding an accepted New York Stock Exchange (NYSE) or National Association of Securities Dealers Automated Quotations (NASDAQ) company—all from the MSN MoneyCentral Web site.
- **Instant Messaging Contacts** provides access to the contacts in your Microsoft Messenger instant messaging program.
- **Person Name** is used to accept a person's name or e-mail address and, assuming you are using Microsoft Outlook, send an e-mail, schedule a meeting, open your Contacts list, or add the name to your Contacts list.

Figure 3-10: Accomplish common tasks using Smart Tags.

When a Smart Tag is added to your field, a drop-down menu will be displayed as your mouse pointer hovers over the field within the record. This menu will provide the previously listed Smart Tag options.

1. Open a table in Design View, and click the field in which you would like to include a Smart Tag.

2. In the General tab in the Field Properties area, click the **Builder** button to the right of the Smart Tags text box. The Smart Tags dialog box will appear (see Figure 3-10).

3. Click any of the Smart Tags that you want to apply to your field, and the available actions (menu choices) will be displayed in the Smart Tag Details area of the dialog box.

4. Click **OK** to return to Design View. Save the table and switch to Datasheet View to experiment with Smart Tags.

Use the Lookup Wizard

There are times when the data to be entered in a field can be found in another table, and/or the data is a series of data points that would benefit from being provided only once to eliminate data entry errors. Rather than selecting a data type for your field, it may be helpful to call upon the Lookup Wizard to create a drop-down list of values from which you can choose.

START THE LOOKUP WIZARD

1. Open a table in Design View, and click the **Data Type** down arrow in the field in which you would like to include a list of lookup data.

2. Scroll to the bottom of the list, and click **Lookup Wizard**. The Lookup Wizard dialog box will appear.

3. Click **I Want The Lookup Column To Look Up The Values In A Table Or Query** to pull data from an existing table or query. Click **Next** and continue through the next page.

   –Or–

   Click **I Will Type In The Values That I Want** if you would like to create your own data list. Click **Next** and skip to "Create Your Own Value List with the Lookup Wizard."

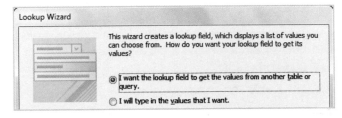

FIND YOUR LOOKUP VALUES IN A TABLE OR QUERY

1. Use steps 1–3 of "Start the Lookup Wizard," and select the first option in step 3.

2. Click **Tables**, **Queries**, or **Both** to display their contents.

3. Select a specific table or query, and click **Next**. A dialog box with the available fields will appear.

4. Select the field you would like to include in the lookup column, and click the single right arrow to add the field to the Selected Fields box, as shown in Figure 3-11. Continue this process until you have chosen all the desired fields. If you would like to remove any of the fields from the selected field box, simply select the field, and click the single left arrow. (Click a double arrow to move all fields at once.) Click **Next**.

5. Choose to sort field(s) by ascending or descending order (Chapter 5 describes sorting in more detail). Click **Next**.

Click to move the selected Available Field to the Selected Fields list

Click to move all Available Fields to the Selected Fields list

Click to remove selected or all fields

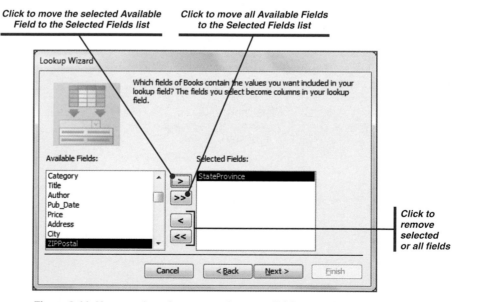

Figure 3-11: You can draw from more than one field to provide lookup data.

6. Adjust the column width for your lookup fields in the next page of the wizard. Do this by placing the mouse pointer near the right edge of the column header. When a double-headed arrow appears, drag the column to the desired width.

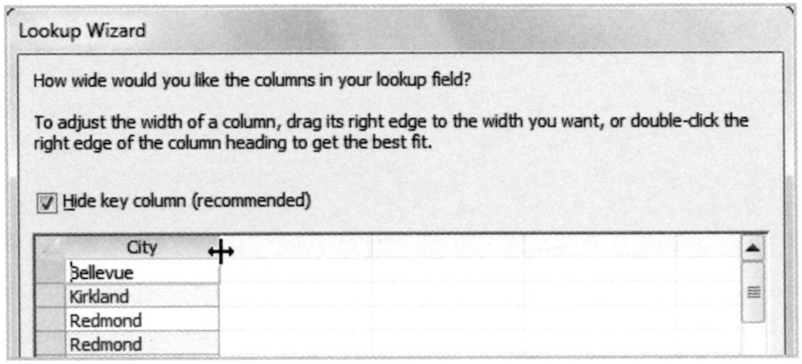

–Or–

Double-click the right edge of the column header to have Access fit the column to the widest entry. Click **Next** when satisfied with the results.

7. Clear the **Hide Key Column** check box if you want to include the primary key in your list of options. Access recommends that you hide this column. Click **Next**.

8. In the final Lookup Wizard dialog box (see Figure 3-12):

   • Accept the default label for the lookup column, or type a new name.

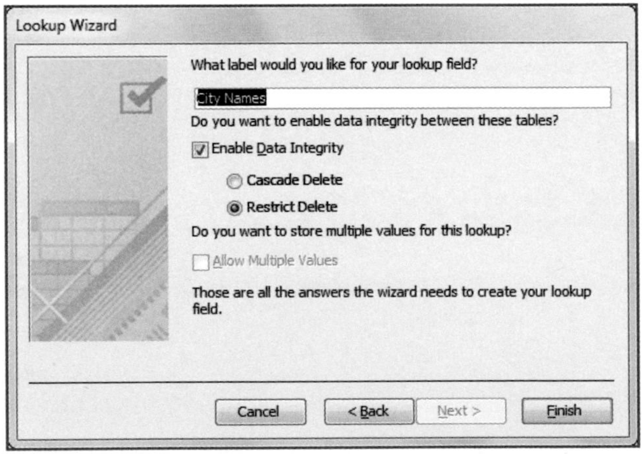

Figure 3-12: You can name your lookup field and select data options.

1
2
3
4
5
6
7
8
9
10

- Click the **Enable Data Integrity** check box and accept the default Restrict Delete to prevent deletions in the source table(s) that would affect the lookup values.

- Click **Allow Multiple Values** (only available if Enable Data Integrity is unchecked) if you want Access to store the values you just entered so that you can choose more than one value for each record. These values will display as a drop-down list of check boxes when the table is in Datasheet View. (See the "Deciding to Use a Multivalued Field" QuickFacts later in the chapter.) Click **Finish**.

9. Save your table and switch to Datasheet View to enter data using the lookup column.

Field Properties	
General Lookup	
Display Control	Combo Box
Row Source Type	Table/Query
Row Source	SELECT [Employees].[ID], [Employees].[City], [Employees].
Bound Column	1
Column Count	3
Column Heads	No
Column Widths	0";1";1"
List Rows	16
List Width	2"
Limit To List	Yes
Allow Multiple Values	No
Allow Value List Edits	Yes
List Items Edit Form	
Show Only Row Source V	No

NOTE

A Lookup field has its own set of properties listed in the Lookup tab in the Field Properties area of Design View.

CREATE YOUR OWN VALUE LIST WITH THE LOOKUP WIZARD

This option allows you to have a set group of values from which you can choose when entering data.

1. Display the Lookup Wizard (see steps 1–3 of "Use the Lookup Wizard").

2. Select **I Will Type In The Values That I Want**, and click **Next**.

3. Type your first value in the empty field, and press **TAB**, as shown in Figure 3-13. Continue entering values until your list is complete. If multiple columns of data are desired, enter the appropriate number in the Number Of Columns text box.

4. Adjust the column width by placing the mouse pointer near the right edge of the column header. When a double-headed arrow appears, drag the column to the desired width.

–Or–

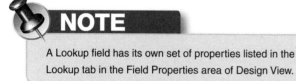

Figure 3-13: Create your own lookup list by typing in the available values.

TIP

You can edit your own value list directly in the Row Source text box of the Lookup tab in Design View; however, lists generated from another table or query need to be edited in their source object.

QUICKFACTS

DECIDING TO USE A MULTIVALUED FIELD

While the ability to use more than one value in a field is useful, as with all parts of your database, think it through carefully before making the decision. In some cases, having more than one value in a field can reduce the functionality of your database should you ever need to move it to another, larger database system, such as Oracle or Microsoft SQL Server. However, if any of the following apply to your database, multiple values may be just what you need. Consider using multiple values in a field when:

- You have a current list of values that are used repeatedly.
- There are a small number of choices a user could make when entering data.
- You work with a database that often accesses a SharePoint site.
- You need to link your database with a SharePoint site.

Double-click the right edge of the column header to have Access fit the column to the widest entry.

5. Click **Next** when satisfied with the results.

6. In the last page of the wizard:
- Accept the default label for the lookup column, or type a new name.
- Click the **Limit To List** check box to select it to prevent users from using values that are not on your list.
- Click the **Allow Multiple Values** check box if you want Access to store the values you just entered so that you can choose more than one value for each record. (See the "Deciding to Use a Multivalued Field" QuickFacts later in the chapter.) Click **Finish**.

7. Save your table and switch to Datasheet View to enter data using the lookup column.

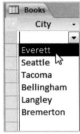

EDIT THE LOOKUP LIST

After entering your data in a lookup list, you may find you need to add an item to this list.

1. Open a table in Datasheet View or Design View, and click the field with the lookup column.

2. In Design View, click the **Lookup** tab in the Field Properties area. In the Row Source text box:
- Add values to the end of your list by typing the values enclosed in double quotation marks ("value") and separated with semicolons ("value1";"value2").

	Field Properties
Display Control	Combo Box
Row Source Type	Value List
Row Source	"Everett";"Seattle";"Tacoma";"Bellingham";"Langley";"Bremerton";""
Bound Column	1

- Delete any values in your list by selecting the entire value, including quotation marks and semicolon, and pressing **DELETE**.

Once you have created a multivalue lookup field from an existing table or query, you cannot change either the data type or the field size of your lookup field without deleting the relationships.

The Calculated data type allows you to create expressions in the Expression Builder that provide the values in the field. To create calculated values, in Design View, click the **Data Type** down arrow in the field in which the value will be contained, and click **Calculated**. See Chapter 5 for more information on using the Expression Builder to create expressions.

3. In Datasheet View, in the Fields tab Properties group (Table Tools), click **Modify Lookups**. The Lookup Wizard opens to the screen where you add values (see Figure 3-13). Add or remove values, and complete the wizard (see "Create Your Own Value List with the Lookup Wizard").

4. Save your table and use Datasheet View to enter data using the lookup column.

Chapter 4
Working in the Table

Data is Access's *raison d'etre* (or reason to be), yet before we can organize the data, retrieve it, present it, or otherwise *use* it, we have to get it into a table. Chapters 2 and 3 described how to create a database, set up a table design, and change the properties of the table fields so that data entered into the table will conform to formatting, input masks, and other rules you establish.

In this chapter you will learn how to add data to a table in Datasheet View, as shown in Figure 4-1, which includes acquiring data from external sources. In addition, you will learn how to format the table to better present the data or emphasize just the data you want to see.

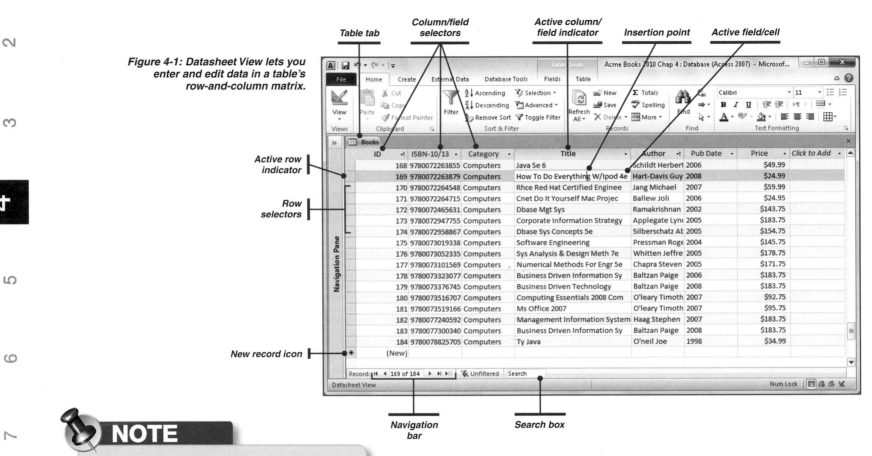

Figure 4-1: Datasheet View lets you enter and edit data in a table's row-and-column matrix.

Table tab

Column/field selectors

Active column/ field indicator

Insertion point

Active field/cell

Active row indicator

Row selectors

New record icon

Navigation bar

Search box

NOTE

The terms *datasheet* and *table* are often confused, and no wonder, because they can refer to the same Access component. Strictly speaking, a datasheet can be one of several matrix-based containers for storing data, for example, a table, the result set of a query, and a datasheet in a form. Most of the techniques described in this chapter for use in tables are also applicable to other forms of datasheets. The same goes for *fields* and *columns*. Fields are the design elements, and columns are the structural elements in a datasheet/table. The confusion usually arises when field names appear in column headers.

Enter and Edit Data

This section will show you ways to populate a designed table with new data you enter. You will also see how to modify data you add to the datasheet by using editing techniques that include moving and copying, locating and replacing data, using a dictionary to flag spelling mistakes, and automatically correcting data as you type. Since data entry is keyboard-intensive, you will learn several shortcuts to move around a datasheet and edit the information you enter without using a mouse.

Enter Data in an Existing Table

You use the keyboard to type new data into the table. You will start adding data in the new record at the end of the datasheet (see Chapter 2 for information on creating a table and adding data to it; Chapter 3 describes how to design a table). The last blank row in the datasheet, identified with a large asterisk in its row selector, is the new record row into which you add new data.

1. Do one of the following:

   ● Click a field in the new record row (see the last row shown in Figure 4-1 with (New) in its first field).

   ● Click the new record button 🔲 on the navigation bar.

   ● In the Home tab Find group, click **Go To** ➡▾ and click **New**.

   ● In the Home tab Records group, click **New**.

   In each case, the first field in the new record row is selected.

2. Type the value you want in the first field, and press **TAB** or **ENTER**. If you do not have a value to add to a field (you do not have to type a value in a field unless it has a field property requiring you to do so), press **TAB** or **ENTER** until the insertion point is in the field you want, or click the next field you want to enter a value into.

   As soon as you start typing in the new record row, a new row is added to the bottom of the table.

Use Keyboard Shortcuts in a Table

Data entry is largely done using the keyboard. Becoming familiar with using the keyboard for other related tasks can be quite a time-saver.

USE THE KEYBOARD TO NAVIGATE

Table 4-1 lists several of the more commonly used keyboard shortcuts for navigating within a table.

USE THE KEYBOARD TO INSERT DATA

Table 4-2 lists several shortcuts for inserting commonly used information and performing other tasks.

TO MOVE...	PRESS...
To the next (to the right) field	**TAB**, **RIGHT ARROW**, or **ENTER** (see the Tip on changing the behavior of using **ENTER** in the datasheet)
To the previous (to the left) field	**SHIFT+TAB** or **LEFT ARROW**
To the last field in the active record	**END**
To the first field in the active record	**HOME**
Up one record at a time in the same field	**UP ARROW**
Up to the first record in the same field	**CTRL+UP ARROW**
Up one screen	**PAGE UP**
Down one record at a time in the same field	**DOWN ARROW**
Down to the last record in the same field	**CTRL+DOWN ARROW**
Down one screen	**PAGE DOWN**
The first field in the first record	**CTRL+HOME**
The last field in the last record	**CTRL+END**
Right one screen	**CTRL+PAGE DOWN**
Left one screen	**CTRL+PAGE UP**

Table 4-1: Shortcuts for Navigating in a Datasheet

TO...	PRESS...
Add a new record	**CTRL++**
Delete the current record	**CTRL+-**
Insert the current time	**CTRL+SHIFT+:**
Insert the current date	**CTRL+;**
Insert the same value from the same field in the previous record	**CTRL+'**

Table 4-2: Shortcuts for Inserting Commonly Used Information

USE THE KEYBOARD TO EDIT DATA

Table 4-3 lists shortcuts for editing data.

USE THE KEYBOARD TO SELECT DATA

Table 4-4 lists shortcuts for selecting data.

Copy and Move Data

You can duplicate or remove data within a table by using the standard copy, cut, and paste techniques, as well as the Office Clipboard (see the "Using the Office Clipboard" QuickSteps). See also "Use Keyboard Shortcuts in a Table" and the "Selecting Records, Fields, and Columns with the Mouse" QuickSteps for ways to select fields and records.

QUICKSTEPS

MOVING THROUGH RECORDS

The navigation bar at the bottom of a table (see Figure 4-2) and the Go To tool in the Find group provide several options for quickly getting to the record you want in a datasheet.

B *I* **U**

- First
- Previous
- Next
- Last
- New

MOVE TO THE FIRST RECORD

Click the **First Record** button on the navigation bar.

Continued . . .

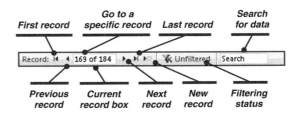

Figure 4-2: The navigation bar provides several ways to quickly locate records.

QUICKSTEPS

MOVING THROUGH RECORDS
(Continued)

–Or–

In the Home tab Find group, click **Go To** and click **First**.

MOVE TO THE LAST RECORD

Click the **Last Record** button on the navigation bar.

–Or–

In the Home tab Find group, click **Go To** and click **Last**.

MOVE TO THE NEXT RECORD

Click the **Next Record** button on the navigation bar.

–Or–

In the Home tab Find group, click **Go To** and click **Next**.

MOVE TO THE PREVIOUS RECORD

Click the **Previous Record** button on the navigation bar.

–Or–

In the Home tab Find group, click **Go To** and click **Previous**.

MOVE TO A SPECIFIC RECORD

Select the record number in the Current Record box, type the record number you want to move to, and press **ENTER**.

TO...	PRESS...
Undo a typing action	CTRL+Z
Cancel typing actions in a record	ESC (pressing once cancels actions in the current field; pressing a second time cancels actions for the record)
Delete the character to the left of the insertion point	BACKSPACE
Delete the character to the right of the insertion point	DELETE
Delete all characters in a word to the right of the insertion point	CTRL+DELETE
Move one character to the right (if this takes you one field to the right, press F2)	RIGHT ARROW
Move one character to the left (if this takes you one field to the left, press F2)	LEFT ARROW
Move to the beginning of the next word to the right	CTRL+RIGHT ARROW
Move to the beginning of the previous word to the left	CTRL+LEFT ARROW
Move to the end of the field	END
Move to the beginning of the field	HOME

Table 4-3: Shortcuts for Editing Data

TO...	PRESS...
Select a character to the right	SHIFT+RIGHT ARROW
Select a character to the left	SHIFT+LEFT ARROW
Select remaining characters in a word to the right	CTRL+SHIFT+RIGHT ARROW
Select remaining characters in a word to the left	CTRL+SHIFT+LEFT ARROW
Select the next field	TAB
Extend the selection above a selected record	SHIFT+UP ARROW
Select a record below a selected record	SHIFT+DOWN ARROW
Select all records	CTRL+A

Table 4-4: Shortcuts for Selecting Data

QUICKSTEPS

USING THE OFFICE CLIPBOARD

The Office Clipboard is shared by all Microsoft Office products. You can copy objects and text from any Office application and paste them into another. The Clipboard contains up to 24 items. The 25th item will overwrite the first one, and the list is cleared when your computer is rebooted.

OPEN THE CLIPBOARD

To display the Office Clipboard, in the Home tab Clipboard group, click the **Dialog Box Launcher** 🔲 The Clipboard task pane will open, as shown in Figure 4-3.

ADD TO THE CLIPBOARD

When you cut or copy text, it is automatically added to the Office Clipboard.

COPY CLIPBOARD ITEMS TO A PLACEHOLDER

To paste one item:

1. Click to place the insertion point in the cell where you want the item on the Office Clipboard inserted.

2. Click the item on the Clipboard to be inserted.

To paste all items:

1. Click to place the insertion point in the cell where you want the items on the Office Clipboard inserted.

2. Click **Paste All** on the Clipboard.

DELETE ITEMS ON THE CLIPBOARD

1. To delete all items, click **Clear All** on the Clipboard task pane.

2. To delete a single item, point to an item, click the arrow next to it, and click **Delete**.

SET CLIPBOARD OPTIONS

1. On the Clipboard task pane, click the **Options** down arrow at the bottom. A context menu is displayed.

Continued . . .

Figure 4-3: The Clipboard task pane allows you to store the last 24 items you copied or cut and paste them into other Office applications.

COPY AND MOVE CHARACTERS

1. In Datasheet View, select the characters you want to copy or move.

2. In the Home tab Clipboard group, click **Copy** 🔳, or right-click the selection and click **Copy**. A duplicate of the selected data is placed on the Clipboard, and the original data is retained.

   –Or–

   In the Home tab Clipboard group, click **Cut** ✂, or right-click the selection and click **Cut**. A duplicate of the selected data is placed on the Clipboard, and the original data is removed.

3. In the destination field, either place your insertion point where you want the new characters inserted or select characters that will be overwritten by the new characters.

4. In the Home tab Clipboard group, click **Paste** (the upper half of the icon); or right-click where you want to add the characters, and click **Paste**.

2. Click an option to select or clear it:

- **Show Office Clipboard Automatically** always shows the Office Clipboard when copying.

- **Show Office Clipboard When CTRL+C Pressed Twice** shows the Office Clipboard when you press **CTRL+C** twice to make two copies (in other words, copying two items to the Clipboard will cause the Clipboard to be displayed).

- **Collect Without Showing Office Clipboard** copies items to the Clipboard without displaying it.

- **Show Office Clipboard Icon On Taskbar** displays the icon on the notification area of the taskbar when the Clipboard is being used.

- **Show Status Near Taskbar When Copying** displays a message about the items being added to the Clipboard as copies are made.

TIP

If you are more comfortable using keyboard shortcuts, you can use **CTRL+C**, **CTRL+X**, and **CTRL+V** for copy, cut, and paste actions, respectively.

CAUTION

Records are usually pasted to the end of the table because most tables have a primary key set to the AutoNumber data type. Any records added to the table are given a unique, sequential number. If you copy or move records within the same table, you may have the same data in two or more records or cause other irregularities in your data.

COPY AND MOVE FIELDS

In Datasheet View, select the fields you want to copy or move (see the "Selecting Records, Fields, and Columns with the Mouse" QuickSteps).

1. In the Home tab Clipboard group, click **Copy**, or right-click the selection and click **Copy**. A duplicate of the selected data is placed on the Clipboard, and the original data is retained.

   –Or–

   In the Home tab Clipboard group, click **Cut**, or right-click the selection and click **Cut**. A duplicate of the selected data is placed on the Clipboard, and the original data is removed.

2. Select an equivalent block of fields where you want the new data. For example, if you selected three adjacent fields in a record that you wanted to copy, ensure that you select three adjacent destination fields where you want the data pasted.

3. In the Home tab Clipboard group, click **Paste**; or right-click the selected fields, and click **Paste**. Any existing data in the destination fields will be overwritten by the new data.

COPY OR MOVE RECORDS

1. In Datasheet View, select the records you want to copy or move.

2. In the Home tab Clipboard group, click **Copy**, or right-click the selection and click **Copy**. A duplicate of the selected records is placed on the Clipboard, and the original records are retained.

   –Or–

   In the Home tab Clipboard group, click **Cut**, or right-click the selection and click **Cut**. A duplicate of the selected records is placed on the Clipboard, and the original records are removed.

3. In the Home tab Clipboard group, click the **Paste** down arrow (the lower half of the icon), and click **Paste Append**. The copied or moved records will be added to the end of the table.

Delete Records and Columns

In Access, unlike most Office programs, when you remove data by deleting records and columns, you cannot undo your actions. However, Access will ask you to confirm your deletions before they are irretrievably gone.

QUICKSTEPS

SELECTING RECORDS, FIELDS, AND COLUMNS WITH THE MOUSE

Start with your table opened in Datasheet View.

SELECT RECORDS

- To select a single record, click the record selector to the left of the record (see Figure 4-1).

    –Or–

- Place the insertion point in the record. In the Home tab Find group, click the **Select** tool, and click **Select** a second time from its menu.

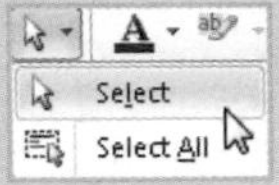

In either case, the record becomes highlighted with an orange border.

- To select adjacent records, point at the first/last row selector in the group you want to select. When the mouse pointer becomes a right-pointing arrow ➡, drag over the selectors of the records. The selected rows are shaded and surrounded by an orange border.

    –Or–

- Select the first row in a contiguous list, press and hold down **SHIFT**, and press the last record in the list.

- To select all records, in the Home tab Find group, click **Select** and click **Select All**.

SELECT DATA IN A FIELD

To select partial data in a field, drag over the characters you want.

SELECT FIELDS

- To select a single field, point at the left or right edge of the field. When the pointer changes to a large cross, click your mouse button.

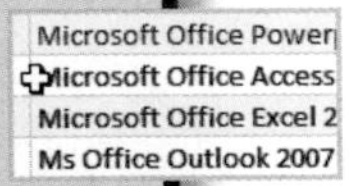

Continued . . .

DELETE RECORDS

1. Select the record(s) you want to delete (see "Selecting Records, Fields, and Columns with the Mouse" QuickSteps for ways to select records).

2. In the Home tab Records group, click **Delete**.

    –Or–

    Right-click the selection and click **Delete Record**.

3. Click **Yes** to confirm your deletion.

DELETE COLUMNS

1. Select the column(s) you want to delete (see the "Selecting Records, Fields and Columns with the Mouse" QuickSteps for ways to select columns).

2. In the Home tab Records group, click **Delete** (the button, not the down arrow).

    –Or–

    Right-click the selection and click **Delete Field**.

3. Click **Yes** to confirm your deletion.

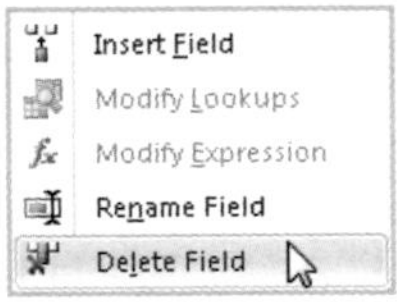

Find and Replace Text

In tables that might span thousands of rows and columns, you need the ability to locate data quickly, as well as to find instances of the same data so that consistent replacements can be made.

FIND DATA

1. Open a table in Datasheet View.

2. In the Home tab Find group, click **Find**, or press **CTRL+F** to open the Find And Replace dialog box, shown in Figure 4-4. If it isn't selected, click the **Find** tab.

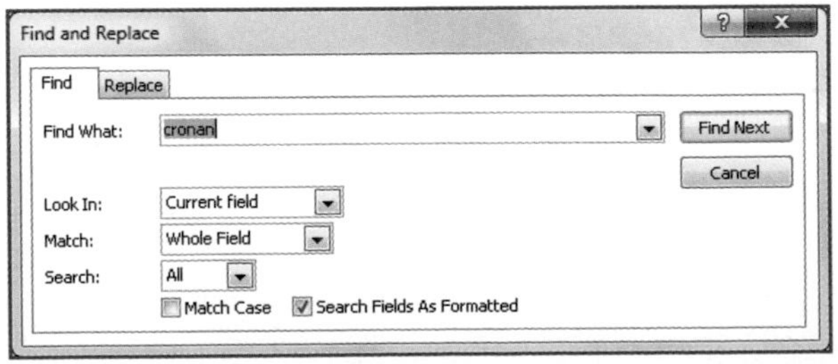

Figure 4-4: The Find tab lets you refine your search based on several criteria.

3. Type the characters you want to find in the Find What text box.

4. Click the **Look In** down arrow, and choose whether to search the entire table or just the field where the insertion point is currently located.

5. Click the **Match** down arrow, and choose one of the following:

   - **Any Part Of Field** to locate fields that contain the searched-for characters embedded in any text within a field. (For example, searching for "pen" would find fields that contained "opening".)

   - **Whole Field** to locate fields that contain only the searched-for characters. (For example, searching for "pen" would find fields that contained only "pen".)

   - **Start Of Field** to locate fields that contain the searched-for characters at the beginning of the field. (For example, searching for "pen" would find fields that contained "Penn Station".)

6. Click the **Search** down arrow to determine the scope of the search. Choose among the following:

   - **All** searches the entire datasheet.

   - **Up** searches from the current insertion point location toward the first record.

   - **Down** searches from the current insertion point location toward the last record.

7. Select the **Match Case** check box to only find fields that match the case of the characters. (For example, searching for "pen" would not find "Penn Station" but would find "pencil".)

8. Note the Search Fields As Formatted check box. This check box may or may not be selected according to whether Access has determined there is an input mask, that is, a type of formatting used in the field (or in the case of a lookup field, in the table or query from which its values are drawn). It's best to simply leave the option as Access has determined. If your search results don't seem to be working as expected, try selecting or clearing the check box. If the search/replace still does not work, try the steps in the accompanying Caution.

9. Click **Find Next**.

CALCULATING DATA IN A FIELD

You can add a row that provides options for performing calculations on the data within a field.

ADD THE TOTAL ROW

1. Open a table in Datasheet View.

2. In the Home tab Records group, click **Totals** Σ . A new row labeled "Total" is added to the bottom of the table.

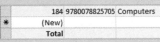

The Total row remains visible at the bottom of the datasheet as you scroll up through your records.

CALCULATE DATA

1. Click the field in the Total row whose data you want to calculate, and click the down arrow that appears.

2. Click the calculation method you want to apply to the data in the column. The result is displayed in the Total row.

REMOVE THE TOTAL ROW

In the Home tab Records group, click **Totals**.

CAUTION

You may not be able to find (and replace) text in tables where an input mask was applied after data was entered and the data doesn't meet the conditions of the input mask. To work around this problem, remove the input mask, perform the find-and-replace action, and reapply the input mask. See Chapter 3 for more information on input masks.

REPLACE DATA

The Replace tab of the Find And Replace dialog box (see Figure 4-4) looks and behaves similar to the Find tab covered earlier.

1. Open a table in Datasheet View.

2. In the Home tab Find group, click **Find** and click the **Replace** tab, or press **CTRL+H**. Either method opens the Find And Replace dialog box with the Replace tab displayed.

3. Type the characters you want to be found and replaced in the Find What text box.

4. Type the replacement characters in the Replace With text box. If specific search criteria are needed, see "Find Data" for the options' descriptions.

5. Click **Find Next** and then click **Replace** to make replacements one at a time.

–Or–

Click **Replace All** to perform all replacements at once.

Verify Spelling

You can check the spelling of selected fields, columns, records, or the entire table using Access's main dictionary and a custom dictionary you add words to. (Both are shared with other Office programs).

1. Open a table in Datasheet View.

2. Select the fields, columns, or records to check. If nothing is selected, the entire table will be checked.

3. In the Home tab Records group, click **Spelling** or press **F7**. When the spelling checker doesn't find anything to report, you are told the spelling check is complete. Otherwise, the Spelling dialog box appears, as shown in Figure 4-5.

Figure 4-5: The Spelling dialog box provides several options to handle misspelled or uncommon words.

TIP

If the correct spelling of a misspelled word is not shown in the Suggestions list box, edit the word in the Not In Dictionary text box, and click **Add** to include it in a custom dictionary that is checked in addition to the main dictionary.

4. With a highlighted word in the Not In Dictionary/Capitalization text box, you may change the characters by picking from the Suggestions list and clicking **Change** or **Change All** to replace the current or all occurrences of the highlighted word. If you have a correct term that is not found in the dictionary, you may:

- Click **Ignore 'Field' Name** to discontinue searching in the current column for misspelled or incorrectly capitalized words.

- Click **Ignore** to disregard the current occurrence of the word shown in the Not In Dictionary/Capitalization text box.

- Click **Ignore All** to disregard all occurrences of the word shown in the Not In Dictionary/Capitalization text box.

5. Click **AutoCorrect** if you want to automatically replace words in the future. (See the next section, "Modify Automatic Corrections," for more information on using AutoCorrect.)

6. Click **Options** to open the Access Options Proofing page (see Figure 4-6), where you can change languages, create and modify custom dictionaries, and set other spelling criteria.

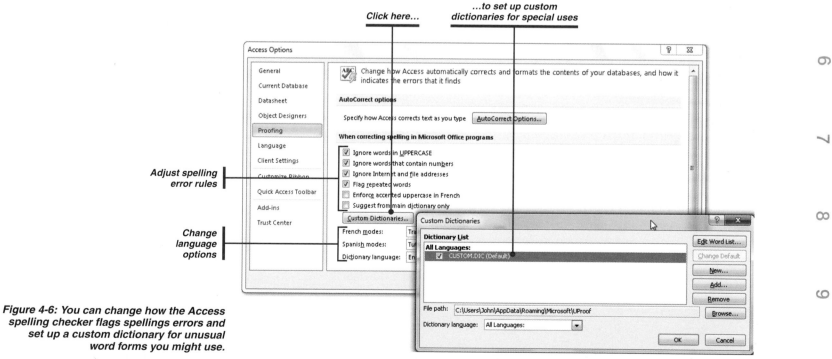

Figure 4-6: You can change how the Access spelling checker flags spellings errors and set up a custom dictionary for unusual word forms you might use.

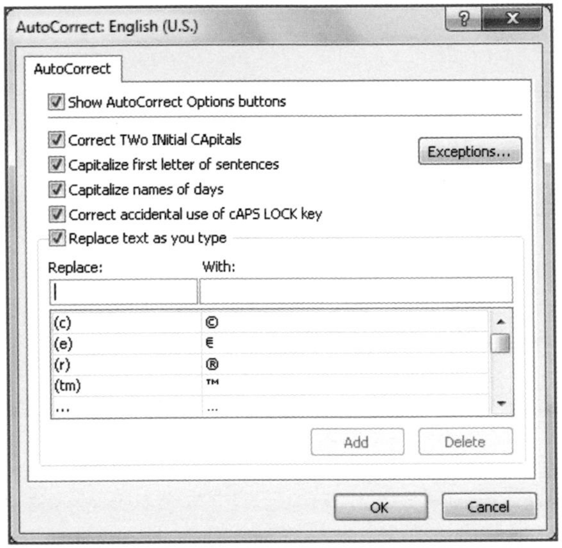

Figure 4-7: AutoCorrect provides several automatic correction settings and lets you add words and characters that are replaced with alternatives.

TIP

Importing data into Access tables is a one-shot process—that is, you get whatever data is in the source at the moment you import. You can maintain a real-time connection to external data if you link it to an Access table. Linking data is covered in Chapter 9. Linking to, and moving data to and from, Microsoft SQL Server tables, is covered in Chapter 10.

Modify Automatic Corrections

Access automatically corrects common data entry mistakes as you type, replacing characters and words you choose with other choices. You can control how this is done.

1. Open a table in Datasheet View.

2. Click the **File** tab, click **Options**, and click the **Proofing** option. On the Proofing page, click **AutoCorrect Options** (see Figure 4-6). The AutoCorrect dialog box appears, as shown in Figure 4-7. As appropriate, do one or more of the following:

   ● Choose the type of automatic corrections you do or do not want from the options at the top of the dialog box.

   ● Click **Exceptions** to set capitalization exceptions.

   ● Click **Replace Text As You Type** to turn off automatic text replacement (this is turned on by default).

   ● Add new words or characters to the Replace and With text boxes, and click **Add**.

   ● Change a current item by selecting the item in the list, edit the With text box entry, and click **Replace**.

   ● Delete replacement text by selecting the item in the Replace and With lists and clicking **Delete**.

3. Click **OK** when you are done.

Acquire Data

In addition to typing data directly into a datasheet, you can enter data by using a form (see Chapter 6) or get existing data into a datasheet by:

● Importing from several different sources into a new or existing Access table

● Copying and pasting

● Collecting data from e-mail replies

Once the data is "safely" in your Access datasheet/table, you have all the tools and features this book describes to format, organize, analyze, retrieve, and otherwise convert the data into the information you want.

dBASE	ODBC-compliant databases
Enterprise Services Web services	SharePoint
Microsoft Access	Text files
Microsoft Excel	HTML documents
Microsoft Outlook	XML files

Import Data from Outside Sources

Most external data sources use a similar initial Get External Data dialog box, shown in Figure 4-8, to determine if you want to add the data to a new table or append it to an existing table. As such, only a few representative sources are covered here. (You can also create a linked table to maintain an update path to the data. Linked tables and linking data are covered in Chapters 9 and 10.) The data types you can import from are shown to the left.

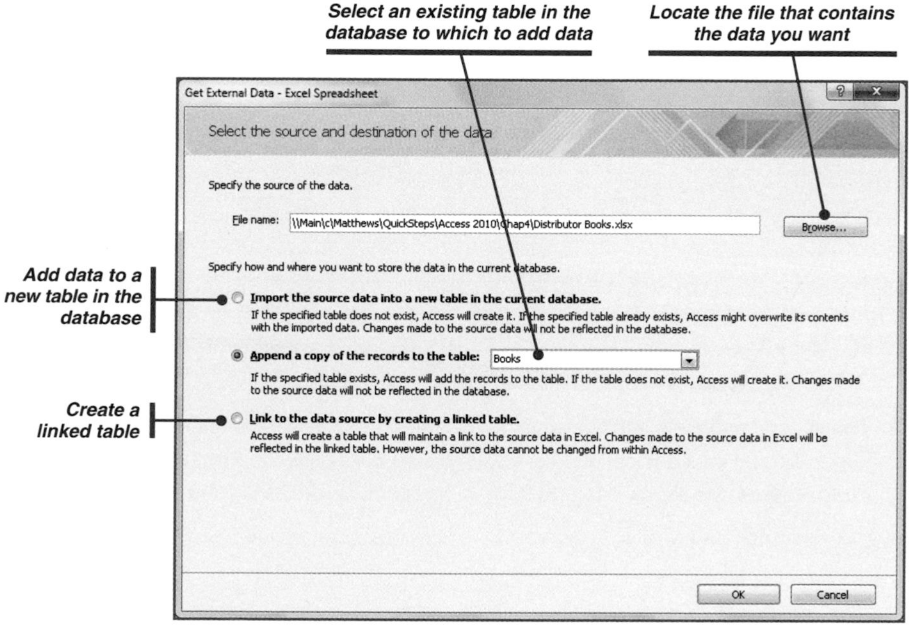

Select an existing table in the database to which to add data

Locate the file that contains the data you want

Add data to a new table in the database

Create a linked table

Figure 4-8: A Get External Data dialog box starts the process of adding data from external sources.

IMPORT DATA FROM TEXT FILES

Text files have file extensions such as .txt and .csv (comma-separated values) that can be formatted using commas, spaces, tabs, and other separators to organize their data. Though the data may not appear to be structured, as shown in Figure 4-9, Access can correctly place the data in columns as long as the data is separated in a consistent and recognizable format.

1. Open the database into which you want to add the data from the text file.

2. In the External Data tab Import & Link group, click **Text File**. In the Get External Data dialog box (see Figure 4-8), locate the text file, and select whether to create a new table or to add the data to an existing table in the database. Click **OK**.

3. In the first page of the Import Text Wizard (see Figure 4-9), preview the file in the lower half of the dialog box. If all appears to be in order, Access has done a good job so far. If not, try choosing the other format. In any case, click **Next** to continue with other options.

NOTE

You can also add data into a table from another table, in either the current database or another Access database, by using an Append query. See Chapter 5 for more information on using queries.

CAUTION

You can click **Finish** at any time in the various import wizards. Doing so certainly expedites the process, but it may overwrite existing data in your currently selected table, causing irreversible changes.

Import Text Wizard

Your data seems to be in a 'Delimited' format. If it isn't, choose the format that more correctly describes your data.

- ⊙ Delimited - Characters such as comma or tab separate each field
- ○ Fixed Width - Fields are aligned in columns with spaces between each field

Sample data from file: \\MAIN\C\MATTHEWS\QUICKSTEPS\ACCESS 2010\CHAP4\CUSTOMERS.TXT.

```
1  "CusID","Last Name","First Name","Company","Address1","Address2","City","ST","ZIP","PH
2  1,"Cummings","Richard","Horizon Manufacturing","11415 W. 15th S.",,"Seattle","WA","981
3  2,"Potter","Sarah",,"1582 S Beacon",,"Edmonds","WA","98040","206-555-1234",,8/22/1992
4  3,"DeMuth","Donald","DeMuth Fabrics","4516 E. Pine",,"Seattle","WA","98113","206-55512
5  4,"Vanderbilt","Jeanette","Pacific NW Trading","Pacific Trade Center, #416","4115 West
6  5,"Farquhar","Eric","Fashions Supreme","C/O Fashion Mart","2237 Fourth Ave. S.","Seatt
7  6,"Fakkema","Edwin","Evans and Fakkma","3497 Westend Ave.","Lake City","WA","98206","
8  7,"Rondell","Mary",,"5517 Lighthouse Drive",,"Clinton","WA","98236","206-555-1513","20
9  8,"Eskenazi","Ralph",,"1956 Dalphin Lane",,"Langley","WA","98260","206-555-6328",,8/3/
10 9,"Stevens","Thomas","Blanchard Mem. Hospital","416 Ninth Avene",,"Bellevue","WA","980
11 10,"Anderson","John",,"53 Summit Drive",,"Redmond","WA","98060","206-555-5459",,11/4/
12 11,"Dailey","Stephan","Minning Machinery","415  Dark Mountain Road",,"Black Diamond","
13 12,"Martinez","Susan",,"5654 Wispering Pines Rd",,"Bow","WA","98435","206-555-5532",,
14 13,"Sato","Yas","Empire Graphics","32 Sentinal Avenue",,"Renton","WA","98334","206-555
```

[Advanced...]   [Cancel] [< Back] [Next >] [Finish]

Figure 4-9: The first step to import data from a text file is to tell Access how it's organized.

4. The second page lets you fine-tune the delimiter used or set fixed-length widths, depending on your choice in the previous dialog box. Click the **First Row Contains Field Names** check box if your text file is set up that way. Click **Next**.

Import Text Wizard

What delimiter separates your fields? Select the appropriate delimiter and see how your text is affected in the preview below.

Choose the delimiter that separates your fields:

○ Tab   ○ Semicolon   ⊙ Comma   ○ Space   ○ Other: [ ]

☑ First Row Contains Field Names   Text Qualifier: [" ▼]

5. In the third page, you can set up field information about each column. Click the field you want to change. To change more detailed field information, click the **Advanced** button (see Figure 4-8). If you do not want to bother with field changes now, you can modify the field information in Access after the data has been imported. Click **Next** when finished.

6. In the fourth page, choose whether and how to assign a primary key to the new table (see Chapter 2 for information on primary keys). This page is omitted if you are appending data. Click **Next**.

7. In the last page, retain or type a name for the new table in the Import To Table text box.

   –Or–

   Verify the name of the table you want to append data into.

   Click **Finish**.

IMPORT DATA FROM SPREADSHEETS

Data created by the spreadsheet program Microsoft Excel is imported using the Import Spreadsheet Wizard.

1. Open the database into which you want to add the data from the text file.

2. In the External Data tab Import & Link group, click **Excel**.

3. In the Get External Data dialog box (see Figure 4-8), locate the spreadsheet file, and select whether to create a new table or to add the data to an existing table in the database. Click **OK**.

Import Spreadsheet Wizard

Your spreadsheet file contains more than one worksheet or range. Which worksheet or range would you like?

◉ Show Worksheets
○ Show Named Ranges

```
Sheet1
Sheet2
Books
2010 P & L
```

---

4. In the first page of the Import Spreadsheet Wizard, choose whether to get data from worksheets or named ranges. Select the item that contains the data, and preview the item in the lower half of the dialog box. Click **Next** to continue with other options.

5. The remaining steps in the Import Spreadsheet Wizard are the same as those in the Import Text Wizard. Continue with step 4 in the previous section, "Import Data from Text Files."

IMPORT ACCESS TABLES

You can import tables (and other Access objects) from other Access databases.

1. Open the database into which you want to add the data from the text file.

2. In the External Data tab Import & Link group, click **Access**. In the Get External Data dialog box (see Figure 4-8), locate the Access database, and select the first option to import Access objects into the database. Click **OK**.

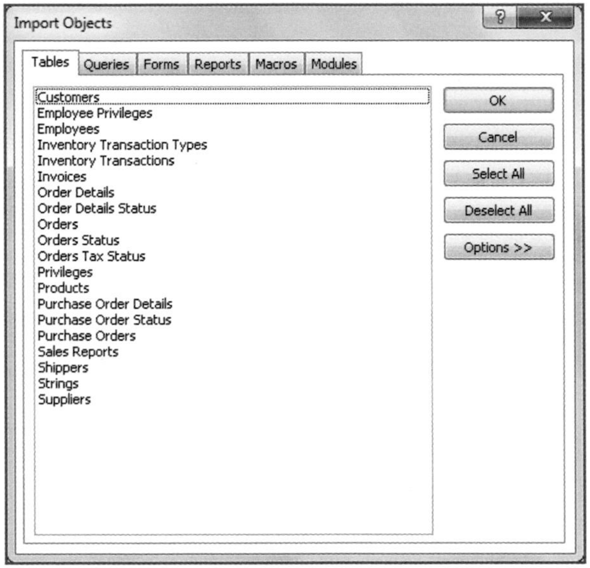

Figure 4-10: You can choose a table, as well as other objects, to import from an Access database.

NOTE

When pasting data into a table, it's important to ensure that the field structure of the source and destination tables are the same so that data isn't lost. For example, if your source record contains more fields than your destination table, the data in the additional fields is simply not added to the destination table. Also, the data types need to be compatible. If there is a data type mismatch, Access will display an error. Also, data unable to be pasted will be added to a Paste Errors table.

3. In the Import Objects dialog box, shown in Figure 4-10, select the table(s) whose data you want. If you need to deselect a choice, either click the table you want deselected or use the **Deselect All** button and start over.

4. Click the **Options** button to display detailed importing options:

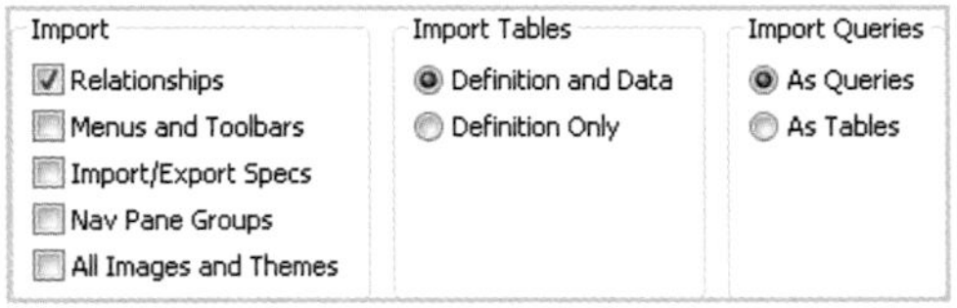

- Under **Import**, select one or more of the features to include with the imported table(s).

- Under **Import Tables**, choose whether to import the table's definition (design) and data or just its definition.

- Under **Import Queries**, select whether you want to import the query or the results of a query (table). Chapter 5 describes queries in more detail.

5. When finished, click **OK**.

6. In the final dialog box, click the **Save Import Steps** check box if you want to repeat the importing steps without working through the wizard. Saved imports are available by clicking **Saved Imports** in the Import & Link group, where you can also create tasks in Microsoft Outlook to remind you to repeat the action. In any case, click **Close**.

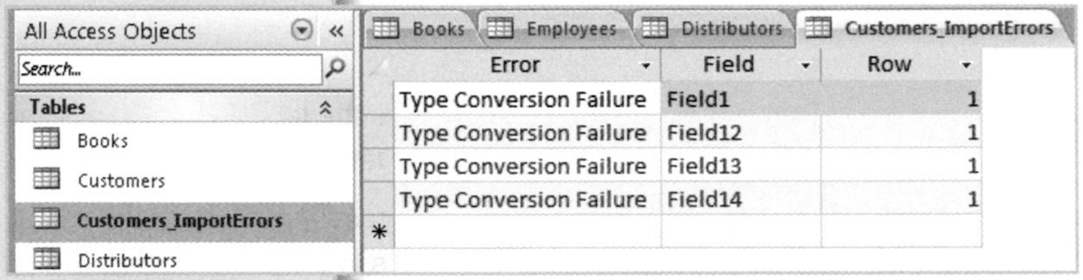

PASTE DATA INTO A TABLE

You can add existing rows (records) or columns of data to your table by pasting them from other data sources.

1. Open the program that contains the data you want.

2. Select the rows or fields you want using the selection techniques of the source program.

3. Copy the data to the Windows Clipboard, either by clicking the **Copy** command from a toolbar or ribbon or by pressing **CTRL+C**.

NOTE

To update existing information in your database, you need to have the e-mail addresses of the recipients already stored in the database.

4. Open the Access table into which you want to place the data in Datasheet View. Do one of the following:

- To paste the data as new records to the end of the datasheet, in the Home tab Clipboard group, click the **Paste** down arrow, and click **Paste Append**.

- To replace records, select the records to be replaced, and in the Home tab Clipboard group, click **Paste**.

- To replace fields, select the fields to be replaced, and in the Home tab Clipboard group, click **Paste**; or right-click the selected fields, and click **Paste**.

Collect Data from Outlook Messages

Office 2010 provides a feature whereby you can send data collection forms to e-mail recipients and then have the data contained in the e-mail responses added to a new or existing Access table.

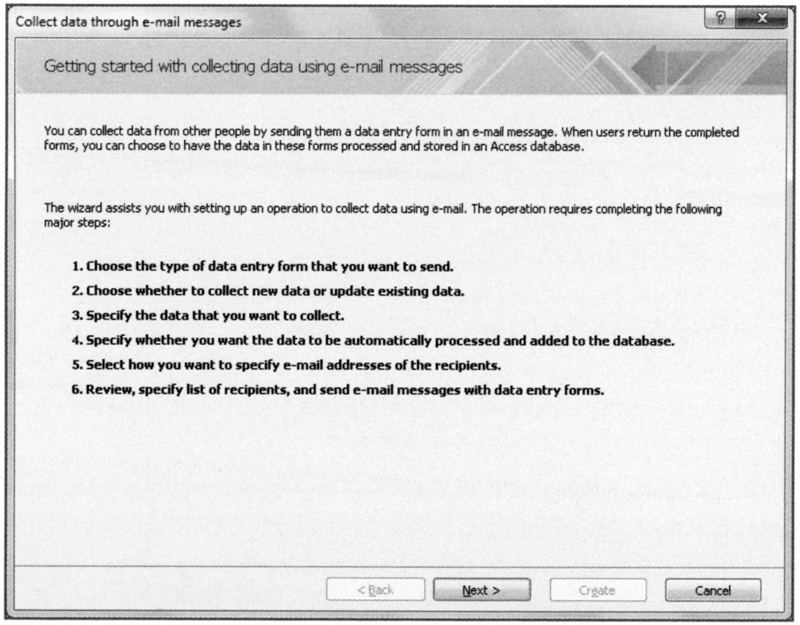

CREATE AND SEND THE DATA REQUEST

1. Open the database that contains the table where you want to collect data.

2. In the Navigation Pane, select the table that will be used to collect data. In the External Data tab Collect Data group, click **Create E-mail**.

–Or–

Right-click the table in the Navigation Pane, and click **Collect And Update Data Via E-mail**.

In either case, the first page of the Collect Data Through E-mail Messages Wizard provides an overview of the process, as shown in Figure 4-11. Click **Next**.

3. In the second page, accept the **HTML Form** option (this is selected by default) as the type of form you want to send, and click **Next**.

4. In the third page, select whether you are collecting new data or updating existing data. Click **Next**.

Figure 4-11: The several steps to create a form for data collection are straightforward and worth the effort.

5. In the fourth page, select the fields from your selected table (see step 1) that you want recipients to provide data for, using the controls shown in Figure 4-12. Click **Next**.

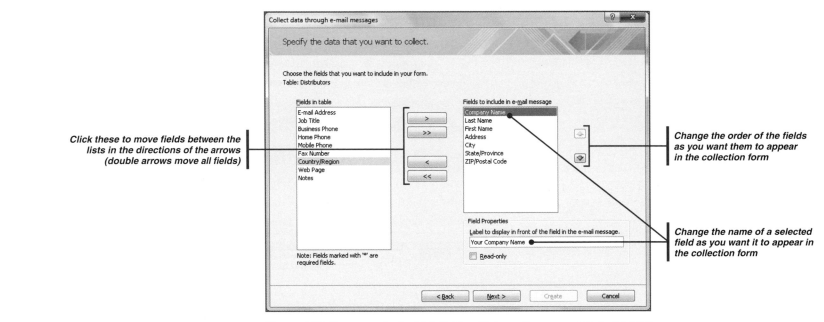

Click these to move fields between the lists in the directions of the arrows (double arrows move all fields)

Change the order of the fields as you want them to appear in the collection form

Change the name of a selected field as you want it to appear in the collection form

Figure 4-12: You can select which fields of information you want your e-mail recipients to provide with their own data.

6. The fifth page lists the Outlook folder where the replies will be stored. Click the **Automatically Process Replies And Add To** *tablename* check box if you want Access to add incoming data directly to your selected table (you can apply this after you receive messages).

7. In the sixth page, select whether you want to add the recipients' e-mail addresses in Outlook or from a field in your database. Click **Next**.

8. In the seventh page, type a subject and message for the recipients, and click **Next**.

9. Click **Create** in the final page to open an Outlook 2010 message form, similar to that shown in Figure 4-13. Review the message, make any changes to the subject or message text, and add recipient addresses, as necessary. Click **Send** when finished.

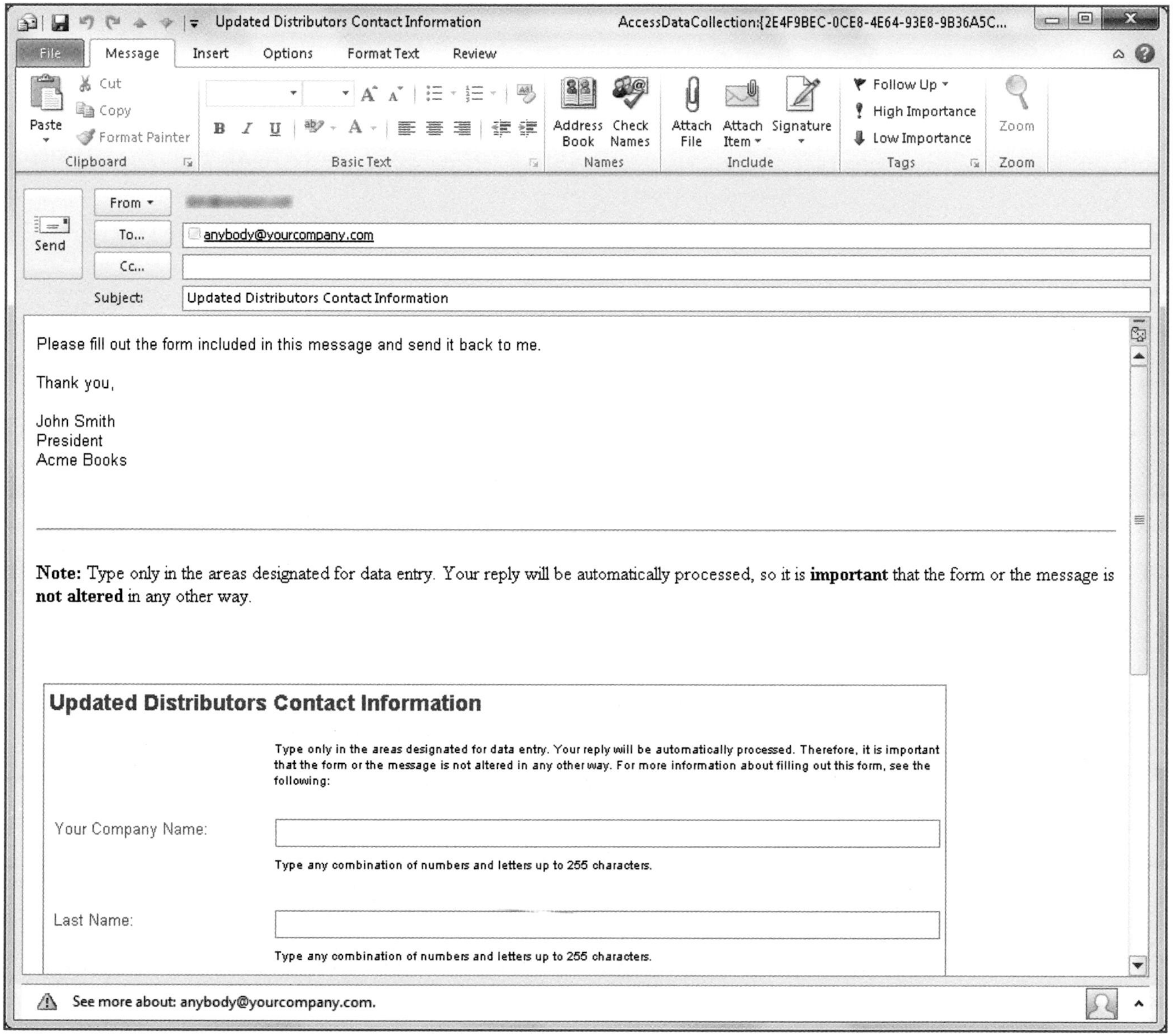

Figure 4-13: Access adds a professionally designed form to your outgoing Outlook 2010 message.

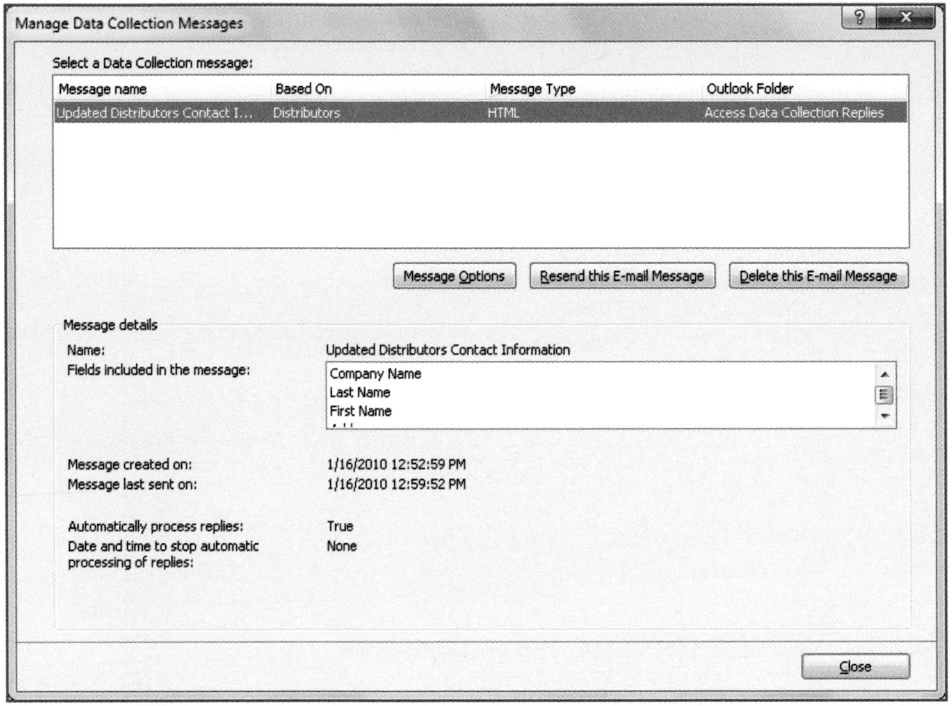

Figure 4-14: E-mail replies from a data collection request are listed and managed in a single location.

MANAGE REPLIES

Replies from your requests for data are automated in one fashion or another, depending on your choice in the Collect Data Through E-mail Messages Wizard. If you chose to automatically add the data to a table, all you really need to do is view the data. If you didn't choose this option, replies are gathered in a common Outlook folder where you can easily manage them.

1. Open the database that contains the table from which you created the data collection message.

2. In the External Data tab Collect Data group, click **Manage Replies**. The Manage Data Collection Messages dialog box appears, shown in Figure 4-14.

   ● To automatically add data to the collection table, select a message and click **Message Options**. Click the **Automatically Process Replies And Add Data To The Database** check box, and select any importing options you want. Click **OK** when finished.

   ● To resend or delete a message, or to view message details, select a message. Use the applicable controls in the dialog box to perform the action you want.

3. Click **Close** when finished.

Arrange a Table

There are several actions you can take to customize how you see the data presented in a table (or datasheet). You can resize rows and columns, hide columns, and format the appearance of the table. (Chapters 2 and 3 describe how to insert and size columns and fields.)

Adjust Column Width

There are several ways to change the width of a column.

- Use the mouse to drag the column to the width you want.
- Type a precise width.
- Let Access choose a default or tailored width.

CHANGE THE WIDTH FOR A SINGLE COLUMN WITH THE MOUSE

1. Point to the right border of the column selector until the pointer changes to a cross.

Title	Aut
Aviation Maintenance Managem	Kinnis
Understanding Health Policy,	Boden

2. Drag the border to the left or right to the width you want.

CHANGE THE WIDTH FOR ADJACENT COLUMNS WITH THE MOUSE

When you change the column width for a group of selected columns, the widths of each column are changed by the same amount.

1. Select the columns whose widths you want to adjust.

2. Drag the right border of any of the selected columns to the left or right to the width you want.

CHANGE THE WIDTH OF COLUMNS PRECISELY

1. Select the column(s) whose width you want to adjust.

2. Right-click the selection and select **Field Width**.

3. In the Column Width dialog box, type a column width (in points), and click **OK**.

LET ACCESS DETERMINE THE COLUMN WIDTH

1. Select the column(s) whose width you want to adjust.

2. Right-click the selection and select **Field Width**.

3. In the Column Width dialog box, click the **Standard Width** check box to have Access change the width based on the default font (see the associated Tip).

–Or–

Click **Best Fit** to change the column(s) width to be just wider than the widest content in each column.

–Or–

Double-click on the right side of a column to have Access resize to best fit.

TIP

To change the field size of a column (the number of characters the field can contain), as opposed to the column width (the width of the column you see in the datasheet), in the Fields tab Properties group (Table Tools), type a value in the **Field Size** text box and click **ENTER**.

Field Size 18

TIP

The default column width is determined by the average number of characters in the default font that will fit in the column. For example, the Calibri 11 pt. font provides for a default column width of 11.75 characters.

Column Width

Column Width: 11.75   OK

☐ Standard Width   Cancel

Best Fit

You can change the default settings for how new datasheets (including tables) appear. Click the **File** tab, click **Options**, and click the **Datasheet** option. Change gridline, cell effects, default column width, and font options. Click **OK** when finished.

QUICKSTEPS

CHANGING HOW THE CURRENT DATASHEET LOOKS

Unlike spreadsheets and Word tables, formatting is applied to an entire datasheet—you cannot format individual fields, rows, or columns when working in Datasheet View. (The one exception is fields with the Memo data type and whose Text Format field property is set to Rich Text, as described in Chapter 8.) The formatting options for the open table (or datasheet) are found in the Home tab Text Formatting group (see Figure 4-15) and the Datasheet Formatting dialog box, shown in Figure 4-16.

CHANGE TEXT ATTRIBUTES

- To change the typeface, click the **Font** down arrow, scroll through the list, and select a new typeface.
- To change the text size, click the **Font Size** down arrow, scroll through the list, and select a new size.

Continued . . .

Move and Hide Columns

You can position columns and hide them from view.

POSITION A COLUMN

1. Click the column selector for the column whose position you want to change in the table.

2. Drag the column selector to the left or right to where you want the column located. You will see a heavy vertical line appear along its left border.

3. Release the mouse button when the heavy vertical line appears where you want the left side of the column located.

Drag a column... *...and place its vertical line where you want the column*

HIDE AND UNHIDE COLUMNS

Hidden columns provide a means to temporarily remove columns from view without deleting them or their contents. (See the "Selecting Records, Fields, and Columns with the Mouse" QuickSteps for information selecting columns.)

1. Select the column(s) to be hidden.

2. In the Home tab Records group, click **More** and click **Hide Fields**.

–Or–

Right-click the selection, and click **Hide Fields**.

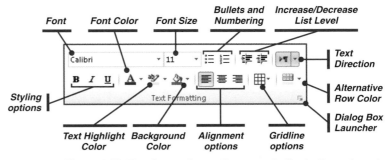

Figure 4-15: Text formatting options are similar to those found in other Office products, such as Word, Excel, and PowerPoint.

QUICKSTEPS

CHANGING HOW THE CURRENT DATASHEET LOOKS *(Continued)*

- To bold, italicize, or underline selected field contents, click the respective Styling button.

- To change text color, click the **Font Color** down arrow, and select a color from the palettes. (Chapter 8 provides more information on working with standard, custom, and theme-controlled colors.) The most recently used color appears on the Font Color button.

ALIGN TEXT IN A COLUMN

Click the **Left**, **Center**, or **Right** alignment buttons in the Font group.

CHANGE BACKGROUND COLORS

To provide contrast to your data, alternating rows in a table can have different colors applied. By default, the colors are drawn from the current formatting theme in effect (see Chapter 8 for more information on using themes). You can change this default appearance by changing either or both of the two colors used in the Datasheet Formatting dialog box, or use the applicable tools in the Text Formatting group.

1. Click the Text Formatting group **Dialog Box Launcher** (the arrow in the lower-right corner of the group):

   - To change the background color, click the **Background Color** down arrow, and select a color from the palettes.

   - To change the color of alternating rows, click the **Alternate Background Color** down arrow, and select a color from the palettes. Click **No Color** to apply the fill/back color as a solid background.

Continued . . .

Figure 4-16: The Datasheet Formatting dialog box, in combination with the Font group, contains options that apply formatting to the entire table.

3. To unhide columns, in the Home tab Records group, click **More** and click **Unhide Columns**.

   –Or–

   Right-click a column selector, and click **Unhide Columns.**

   In either case, in the Unhide Columns dialog box, click the check box next to hidden column(s) you want to show, and click **Close**.

Hidden fields

QUICKSTEPS

- To change the color of the gridlines, click the **Gridline Color** down arrow, and select a color from the palettes.

2. Click **OK** when finished.

CHOOSE A GRID APPEARANCE

In the Text Formatting group, click the **Gridline** down arrow, and select the combination of vertical and horizontal gridlines you want from the menu.

ADD EFFECTS TO CELLS

1. Click the Text Formatting group **Dialog Box Launcher** (the arrow in the lower-right corner of the group).

2. Under Cell Effect, select a type of effect. The result appears in the Sample area.

3. Click **OK** when finished.

FORMAT MEMO FIELDS

Some text-formatting options only apply to fields whose data type is Memo and whose Text Format property is set to Rich Text:

- Use **Bullets And Numbering** to create unordered and ordered lists.

- Use **Increase/Decrease List Level** to indent or promote lists.

- Use **Text Direction** to establish a left-to-right (default) or right-to-left (used in several Middle Eastern and Asian countries) text direction.

- Use **Text Highlight Color** to highlight selected text.

Lock and Unlock Columns

You can lock (or *freeze*) one or more columns to the leftmost side of the table so that they are visible no matter where in the table you might be.

1. To lock columns, select the column(s) you want to lock. Then, in the Home tab Records group, click **More** and click **Freeze Fields**.

   –Or–

   Right-click a column selector, and click **Freeze Fields**.

2. To unlock frozen columns, in the Home tab Records group, click **More** and click **Unfreeze**.

   –Or–

   Right-click a column selector, and click **Unfreeze All Fields**.

   In either case, you will have to move the columns back to their original locations (see "Move and Hide Columns" earlier in the chapter).

Adjust Row Height

You can adjust the height of all rows in the table by using the mouse, typing a precise value, or choosing a default height.

To change row height with the mouse, point at the bottom border of a record selector. When the pointer changes to a cross, drag the border up or down to the height you want.

1. To change row height precisely, right-click a row selector, and click **Row Height.**

   –Or–

   In the Home tab Records group, click **More**, and click **Row Height.**

2. In the Row Height dialog box, type a row height. To use the default row height (14.25 pts is the default height for the 11 pt Calibri font), click the **Standard Height** check box. Click **OK**.

Chapter 5

Retrieving Information

A great deal of Access is geared toward getting data into tables. In earlier chapters, you learned how to create tables, set field properties, and enter the data. Those are all worthwhile skills you need to develop, but the *value* of data lies in finding ways to extract from it just the information you want for a particular need. In this chapter you will learn how to organize data by sorting; how to filter data so that you see only the fields you want; how to create queries, which can do everything filters do and much more; and how to use the Expression Builder to help you choose the components that comprise an expression.

Sort Data

Sorting allows you to reorganize your data by taking values in one or more fields and placing their corresponding records in an ascending or descending order. There are no permanent changes made to the data, data in each record is unchanged, and you can easily return your data to the view you started with.

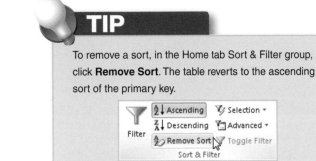

TIP

To remove a sort, in the Home tab Sort & Filter group, click **Remove Sort**. The table reverts to the ascending sort of the primary key.

NOTE

The label next to many ascending and descending sort buttons and commands changes according to the data type of the field being sorted. For example, when performing an ascending sort, a Text data type label reads "Sort A To Z"; when sorting a Number data type, the label reads "Sort Smallest To Largest"; and when sorting a Date/Time data type, the label reads "Sort Oldest To Newest."

Sort Records in a Table

Typically, records are sorted sequentially by the primary key as they are entered. You can alter this *sort order* by choosing to sort all records based on the values in a different field, or even in multiple fields.

SORT ON ONE COLUMN

1. In the database whose data you want to sort, open the table in Datasheet View (see Chapter 4).

2. Right-click anywhere in the column for the field that you want to sort your data on. Click ⌷ to sort ascending—from smaller to larger numbers, oldest to newest dates and times, and alphabetically from A to Z. See the accompanying Note that describes which labels you will see next to the icon.

   –Or–

   Click ⌷ to sort descending—from larger to smaller numbers, newest to oldest dates and times, and alphabetically from Z to A.

   (Alternatively, in the Home tab Sort & Filter group, click the **Ascending** or **Descending** buttons.)

   In all cases, records are reordered in the table to conform to the sort. A small up arrow (ascending sort) ⌷ or down arrow (descending sort) ⌷ appears next to the right side of the column header.

3. When you close the table, you will be asked if you want to change the table design. Clicking **Yes** will save the sort order. The next time you open the datasheet, the data will display with its new sort order.

SORT ON MULTIPLE FIELDS

You can sort on two or more fields by sorting them in a specific order. First, sort the most specific (or *innermost*) field. Sort the least specific (or *outermost*) field last, and sort any intermediate fields in the most-to-least hierarchy. For example, if you wanted an ascending sort for the prices in several categories of books, you would first perform an ascending sort of the Price field, and then perform an ascending sort of the Category field. Records are then organized by category, with the list prices in an ascending sort within each category. Figure 5-1 shows the results of this example.

The least specific, or outermost, field is sorted last

Records are first sorted by the most specific, or innermost, field

	ID	ISBN-10/13	Category	Title	Author	Pub Date	Price	On Hand	Total Sales
	43	0809223406	Business	Getting Your Foot In The Doo	Sullivan	2001	$12.95	18	543
	17	0071418717	Business	Hope Is Not A Strategy Pb	Page	2003	$14.95	23	745
	18	0071421947	Business	50 High Impact Speeches & Re	Kador	2004	$14.95	43	341
	29	007146252X	Business	What The Best Ceo's Know	Krames	2005	$14.95	23	542
	32	0071466606	Business	Instant Advertising	Sugars	2005	$16.95	42	544
	33	007146672X	Business	The Business Coach	Sugars	2005	$16.95	28	744
	31	0071466592	Business	Instant Cashflow	Sugars	2005	$16.95	48	238
	34	0071467858	Business	Words That Sell, Revised	Bayan	2006	$16.95	29	666
	26	0071449124	Business	How Buffett Does It	Pardoe	2005	$16.95	43	234
	13	0071408959	Business	Options Strategist	Allaire	2003	$29.95	21	321
	22	0071429697	Business	Accounting For M&A, Equity &	Morris	2004	$49.95	3	433
	10	0071369988	Business	How To Measure Human Res Mg	Fitz-Enz	2001	$49.95	32	567
	42	0786310251	Business	Black Scholes & Beyond:Optio	Chriss	1996	$65.00	14	521
	6	0071343105	Business	Astd Hndbk Training Dsgn	Piskurich	1999	$79.95	23	643
	62	9780071490870	Computers	Ty Compu For The Over 50s	Reeves Bob	2007	$12.95	23	854
	49	9780071461511	Computers	Ty Php W/Mysql W/Mysql	Mcbride Nat	2005	$12.95	23	643
	98	9780071598415	Computers	Ty Basic Mac Skills	Lawton Rod	2008	$12.95	34	234
	130	9780072232301	Computers	Ms Office Powerpoint 2003 Quic	Matthews Carc	2004	$16.99	34	321
	50	9780071482981	Computers	Digital Photo Quicksteps 2e	Sahlin Doug	2007	$16.99	45	345
	160	9780072263701	Computers	Microsoft Office Powerpoint 20	Matthews Carc	2006	$16.99	48	238

Record: 1 of 184   No Filter   Search

Figure 5-1: You can sort a table on one or more fields to present the data in just the form you need.

NOTE

Sorting on multiple fields by the innermost and outermost concepts is a *complex* sort, since you can select an ascending or descending sort for each field. If you want to sort multiple fields so that they are all ascending or all descending, move the columns so that they are adjacent, with the leftmost being the outermost field and the rightmost the innermost field. Select the columns (see Chapter 4 for information on moving and selecting columns), and select an ascending or descending sort.

1. In the database whose data you want to sort, open the table in Datasheet View (see Chapters 2 and 3).

2. Right-click the innermost field, and click an ascending or descending sort.

3. Repeat step 2 for any other fields you want to sort on, ending with the outermost field.

4. When you close the table, you will be asked if you want to change the table design. Clicking **Yes** will save the sort order. The next time you open the table, the data will display with its new sort order.

Sort Records in a Form

You can sort records using a form in Form view, and then move through them in the new sort order.

1. In the database whose data you want to sort, open the form in Form view (see Chapter 6 for information on working with forms).

2. Right-click the field in the form that you want to sort on. Click **Ascending** ⬆ to sort ascending—from smaller to larger numbers, oldest to newest dates and times, and alphabetically from A to Z.

   –Or–

   Click **Z-A** ⬇ to sort descending—from larger to smaller numbers, newest to oldest dates and times, and alphabetically from Z to A.

   Depending on your choice of sort order, you will see either the first or last record in the table or form, as shown in Figure 5-2.

NOTE

You can filter records in a datasheet/subdatasheet, form/subform, or query. The procedures, figures, and illustrations in this chapter use tables as the primary example object. However, the filtering techniques work similarly for each object.

TIP

All filters are "saved" with the table or form in which they were created until they are replaced with a new filter. When you close the table or form, you will be asked if you want save changes to the design of the object. Clicking **Yes** will retain the filter for the next time you open the object. Also, if you switch views when a filter is applied, for example, switching from Datasheet View to Form View, the filtering in place is retained. (Of course, you can easily remove the filter.) Advanced filters can also be saved as a query and be run irrespective of subsequent filters you've created. See "Save an Advanced Filter," later in the chapter.

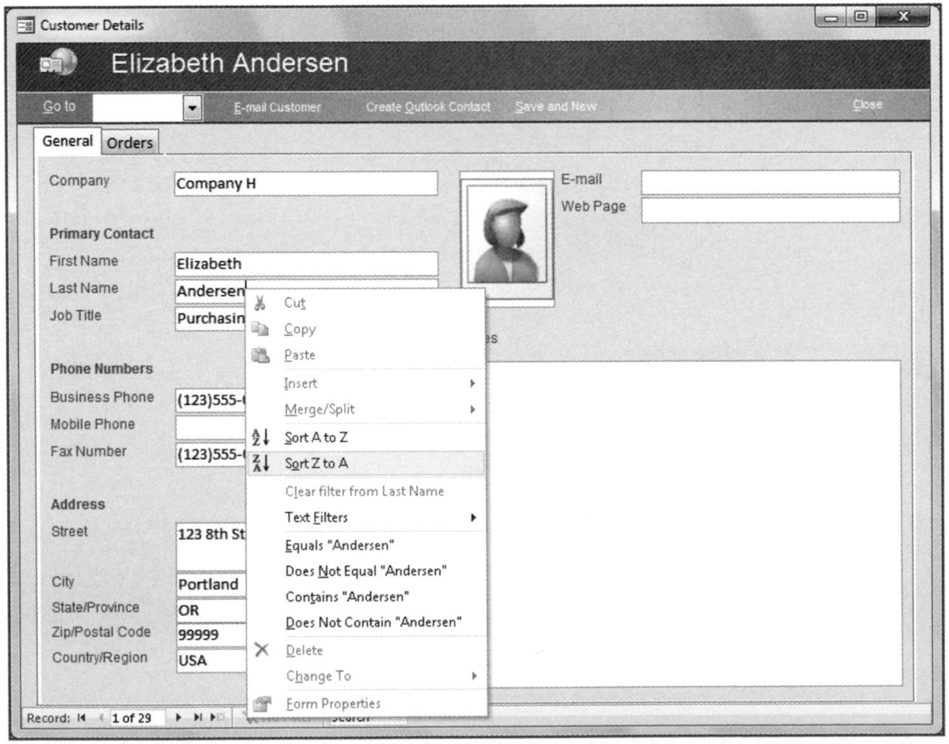

Figure 5-2: Performing a descending sort on the Last Name field reorders the records, with last names at the end of the alphabet now appearing first in the new sort order.

$65.00	14	521
$79.95		
$12.95	✂ Cut	
$12.95	🗐 Copy	
$12.95	📋 Paste	
$16.99	↕ Sort Smallest to Largest	
$16.99	↕ Sort Largest to Smallest	
$16.99		
$16.99	Clear filter from Price	
$16.99	Number Filters ▸	
$16.99	Equals 79	
$16.99	Does Not Equal 79	
$16.99	Less Than or Equal To 79	
$16.99	Greater Than or Equal To 79	

Filter Data

Filtering by one of several methods lets you focus on specific records you want to see while hiding from view the rest of the data in the table. Setting up a filter can be as simple as selecting a value in a field (table column) and clicking a button, or you can apply complex criteria to multiple columns and save the filter design as a *query* (working with queries is discussed later in the chapter). In a filter, you enter a value (and/or add *criteria*) in a field that you want to find in all other records that have the same value (or that meet the criteria you set) in the same field. For example, you might want to find all salespersons that have the value "Washington" in their Territory field. You would filter on "Washington" in the Territory field, and only those records that satisfied that criteria would be displayed. The record for a salesperson named "Joe Washington" whose territory is New York would not be displayed, since "Washington," in this case, is not in the filtered field (Territory).

Filter by Selecting

Filtering by selecting values is the easiest filter to perform, especially in small databases. The main reason for using this filter is that you can quickly locate the value on which the filter is based. Access offers several filtering options based on common criteria applicable to the data type of the column or field. You can identify data that contains a filter by looking for icons displayed in the column header that contains the filtered value 🏷 and on the navigation bar at the bottom of a table in Datasheet View `Record: ◄ ◄ 1 of 5 ► ►I ►✲ 🏷 Filtered   Search` or a form in Form view.

HIGHLIGHT A VALUE OR PORTION OF A VALUE

1. Open a table in Datasheet View or a form in Form view.

2. Select the value in the field that you want to filter on, as shown in Figure 5-3. The part of the value you select will determine the breadth and focus of the options made available.

3. Right-click the value and click one of the most common filtering criteria in the context menu.

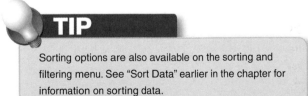

Figure 5-3: Selecting a field and choosing a filter is a quick and easy way to view only the data you want.

–Or–

In the Home tab Sort & Filter group, click **Selection** and click one of the common filters.

In any case, the filtered records are displayed, as shown in Figure 5-3.

4. To remove or delete the filter and return the data to its prefiltered state, see the "Removing, Clearing, or Reapplying a Filter" QuickSteps later in the chapter.

⍬ Selection▾		⍅ New
Equals "2008"		
Does Not Equal "2008"		
Contains "2008"		
Does Not Contain "2008"		

TIP

Sorting options are also available on the sorting and filtering menu. See "Sort Data" earlier in the chapter for information on sorting data.

FILTER BY SELECTING FIELD VALUES

1. Open a table in Datasheet View or a form in Form view.

2. In the Home tab Sort & Filter group, click **Filter**.

   –Or–

   In Datasheet View, click the column header down arrow Pub Date ▾ .

   In either case, a sorting and filtering menu appears.

3. Click **Select All** in the values list to remove the check marks next to all values in the column.

4. Click the values whose records you want to display. Click **OK** to display the filtered records.

FILTER BY EMPTY CELLS

1. Open a table in Datasheet View or a form in Form view.

2. In the Home tab Sort & Filter group, click **Filter**.

   –Or–

   In Datasheet View, click the column header down arrow.

   In either case, a sorting and filtering menu appears.

3. Click **Select All** to remove the check marks next to all values in the column.

4. Click **(Blanks)** at the top of the values list. Click **OK**, and those records with blank values in the column will be displayed.

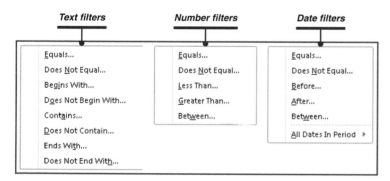

Text filters   **Number filters**   **Date filters**

Figure 5-4: Filtering options that accept criteria in a dialog box vary according to the field's data type.

Filter for an Input

You can type a value, operators, and wildcards in a text box to quickly filter your data.

1. Open a table in Datasheet View or a form in Form view.

2. Right-click the value in the field that you want to filter on.

   –Or–

   In the Sort & Filter group, click **Filter**.

3. Click *Data type* **Filters** (such as Text Filters or Number Filters) to see a more expanded list of filters based on the data type of the field, as shown in Figure 5-4.

NOTE

Filtering by exclusion—that is, displaying all records that *don't* contain the filtered-on value in the same field—is performed in the same way as described in "Highlight a Value or Portion of a Value" earlier in the chapter, except for the command to start the filter. In this case, click the **Does Not Equal** *Value* to start the filter.

Number Filters	▶
Equals $9.95	
Does Not Equal $9.95	
Less Than or Equal To $9.95	
Greater Than or Equal To $9.95	

4. Click the filter you want, and a custom filter dialog box appears, with one or two text boxes to accept the value you want to filter on, or you can type additional criteria (see "Use Operators and Wildcards in Criteria" later in the chapter).

Between Numbers

Smallest:	
Largest:	

OK   Cancel

5. To remove or delete the filter and return data back to its prefiltered state, see the "Removing, Clearing, or Reapplying a Filter" QuickSteps later in the chapter.

Filter by Form

You can create a filter by choosing a value to filter on from a drop-down list of all values in the field, or you can type the value and/or add operators and wildcards. (See "Use Operators and Wildcards in Criteria" later in the chapter.)

1. Open a table in Datasheet View or a form in Form view.

2. In the Home tab Sort & Filter group, click **Advanced** and click **Filter By Form**. You will see a one-line blank record in Datasheet View, or you will see a blank set of fields in Form view.

Advanced ▾		
Clear All Filters		
Filter By Form		
Apply Filter/Sort		
Advanced Filter/Sort...		

3. Click the field you want to filter on in the record that appears. A down arrow will appear at the right end of the field, as shown here for Datasheet View, and for Form view in Figure 5-5. Click the down arrow and select the value you want to filter on from the drop-down list.

Pub Date	Price	On Hand
	▾	
	9.95	
	10.95	
	12.95	
	14.95	

–Or–

Type the value you want to filter on in the field.

–Or–

Type operators and wildcards in addition to typed or selected values.

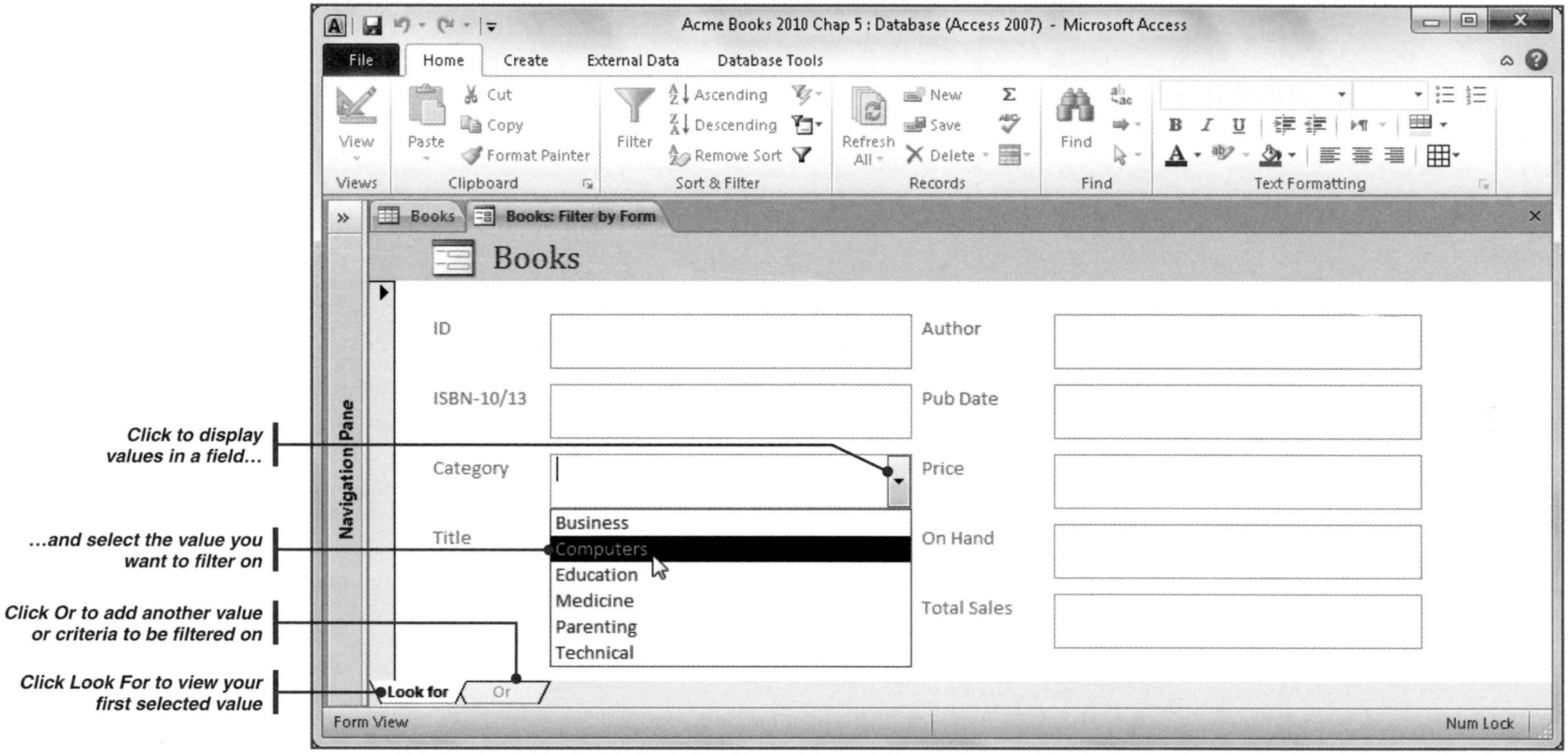

Figure 5-5: *You can select a value to filter on from a list, or you can type a value and other criteria.*

Click to display values in a field...

...and select the value you want to filter on

Click Or to add another value or criteria to be filtered on

Click Look For to view your first selected value

TIP

To clear values that are displayed in the table or form, right-click a cell or field, and click **Clear Grid**.

4. Click **Toggle Filter** in the Sort & Filter group to apply the filter.

5. To remove or delete the filter and return data back to its prefiltered state, see the "Removing, Clearing, or Reapplying a Filter" QuickSteps.

COMPARISON OPERATOR	DESCRIPTION
>	Greater than
>=	Greater than or equal to
<	Less than
<=	Less than or equal to
=	Equal to
<>	Not equal to
Between	The inclusive values between two values (for example, "between 9 and 12" would return 9, 10, 11, and 12)

Table 5-1: Comparison Operators

NOTE

You can select directly from menus filters that use most of the common comparison operators. See "Highlight a Value or Portion of a Value" earlier in the chapter.

TIP

For a complete listing of operators, use the Expression Builder, described later in this chapter.

Use Operators and Wildcards in Criteria

You can "juice up" how records are filtered by using *operators* and *wildcards*. These are symbols and other characters that tell the filter or query to return certain results. For example, if you use "12.95" in a Price field, the filter or query would return only those records that contained a $12.95 price. If you entered the greater-than-or-equal-to operator—">=12.95"—Access would return those records greater than or equal to $12.95.

USE COMPARISON OPERATORS

Table 5-1 provides a list and descriptions of common operators you can use to compare values.

USE ARITHMETIC OPERATORS

Table 5-2 provides a list and descriptions of common operators you can use to calculate a value.

ARITHMETIC OPERATOR	DESCRIPTION
+	Addition
*	Multiplication
/	Division
-	Subtraction

Table 5-2: Arithmetic Operators

USE LOGICAL OPERATORS

Table 5-3 provides a list and descriptions of common operators you can use to apply logical comparisons.

LOGICAL OPERATOR	DESCRIPTION
AND	Both values must be satisfied
OR	Either value must be satisfied
NOT	The value is not satisfied

Table 5-3: Logical Operators

USE WILDCARDS

Wildcards are characters that act as placeholders in expressions used in filters or queries when you are trying to find a particular word or string of characters and only know limited information about the value. Typically used in text fields, you can use them in other data types. Table 5-4 lists the most commonly used wildcards.

WILDCARD	DESCRIPTION
*	Used as a placeholder for all characters that occupy the space. For example, filtering on a value of *son would return values that started with any characters as long as they ended in "son," such as Robertson and comparison.
?	Used as a placeholder for a single character. For example, filtering on a value of r??der would return values that contained any characters in the second and third positions, such as reader and Ridder.
[ ]	Returns values that match any characters you type between the brackets. For example, the[mr]e would return there and theme, but not Thebe.
!	Returns values that don't match the characters you type between brackets. For example, the[!mr]e would return Thebe, but not there or theme.
-	Returns values that match a range of characters between brackets. For example, the[m-z]e would return there and theme, but not Thebe.
#	Used as a placeholder, similar to?, but used to replace a single numeric character.

Table 5-4: Common Wildcards

QUICKSTEPS

REMOVING, CLEARING, OR REAPPLYING A FILTER

When you *clear* a filter, you permanently strike it from the object it's associated with. When you merely *toggle* a filter, it can be reapplied. To re-create a cleared filter, you have to start from scratch.

REMOVE A FILTER

1. Open the table or form that contains the filter you want to remove.

Continued . . .

Use Advanced Filters

Advanced filters allow you to easily use multiple criteria in multiple fields (columns) to find and sort records.

You can also use *expressions* to set up criteria. Expressions used in filters are typically short combinations of values, operators, wildcards, and other terms that return a value. Access has an Expression Builder tool that you can use to build the expression using lists and buttons. (Right-click a criteria field in the advanced filter, and select **Build** to open the Expression Builder window.) See the "Using the Expression Builder" QuickSteps for more information.

QUICKSTEPS

REMOVING, CLEARING, OR REAPPLYING A FILTER *(Continued)*

2. In the Home tab Sort & Filter group, click **Toggle Filter** 🔽 .

   –Or–

   Click the **Filtered** icon 🔽 **Filtered** on the navigation bar.

   In either case, the data is returned to its prefiltered state.

REAPPLY THE MOST RECENT FILTER

1. Open the table or form that contains the filter you want to reapply.

2. In the Home tab Sort & Filter group, click the **Toggle Filter** button.

   –Or–

   Click the **Unfiltered** icon 🔽 **Unfiltered** on the navigation bar.

   In either case, the data is filtered according to the criteria used in the most recent filter.

CLEAR A FILTER

1. Open the datasheet or form that contains the filter you want to delete.

2. In the Home tab Sort & Filter group, click **Advanced** and click **Clear All Filters** (this option, as the label implies, clears the current filter and any saved filters).

   –Or–

   Select a cell in the column that contains the filter, right-click the cell, and click **Clear Filter From Field Name**.

CREATE AN ADVANCED FILTER

1. Open a table in Datasheet View or a form in Form view.

2. In the Home tab Sort & Filter group, click **Advanced** and click **Advanced Filter/Sort**. The advanced filter design tab opens with a default name, including the table name and a sequential filter number.

3. Click the **Field** down arrow in the leftmost column of the grid in the lower half of the tab. Select the first field that you want to search. (See "Work in the Grid" later in this chapter for other ways to choose the field you want.)

4. If you want to sort your results, click the **Sort** field, and open its drop-down menu. Click the sort order you want.

5. In the Criteria field, type the first criteria you want to apply in the current field. (See "Use Operators and Wildcards in Criteria" earlier in the chapter.) Press **ENTER** (the criteria, not the operator, is surrounded by double quotes).

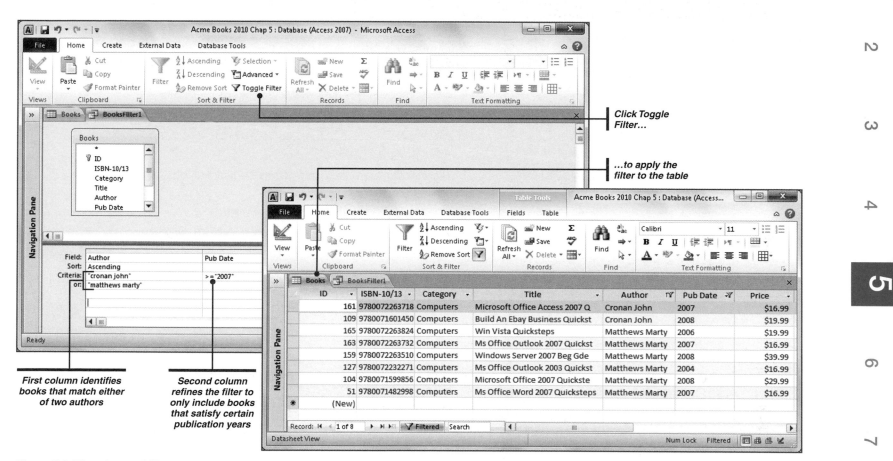

Figure 5-6: *The advanced filter pane lets you set up complex filters and sort the results.*

Click Toggle Filter...

...to apply the filter to the table

First column identifies books that match either of two authors

Second column refines the filter to only include books that satisfy certain publication years

6. Type a second criteria, as necessary, in the "or" field. Records that satisfy either condition will be returned. Repeat for any other criteria you want to add.

7. To apply additional criteria in the form of an AND operator (the value has to satisfy the criteria in the column(s) to the left as well as the present column), repeat steps 3–6 to apply criteria in multiple fields, as shown in Figure 5-6.

8. In the Home tab Sort & Filter group, click **Toggle Filter** to display the results.

5

TIP

To clear any existing criteria in the grid, in the Sort & Filter group, click **Advanced** and click **Clear Grid**; or right-click an area of the pane outside the grid, and click **Clear Grid.**

TIP

You can identify many queries by their icons in the Navigation Pane (the same icons are displayed with each query type in the Query Type group of the Query Tools Design tab). For example, Select queries show overlapping datasheets, Action queries show an exclamation point (!) along with a specific identifier, Append queries add a cross, Delete queries add an X, Make-Table queries add a table, Update queries add a pencil, and Crosstab queries show a PivotTable.

SAVE AN ADVANCED FILTER

You can save a filter you set up in the advanced filter pane as a query and run it at a future time.

1. Set up the filter in the advanced filter pane.

2. Prior to applying the filter, in the Sort & Filter group, click **Advanced** and click **Save As Query**.

–Or–

Right-click an area of the pane outside the grid, and click **Save As Query**.

3. In the Save As Query dialog box, type a name for the query. Click **OK**. (To run the query, see "View the Query Results" later in the chapter.)

Work with Queries

Queries offer the most powerful and flexible way to work with the data in your database. They allow you to retrieve, change, add to, and analyze data from one or more tables or other queries. Queries respond to the criteria you set and display the resultant data in a table or datasheet. The *Select* queries family—such as Simple, Find Duplicates, and Find Unmatched—do so without changing any underlining data. *Action* queries (such as Make-Table, Update, Append, and Delete) cause the underlying data to change. You can also *join* data from multiple tables and analyze data by using Crosstab queries (see Chapter 10 for information on Crosstab queries).

Create a Simple Query with a Wizard

The easiest way to create a Select query is to let Access guide you using the Simple Query Wizard. The operant word in the wizard name is "Simple."

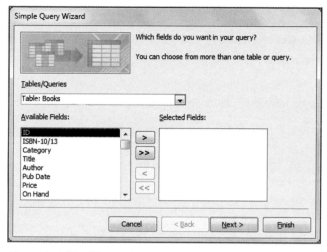

Figure 5-7: *The Simple Query Wizard lets you select the fields of data you want from tables or queries in the database.*

The wizard doesn't try to help you establish criteria, other than letting you choose what fields (columns) you want to include. After finishing the query, you will most likely need to modify the design (see "Create or Modify a Query in Design View" later in the chapter).

1. Open the database in which you want to create the query.

2. In the Create tab Macros & Code group, click **Query Wizard**.

3. In the New Query dialog box, click **Simple Query Wizard**, and click **OK**.

4. In the first page of the Simple Query Wizard, shown in Figure 5-7, click the **Tables/ Queries** down arrow, and select the table or query from where you first want to select the fields that will appear in your query results.

5. Move the fields you want from the Available Fields list to the Selected Fields list by either double-clicking the fields you want or by using the select/remove buttons between the two lists to add or remove fields (single arrows move the selected field; double arrows move all fields).

6. Repeat steps 4 and 5 if you want to include fields from other tables or queries. Click **Next** when finished adding fields.

7. Depending on the fields you have selected, you may see a dialog box that provides options for viewing your data, such as a summary of calculated values or whether to view all fields in all records that meet your criteria. Make your selection, select any summary options, and click **Next** when finished.

8. In the last page of the wizard, type a title or name for the query, and choose whether to open (run) the query as is or to modify its design. Click **Finish** when done. Depending on the choice you selected, the new query will appear as a table or datasheet with the resultant fields you selected earlier in the wizard.

   –Or–

   The new query will open in Design View, ready for adding criteria and making other changes.

In either case, the new query will be listed under the Queries group in the Navigation Pane.

Create or Modify a Query in Design View

Queries use a Design View pane, shown in Figure 5-8, where you can modify an existing query (for example, a query created using the Simple Query Wizard) or start one from scratch.

1. Open the database where you want to create or modify a query.

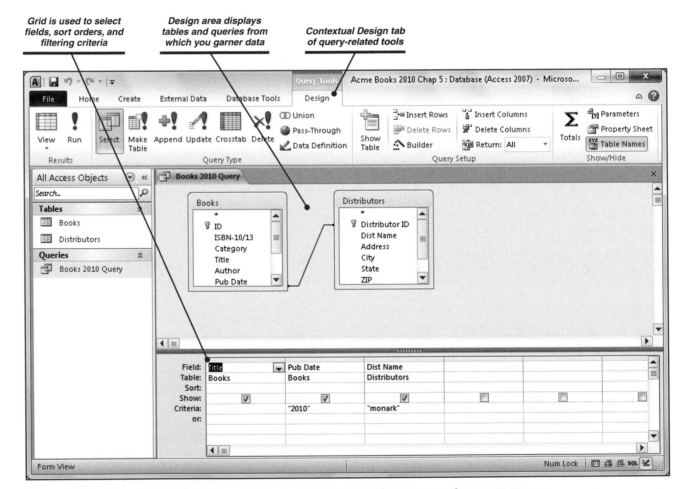

Figure 5-8: The Query Design View pane provides everything you need to set up or change a query.

Figure 5-9: **Add tables and queries to the design area.**

2. In the Create tab Macros & Other group, click **Query Design**. In the Show Table dialog box (see Figure 5-9), select the tables and/or queries that will be included in the query (press **CTRL** while clicking objects to select multiple objects), and click **Add**. Click **Close** to open the query in Design View.

   –Or–

   In the Navigation Pane, display the Queries group, right-click the name of the query you want to change, and click **Design View**. The query opens in Design View, and the ribbon displays the Design tab (Query Tools).

   –Or–

   Switch an open query from Datasheet View to Design View by clicking the **Design View** icon  in either the Home tab Views group or from the views area on the status bar.

WORK IN THE DESIGN AREA

The top portion, or *design area*, of the query Design View pane displays the fields, tables, and queries that you want the query to use in performing the actions you ask of it. (Existing queries will show their associated tables and queries; new queries will show a blank palette unless tables and queries were added.)

1. If not displayed, click **Show Table** in the Design tab (Query Tools) Query Setup group to display the Show Table dialog box (see Figure 5-9). Choose which tables and/ or queries you want to include (press **CTRL** while clicking objects to select multiple objects).

2. Click **Add**. The objects are added to the design area. Click **Close** when finished.

3. In the Design tab Query Type group, click the query you want. (The query names pretty much describe their usage; if you want more information on the purpose of each query, point to its icon and a tooltip will describe its function.) Depending on your selection, you will see a tailored grid at the bottom of the pane and/or be presented with a dialog box requesting more information from you, as shown in Figure 5-10.

4. To remove an object from the design area, right-click the object and select **Remove Table**.

Append dialog box

Append To
Table Name: [▼]   OK
○ Current Database   Cancel
○ Another Database:
File Name: [   ]
                              Browse...

*Figure 5-10: **Append and Make-Table queries obtain information from you in order to add query results to existing or new tables.***

TIP

A popular use for queries is to calculate a total. Click **Totals** in the Design tab (Query Tools) Show/Hide group to add a Total row to the grid. Click the **Total** field in the column where you want to apply it, click the **Group By** down arrow that appears, and choose the type of total you want. If you choose **Expression**, type the expression in the Criteria field; or right-click the field, and select **Build** to use the Expression Builder (see the "Using the Expression Builder" QuickSteps later in the chapter).

Price
Books
Group By   ▼
Group By
Sum
Avg
Min
Max
Count
StDev
Var
First
Last
Expression
Where

TIP

You can simultaneously move all fields in a table or query from the design area to the columns in the grid, rather than dragging them or choosing them individually. From the top of each field list in the table or query object, drag the asterisk (*) to the first field in the grid (see the Books and Distributors tables in Figure 5-8).

WORK IN THE GRID

The lower portion of the query Design View pane (see Figure 5-8), or *grid*, contains columns that you set up, on a field-by-field basis, using the fields from the tables and queries in the design area. Each column has several parameters you can apply to fully build your query.

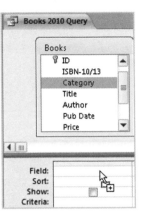

Books 2010 Query

Books
 ♀ ID
   ISBN-10/13
   Category
   Title
   Author
   Pub Date
   Price

Field:
Sort:
Show:
Criteria:

1. If working with a blank grid, add the first (or only) field to the leftmost column by locating it in the table or query in the design area and dragging it into the field labeled "Field." You can also click the field in the grid, click the down arrow that appears, and select the field you want.

2. To display the name of the table that the field came from, click **Table Names** in the Show/Hide group.

   –Or–

   Right-click the field and click **Table Names**.

   In either case, a row labeled Table is added under the Field row.

   Σ   [?]   Property Sheet
   Totals Parameters Table Names
                 Show/Hide

3. If you want to sort your results, click the **Sort** field, click its down arrow, and select the sort order you want.

4. Select the **Show** check box if you want the values from this field to display after the query is run.

5. Type expressions, values, or other criteria in the Criteria field, or click **Builder** in the Query Setup group to have the Expression Builder help you construct an expression (see the "Using the Expression Builder" QuickSteps later in the chapter).

6. Repeat steps 1–5 for other fields you want to include in the query.

7. Modify the structure of the grid by changing the number of rows and columns using the applicable Insert and Delete tools in the Query Setup group. (See Chapter 4 for information on selecting, inserting, and deleting rows and columns in a table.)

   Show Table   Insert Rows   Insert Columns
                 Delete Rows   Delete Columns
                 Builder   Return: All ▼
                      Query Setup

View the Query Results

In order to view the results of a query, you can *run* it from Design View, *switch* to Datasheet View, or *open* a saved query in the Navigation Pane.

1. With the query in Design View, click **Run** in the Results group.

   –Or–

   Switch to Datasheet View by clicking the **View** button in the Results group or clicking **Datasheet View** in the Views area at the right end of the status bar.

2. Depending on the query type you are using, you will either see the results displayed in a table or datasheet, or you will need to supply additional criteria in a dialog box.

Save and Close a Query

Queries, unlike advanced filters, can be saved as objects to be used over and over again (of course, you can save the advanced filter as a query and use it "over and over" again).

SAVE A QUERY

You can save the query in Design View or in Datasheet View with the query results.

1. Right-click the tab corresponding to the query's name, and click **Save**.

   –Or–

   Press **CTRL+S**.

2. If the query is new, type a query name in the Save As dialog box, and click **OK**. The query will be displayed in the Queries group in the Navigation Pane. For an existing query, click **Yes** to save design changes.

CLOSE A QUERY

1. Right-click the tab corresponding to the query's name.

   –Or–

   In Design View, right-click a blank spot in the design area.

2. Click **Close**.

3. If changes to the query have not been saved, click **Yes** when prompted. In addition, if the query is new, type a query name in the Save As dialog box, and click **OK**.

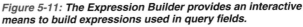

QUICKSTEPS

USING THE EXPRESSION BUILDER

The Expression Builder, shown in Figure 5-11, provides listings and buttons for the expression terms that you select to build your own criteria.

CREATE OR EDIT AN EXPRESSION

In query Design View or in an advanced filter, right-click a criteria field, and click **Build**.

–Or–

In query Design View, place the insertion point in a criteria field, and click **Builder** in the Design tab (Query Tools) Query Setup group.

ADD AN EXPRESSION ELEMENT, CATEGORY, OR VALUE

1. Select the folders containing database objects, functions, constants, operators, and common expressions you want. In the middle pane appear categories of elements, such as fields within tables or collections of operators.

2. Select the expression category in the middle pane to view its values (if it has them) in the rightmost pane. In any case, double-click the category or value you want from the middle or right pane to add it to the build area at the top of the dialog box.

3. Repeat steps 1 and 2 to add other terms to the expression.

4. Once in the build area, you can edit the expression by typing elements in addition to choosing them from the Expression panes. In most cases, however, the Expression Builder will correctly set up the build area expression for you if you select the elements, categories, and values in the correct sequence.

Continued . . .

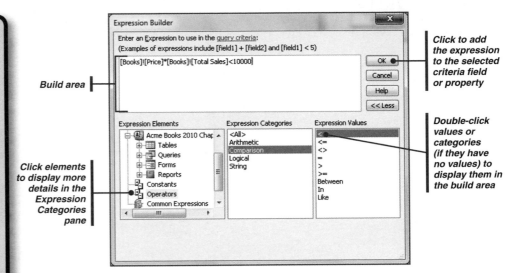

Figure 5-11: The Expression Builder provides an interactive means to build expressions used in query fields.

Set Query Properties

You can fine-tune several characteristics of a query by changing the attributes of its properties, as shown in Figure 5-12.

OPEN THE QUERY PROPERTY SHEET

The property sheet can be used to display both field properties and query properties. Once you have the property sheet displayed, make sure you are viewing the query properties list.

Open the query in Design View, and click **Property Sheet** in the Design tab (Query Tools) Show/Hide group.

–Or–

Right-click a blank area in query Design View (avoid objects in the design area and the grid), and click **Properties**.

USING THE EXPRESSION BUILDER
(Continued)

5. You can also work completely in the build area by typing the elements you want. When you type a letter, a drop-down list of available functions and other elements such as fields appears from which you can select.

> Enter an Expression to use in the query criteria:
> (Examples of expressions include [field1] + [field2] and [field1] < 5)
>
> b|
> 📇 Book Price Query
> 📑 Books
> 📇 Books 2010 Query
> ⨍ BuildCriteria

BUILD A SIMPLE EXPRESSION

To build the expression shown in Figure 5-11, which returns the records (or book titles, in this case) of those books whose total sales in dollars (price times sales) is less than $10,000, you would:

1. In the Expression Builder's Expression Elements pane, click the **plus sign** (+) next to the Acme Books 2010 database to view its objects, and then do the same for the Books table.

2. Click **Books** in order to view its fields in the Expression Categories pane, and then double-click **Price** to place the Price field in the build area.

3. In the Expression Elements pane, click **Operators**, click **Arithmetic** in the Expression Categories pane, and then double-click the * to place the operator for multiplication in the build area (you could also type the character from the keyboard).

4. Repeat steps 1 and 2 to place the Total Sales field in the build area.

Continued . . .

Property Sheet	
Selection type: Query Properties	
General	
Description	
Default View	Datasheet
Output All Fields	No
Top Values	All
Unique Values	No
Unique Records	No
Source Database	(current)
Source Connect Str	
Record Locks	No Locks
Recordset Type	Dynaset
ODBC Timeout	60
Filter	
Order By	
Max Records	
Orientation	Left-to-Right
Subdatasheet Name	
Link Child Fields	
Link Master Fields	
Subdatasheet Height	0"
Subdatasheet Expanded	No
Filter On Load	No
Order By On Load	Yes

*Figure 5-12: **The Query Properties property sheet lists several query properties whose settings you can choose or modify.***

–Or–

Press **ALT+ENTER**.

In each case, the property sheet displays on the right side of the query tab, listing query properties (see Figure 5-12).

SET OR MODIFY A PROPERTY

Click the box to the right of the property you want to set or change. Depending on the property, type the setting you want to add or change.

–Or–

Click the down arrow that appears, and select the setting from the drop-down list.

USING THE EXPRESSION BUILDER

(Continued)

5. Repeat step 3 to place the less than (<) operator in the build area.

6. Type the value 10000.

7. Delete the <<Expr>> characters that appear in the build area by selecting them and pressing **DELETE**.

ADD THE EXPRESSION TO THE CRITERIA FIELD

Click **OK** in the Expression Builder dialog box.

NOTE

If you right-click a table or query in the design area and select **Properties**, you will see "Field List Properties" instead of "Query Properties" in the property sheet.

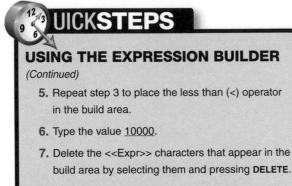

TIP

You can cycle through the options available to a property (for those that have options) by double-clicking the property name.

CHOOSE ONLY TOP OR BOTTOM VALUES

When running a query that returns a large number of results, you can choose to only have returned a certain number or percentage of the top or bottom numeric values or newest or oldest dates (to display the bottom values, sort the applicable field in descending order).

1. In query Design View, open the property sheet (see "Open the Query Property Sheet"), and display the query properties.

2. Click the **Top Values** property, and then click its down arrow. Click the number of top values to display, or click **5%** or **25%** to display the top values based on those percentages of the total values.

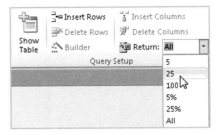

–Or–

In the Design tab (Query Tools) Query Setup group, click the **Return** down arrow, and click the number of values to display or a percentage of the total values.

3. Run the query.

Chapter 6

Creating Forms and Using Controls

You use forms to enter data or to display the information you have already entered in a more attractive format than the datasheets used in tables. This chapter explains the several ways you can create a new form. Access 2010 provides several form tools, a Form Wizard, and you can create a form from scratch in Design View (see Chapter 10 to see how to construct a tabbed navigation form). You also will learn how to modify form designs to meet your needs and how to choose the appropriate *controls*, or building blocks, of a form and set their properties.

Create Forms

Access forms have many uses. Mainly used for data entry and viewing, they are also utilized as user-interactive elements that offer the user additional choices or request additional information.

NOTE

In this chapter, objects are displayed with tabs instead of with overlapping windows. Some instructions may not apply when you use the overlapped windows display. See Chapter 1 for information on changing how objects are displayed.

TIP

You can change the positions of the form and datasheet in a split form using the Split Form Orientation Property. See "Work with Split Form Properties."

QUICKFACTS

UNDERSTANDING FORM VIEWS

Three views are available when you use a form. These are Form View, Layout View, and Design View. Each has its uses.

USE FORM VIEW

Form View allows you to enter data more efficiently. With Form View, you can:

- Sort and filter your data
- Quickly find specific records
- Change the formatting of specific text boxes
- Check spelling of the data within the form (and its underlying table)

Continued . . .

Whatever method you choose to create a form, you can tailor its appearance and behavior to exactly match the end use for the form.

Create a Form Using the Form Tool

The Form tool lets you create a form with one mouse click. Because forms are often created to make data entry more efficient, the Form tool simply places each field from the table or query you select into an easy-to-read format.

To create a form with the Form tool:

1. Select a table or query in the Navigation Pane.

–Or–

Open a table or query in Datasheet View.

2. In the Create tab Forms group, click **Form**. A new form is displayed in Layout View, named the same as the table or query on which it is based. Each field in the table or query is represented in the form with a label (field name) and is populated with the data in the first record of the table or query. Also, the Form Layout Tools contextual tabs containing tools to design, arrange, and format the form are displayed above the ribbon, as shown in Figure 6-1.

Work with the Split Form Tool

Access includes a tool that displays both a Form View as well as the Datasheet View of the table with which you are working. The two views are coordinated so that you can make changes in either the Form View or the Datasheet View.

CREATE A SPLIT FORM

1. In the Navigation Pane, select the table or query on which the form will be based.

–Or–

Open the table or query by dragging it to the Access work area.

UNDERSTANDING FORM VIEWS

(Continued)

USE LAYOUT VIEW

Layout View is the view you first see when using the Form tool (see Figure 6-1). With it, you can:

- See the data as you are working with the form so that you can make changes that fit your requirements

- Add and edit controls to the form

- Add fields using the Field list (see "Adding Fields with the Field List" QuickSteps later in this chapter)

USE DESIGN VIEW

Design View allows you to see more parts of your form; however, unlike Layout View, you don't see any of your data. With Design View, you can:

- Add labels, lines, rectangles, and other such controls to your form.

- Edit text boxes directly within each text box, without using a property sheet. (See Chapter 5 for information about property sheets.)

- Add new fields and controls to your form right on the design grid.

- Resize sections of your form, such as the form header or footer.

SWITCH VIEWS

To switch between views in your form, right-click your form tab, and click the view with which you want to work.

–Or–

Click an icon in the Views area of the status bar.

2. In the Create tab Forms group, click **More Forms**, and then click **Split Form** from the menu.

3. Your new form appears in Layout View, with the underlying data at the bottom of the Access work area in Datasheet View, as well as the property sheet, as shown in Figure 6-2.

4. To move the form separator line (called a *splitter bar*) up or down, place your mouse on the line until you see the double-headed arrow. Hold down the mouse button, and drag up or down to move the splitter bar and display more of either view.

WORK WITH SPLIT FORM PROPERTIES

You can set several properties of your new split form from the property sheet in Design View or for certain properties (Split Form Size/Datasheet/Printing), also in Layout View. From within your split form:

1. Press **F4** to open the property sheet if it's not already open. "Form" should be displayed at the top of the property sheet. If not, click the down arrow, and click **Form**.

2. Click the **Format** tab, and set these properties:

- Click **Split Form Size** to type an exact width and/or height of the form portion (not the datasheet), or allow changes using the splitter bar by typing Auto. The orientation of the datasheet (see next) dictates whether you are specifying its width (left or right) or height (above or below).

- Click **Split Form Orientation** to set the location of the datasheet. It can be on the left, the right, above, or below the form.

- Click **Split Form Datasheet**, and click **Allow Edits** to enable editing directly on the datasheet. Click **Read Only** to prevent editing on the datasheet.

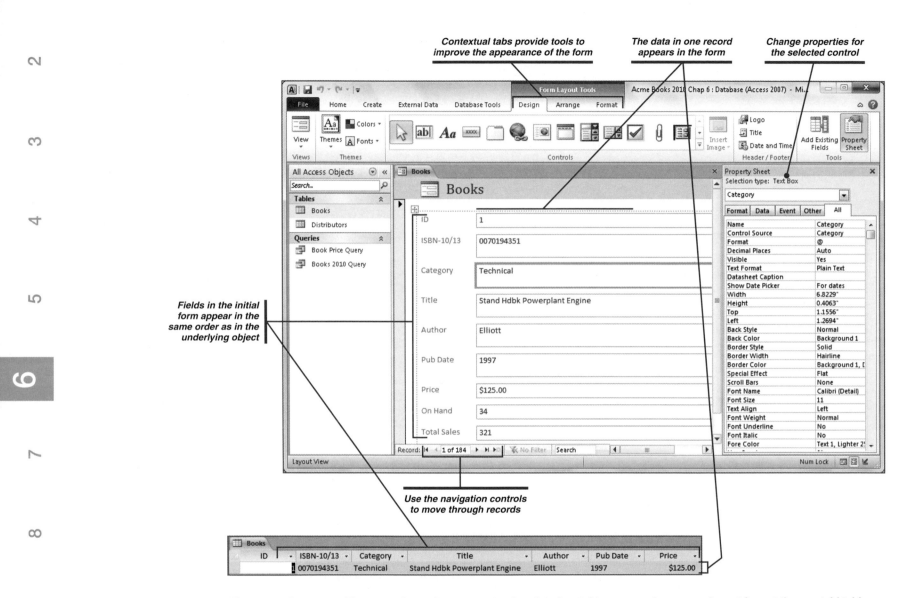

Contextual tabs provide tools to improve the appearance of the form

The data in one record appears in the form

Change properties for the selected control

Fields in the initial form appear in the same order as in the underlying object

Use the navigation controls to move through records

Figure 6-1: Forms provide a record-at-a-time means to view data in a table or query in a more elegant format than a staid table or datasheet.

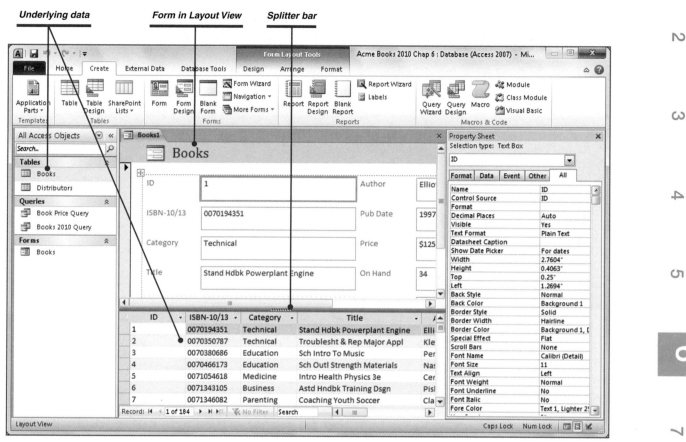

Underlying data   Form in Layout View   Splitter bar

Figure 6-2: *The Split Form tool allows you to see both your form and its underlying data.*

To see more of the form and its data, close the property sheet by clicking **Close** ☒ in its upper-right corner, by clicking **Property Sheet** in the Design tab (Form Layout Tools) Tools group, or by pressing **F4**.

● Click **Split Form Printing** to specify whether the datasheet or form is printed when the user prints the form.

● Click **Save Splitter Bar Position**, and click **Yes** in order to retain the last position of the splitter bar; or click **No** to hide the splitter bar and prevent its change.

Create a Form with Multiple Records

The Form tool creates a form that displays one record at a time. If you need a form that displays more than one record, you can use the Multiple Items tool.

With a multiple-item form, you can show all of your records, but also add a logo or other graphics, change text box sizes, or add controls—things you cannot do in a table or datasheet.

1. From the Navigation Pane, open the table or query with which you want to work.

2. In the Create tab Forms group, click **More Forms**, and click **Multiple Items**.

3. Your new form is displayed in Layout View with all the records from the table or query you selected, as shown in Figure 6-3.

4. Make any changes you want for this form. See "Modify the Form Design" later in this chapter for more information.

5. Right-click the form tab, and click **Save** to display the Save As dialog box. Type a name for this form, and click **OK**.

6. Right-click the form's tab again, and click **Close** to close your new form.

Employ the Form Wizard

If you have used earlier versions of Access, you are familiar with the Form Wizard. You can still use the Form Wizard in Access 2010. The wizard helps you specify how your information is sorted and displayed, and you can use fields from several related tables or queries. (For more information on establishing relationships, see Chapter 2.)

1. To start the Form Wizard, in the Create tab Forms group, click **Form Wizard**.

*Figure 6-3: **A multiple-item form combines a table appearance with form features.***

QUICKSTEPS

CREATING A MULTIPLE-TABLE FORM

You can choose fields from more than one table if the tables are related (see Chapter 2).

1. In the Create tab Forms group, click **Form Wizard**.

2. Click the **Tables/Queries** down arrow, and select the main table from the Tables/Queries list.

3. Double-click each field you want. The fields are moved to the Selected Fields list box.

4. Select the related table from the Tables/Queries list.

5. Select the fields from that table.

6. Click **Finish** or click **Next** to continue the wizard (see "Employ the Form Wizard").

TIP

If you use fields from multiple data sources, you will see an additional dialog box in the Form Wizard where you can choose how to display the fields from each data source, each in their own form. A *linked form* is viewed by clicking a link in the main form, while a *subform* is a section within the main form (see Figure 6-5).

2. In the first Form Wizard page, click the **Tables/Queries** down arrow, and select the table or query you want as the basis for the form, as shown in Figure 6-4.

3. Move the fields you want from the Available Fields list to the Selected Fields list by either double-clicking the fields you want or by using the select/remove buttons between the two lists (single arrows move the selected field; double arrows move all fields). Click **Next** when finished adding fields. (See the "Creating a Multiple-Table Form" QuickSteps for information on adding fields from more than one table or query.)

4. The next Form Wizard dialog box offers you layout choices. Choose the layout you want, and click **Next**.

5. In the final page of the Form Wizard, type a title for the form. Click **Open The Form To View Or Enter Information** to start entering data at once.

   –Or–

   Click **Modify The Form's Design** to change to Design View, where you can edit the design. See "Create a Form in Design View" later in the chapter.

6. Click **Finish**. The completed form resembles that shown in either Figure 6-1 or Figure 6-5. For information on working with subforms, see the "Linking a Form to a Subform" QuickSteps.

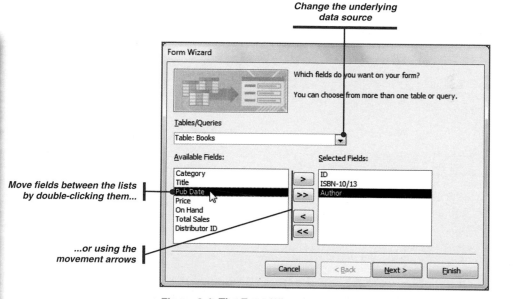

Figure 6-4: *The Form Wizard allows you to select the fields you want to include in a form.*

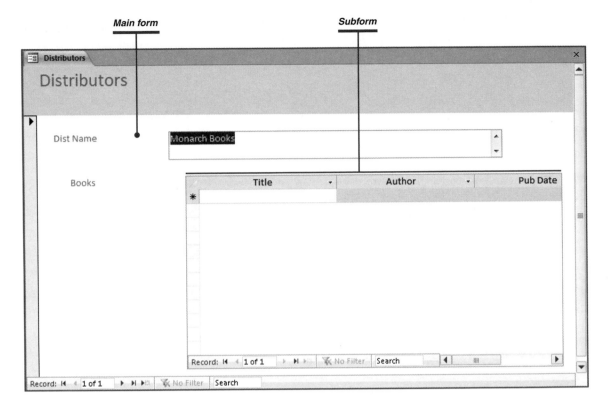

Main form

Subform

*Figure 6-5: **By using data from multiple sources, you can create a subform to display within the main form.***

TIP

If the form is unintentionally blank, there may not be any data in the table or query you chose as the basis for the form. Open the table to check for data. If you based the form on a query, the query may not return any records because of conflicting criteria. Run the query to see if any records are returned. (See Chapter 5 for more information on working with queries.)

Use the Blank Form Tool

If you have only a few fields with which you want to work, you can quickly create a form using the Blank Form tool.

1. In the Create tab Forms group, click **Blank Form**.

2. A blank form window opens in Layout View, as shown in Figure 6-6. The Field List pane opens on the right side of the Access work area, displaying each table in your database.

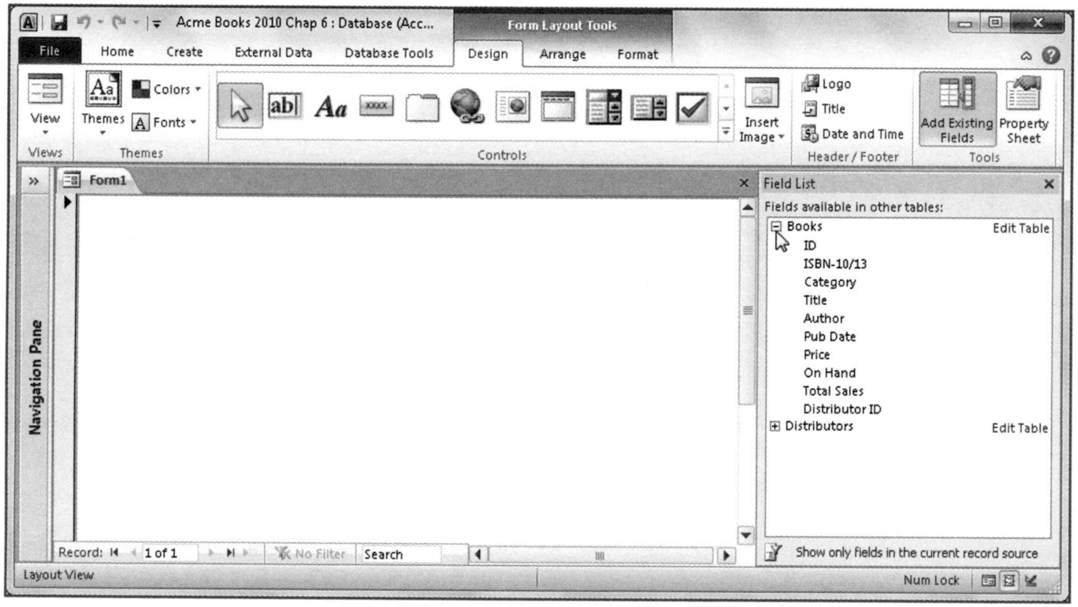

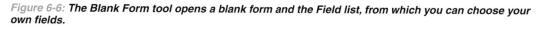

Figure 6-6: *The Blank Form tool opens a blank form and the Field list, from which you can choose your own fields.*

3. Click the plus sign to the left of the table with which you want to work. The Field list displays each of the fields within that table (see Figure 6-6).

4. Double-click each field in the Field list in the order you want them displayed to place them on the form. (See the "Adding Fields with the Field List" QuickSteps for other ways to add fields.)

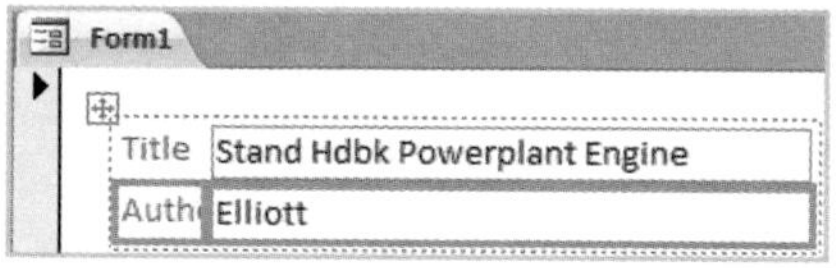

5. Right-click the form tab, and click **Save** to display the Save As dialog box. Type a name for this form, and click **OK**.

6

TIP

If you don't want the form fields in the same order as in your table or query, select the fields one at a time in the order in which you want them on your form.

Create a Form in Design View

You can begin designing a new form without the help of the form tools or the wizard. You also have the option of choosing a table or query as the basis for the new form or creating a form not linked to existing data at all.

1. In the Create tab Forms group, click **Form Design**. A blank form grid opens with the Field List pane on the right side of the Access work area.

2. Click the plus sign to the left of the table you want to use as the basis for your new form. The Field list displays each of the fields within that table. See also the "Adding Fields with the Field List" QuickSteps.

ADD FIELDS USING CONTROLS

In the previous section, we chose the field and Access provided the controls (label and text box). Now we'll talk about adding the control (the empty container) for a field. Later, we will assign a field (bound control) to it with a

1   2   3   4   5   7   8   9   10

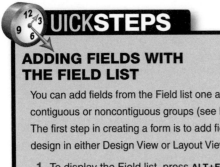

ADDING FIELDS WITH THE FIELD LIST

You can add fields from the Field list one at a time or by contiguous or noncontiguous groups (see Figure 6-7). The first step in creating a form is to add fields to the design in either Design View or Layout View.

1. To display the Field list, press **ALT+F8**.

–Or–

In the Design tab Tools group, click **Add Existing Fields** (the Design View group, shown here, contains a few more tools than the Layout View group).

2. To add one field, drag its field name from the list to the design grid.

–Or–

Double-click the field.

–Or–

Right-click the field and click **Add Field To View**.

3. To add a contiguous group of fields, click the first field name, hold down **SHIFT**, and click the last field name in the group. Then drag the group to the form design.

4. To add a group of noncontiguous field names, hold down **CTRL** while clicking each field name. Then drag the group to the form design.

Continued . . .

---

wizard or with a property sheet. You can also use the controls to add command buttons, list and combo boxes, and other controls. For more information on controls, see "Use Controls" later in this chapter.

1. Open the form, right-click the form tab, and click **Design View** to display the form grid design.

2. In the Design tab Controls group, click the **More** button, and verify that **Use Control Wizards** is selected ; if not, click it to have Access provide assistance when available.

3. In the Design tab Controls group, click the control you want to place on your form from those displayed on the ribbon.

–Or–

Click the **More** button to display the menu of controls.

In either case, a small icon appears by your mouse pointer.

4. Click the position on the grid approximately where you want the control on the form. If there is a wizard associated with this control, follow its steps.

5. After you have added all the controls you want, right-click the form's tab, and click **Save**.

MODIFY THE FORM DESIGN

When you have completed the form design—either with the help of the Form Wizard or on your own—you can still make changes to it. Forms have many

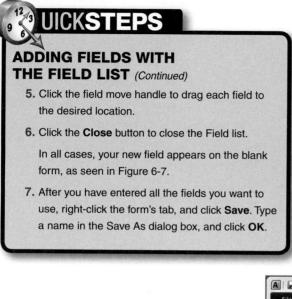

UICKSTEPS

ADDING FIELDS WITH THE FIELD LIST *(Continued)*

5. Click the field move handle to drag each field to the desired location.

6. Click the **Close** button to close the Field list.

   In all cases, your new field appears on the blank form, as seen in Figure 6-7.

7. After you have entered all the fields you want to use, right-click the form's tab, and click **Save**. Type a name in the Save As dialog box, and click **OK**.

properties that determine their appearance and behavior. There are properties for the form itself, properties for controls, properties for the title, and so forth. Verify that "Form" is in the Selection box at the top of the property sheet. For ways to change properties, see the "Selecting a Form Section" QuickSteps later in the chapter.

1. Open the form in Design View.

2. In the Design tab Tools group, click **Property Sheet**.

Grid *Field text box controls* *Display the Field list*

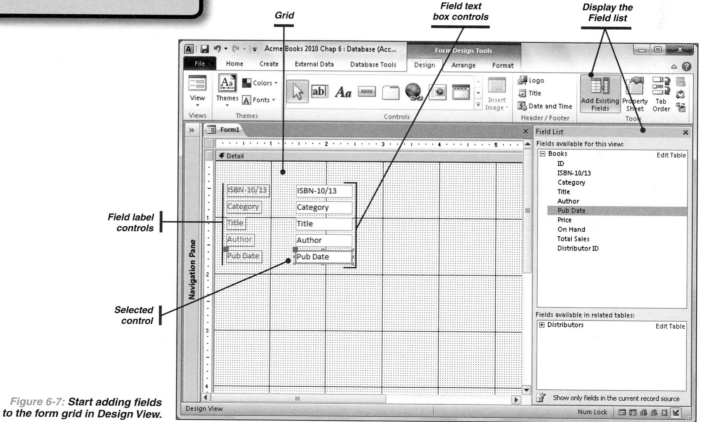

Field label controls

Selected control

Figure 6-7: **Start adding fields to the form grid in Design View.**

TIP

You can size the grid by dragging the lower-right corner or the right or bottom borders.

NOTE

When you select and place many of the controls in the form design, you launch a wizard that guides you through the process. You must have selected the Control Wizards tool by clicking it for these wizards to start. See "Add Fields Using Controls" earlier in the chapter.

TIP

The default form font and color characteristics are defined by the current *theme* that is applied to the database. Themes, which provide collections of complementary colors and fonts across Office programs, are described in Chapter 8.

Special Effect	Flat
Font Name	Cambria (Hea
Font Size	Cambria
Text Align	Calibri (C
Font Weight	Agency F
Font Underline	Aharoni
Font Italic	Algerian
Fore Color	Andalus
Line Spacing	Angsan
	Angsana

3. Click the **Format** tab. Figure 6-8 shows a partial list of the format properties you can set for your form. Other tabs in the property sheet offer data, event, and other properties.

4. Select the property from the list, and enter a value; or click the property's down arrow, and choose from the list of options.

5. When you have finished, right-click the form tab, and click **Layout View** to see how your changes affect your form.

Add Elements to a Form

You can add elements such as a title and the date and time to your form.

ADD A TITLE

Titles are located in a form header. If you did not use the Form Wizard to create a title, you can manually add a title and create a form header.

1. Open the form in Design View.

2. In the Design tab Header/Footer group, click **Title**. A title is created in the form header, as seen in Figure 6-9. By default, the caption is "Form1."

3. Click inside the caption, and type a title name. Press **ENTER** to save your new title.

CHANGE THE APPEARANCE OF A TITLE

1. In Design View, right-click the label box for your title, and click **Properties** to display the property sheet, if it is not shown.

2. Click the **Format** tab. From the Properties list, click the text-related property you want to change (such as Font Name), and then click its down arrow to select an option.

3. Press **ENTER** or **TAB** to accept any changes you have made. You might need to increase the size of the control to accommodate an increased font size (working with controls is described later in the chapter).

Property Sheet ✕

Selection type: Form

Form ▼

Format	Data	Event	Other	All

Caption	
Default View	Single Form
Allow Form View	Yes
Allow Datasheet View	Yes
Allow PivotTable View	Yes
Allow PivotChart View	Yes
Allow Layout View	Yes
Picture Type	Embedded
Picture	(none)
Picture Tiling	No
Picture Alignment	Center
Picture Size Mode	Clip
Width	6.1694"
Auto Center	No
Auto Resize	Yes
Fit to Screen	Yes
Border Style	Sizable
Record Selectors	Yes
Navigation Buttons	Yes
Navigation Caption	
Dividing Lines	No
Scroll Bars	Both
Control Box	Yes
Close Button	Yes
Min Max Buttons	Both Enabled
Moveable	No
Split Form Size	Auto
Split Form Orientation	Datasheet on Top
Split Form Splitter Bar	Yes
Split Form Datasheet	Allow Edits
Split Form Printing	Form Only
Save Splitter Bar Position	Yes
Subdatasheet Expanded	No
Subdatasheet Height	0"
Grid X	24
Grid Y	24
Layout for Print	No
Orientation	Left-to-Right
Palette Source	(Default)

*Figure 6-8: **Set the form properties with the property sheet.***

Clicking Title...

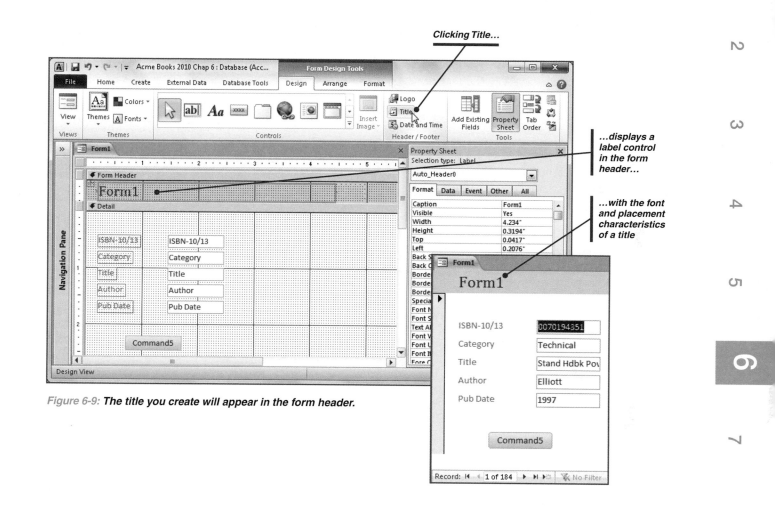

...displays a label control in the form header...

...with the font and placement characteristics of a title

Figure 6-9: *The title you create will appear in the form header.*

INCLUDE THE DATE AND/OR TIME ON A FORM

On occasion, you may need to include a date and time on your forms. The date and time that appear are the system date (the date on your computer) at the time the form is opened.

QUICKSTEPS

SELECTING A FORM SECTION

Before you can work on a particular section of a form (or report), you need to select it.

SELECT THE FORM

- To select the form itself, click the form selector (the small square at the intersection of the horizontal and vertical rulers). A small black square appears when the form is selected.

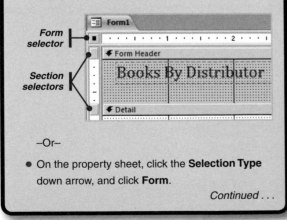

–Or–

- On the property sheet, click the **Selection Type** down arrow, and click **Form**.

Continued . . .

1. Open the form in Design View.

2. In the Design tab Header/Footer group, click **Date And Time** to open the Date And Time dialog box.

3. Click **Include Date** to display the date. Choose from the three available formats, as seen in Figure 6-10. An example of how the format will look is shown in the Sample area.

4. Click **Include Time** if you want to display the time as well. Choose from the three available time formats.

5. Click **OK** to close the dialog box. The date (and time, if you included it) controls appear in the form header.

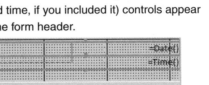

Figure 6-10: **You can choose to display both the date and time on your form.**

6. Right-click the form tab, and click **Save** to save the changes to your form.

Use Controls

Form designs include three types of controls:

- **Bound** controls contain data stored directly in an Access table. For example, text boxes, combo boxes, and list boxes are bound controls. See "Add Bound Controls" in the next section.

- **Unbound** controls are design elements unrelated to table data. For example, labels, command buttons, images, lines, and rectangles are unbound controls. These are discussed in the section, "Add Unbound Controls."

- **Calculated** controls are a type of bound control that contain data that is an *expression* of several elements, similar to a formula in Microsoft Excel. See "Add a Calculated Control" later in the chapter.

The main control types used in Access 2010 can be found on the Design tab (Form Design Tools) Controls group, and are shown in Table 6-1.

QUICKSTEPS

SELECTING A FORM SECTION
(Continued)

SELECT FORM SECTIONS

The form header, footer, and detail sections also have selectors at the intersection of the section bar and the vertical ruler.

- Click the selector for the section you want. The section bar is reverse-highlighted (white text appears on a black background).

  –Or–

- On the property sheet, click the **Selection Type** down arrow, and click the section (or control) from the list.

CONTROL NAME	DESCRIPTION
Text box	A control that displays the values stored in fields in the underlying table or query, including calculated fields
Label	A block of text, such as a title, a description, or instructions for the user
Button	A command button that starts an action—such as opening a report, running a macro, or initializing a VBA procedure
Tab	A control that can be used to create a form with several pages so that the user can move from section to section by clicking the tab
Hyperlink	A control used to insert a link, whether to another location or file on the user's computer, a Web site, or an e-mail address
Web Browser	A control that uses a Hyperlink Builder to display Web content in your applications (see Figure 6-11)
Navigation	A control to provide tabbed navigation without using any code
Option Group	A set of mutually exclusive options within a frame (can contain toggle buttons, option buttons, or check boxes)
Insert Page Break	A control used to start a new screen on your form or a new page on a printed form
Combo Box	A control that displays a drop-down list of values, with a text box for data entry
Chart	A control that starts a Chart Wizard used to display Access data in chart form
Line	A control that allows you to emphasize information on a form
Toggle button	A button that shows an on or off position
List box	A control that displays a list of choices for user interaction (this can represent a field value or search criteria)
Rectangle	A control that can be used for graphic effects
Check box	A control that specifies a Yes/No value from the underlying record source
Unbound object frame	A control used to display an OLE object
Attachment	A control that allows the form to access the files stored in the underlying database as attachments
Option Button	A control that displays a Yes/No value
Subform/subreport	A control that displays data from more than one table
Bound Object Frame	A control for objects that are stored in a field in the underlying table's data
Image	An unbound picture, such as a company logo, that has no ties to the underlying data in the form

Table 6-1: Controls Commonly Used in Form Design

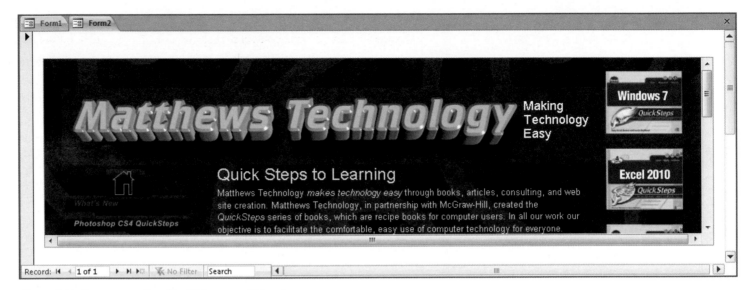

Figure 6-11: *You can easily add a Web page within a form.*

Add Bound Controls

You can set up bound controls from a wizard or manually using the Field list. The easiest way to add table or query data to the design is to use the Field list, as described in the "Adding Fields with the Field List" QuickSteps earlier in this chapter. To add other types of controls, see "Add Fields Using Controls" earlier in the chapter:

ADD A COMBO BOX CONTROL WITH THE WIZARD

Combo and list boxes are both bound to the underlying table data. The only difference between them is the amount of space they take up in the form.

- A list box displays a number of values in the field. How many values depend on the height of the control you draw in the form design. If not all values fit in the box, a scroll bar is added.

- A combo box displays a single value with a down arrow that expands the list. Again, if there are more values than fit in the drop-down list, a scroll bar is added.

TIP

You can change the size of the design area sections by dragging the top of the section bars up or down.

Control wizards are available for many of the control types. For example, you can add a combo box control that shows a list from which the user can choose, based on values in the underlying table or query or on values you create.

1. Open a form in Design View or Layout View. In the Design tab Controls group, click **Combo Box** ▦ (you might have to click the **More** button to see the tool). Your mouse pointer turns into a crosshair, with a combo box icon.

2. Click or drag a rectangle on your form design where you want this list located. When you release the mouse button, you will see both a label and an unbound control box, and the Combo Box Wizard appears, as seen in Figure 6-12.

3. Click **I Want The Combo Box To Look Up The Values In A Table Or Query** if you want your list based on information in the underlying data source.

   –Or–

   Click **I Will Type In The Values That I Want** if you want to add values manually.

   In either case, click **Next** (the rest of these steps assume you are using data from a table or query; the steps to add values are similar and easily followed).

4. Select the table or query where the values are stored. Click **Next**.

5. Select the field(s) you want to see in the list (each field appears as a column so generally only one field is required), and click **Next**.

6. Set the sort order for your items, if you choose. Click **Next** to continue.

7. Double-click the right edge of the column border to adjust the column widths to fit the field values, and choose whether to show or hide (recommended) the primary key field. Click **Next**.

Combo box label   *Combo box control*

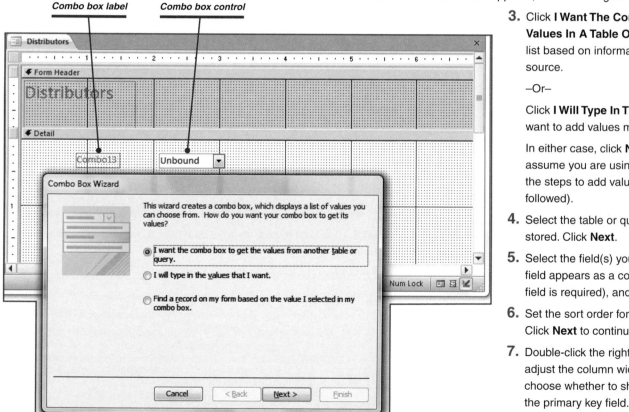

Figure 6-12: **Use the Combo Box Wizard to easily set up a combo box control.**

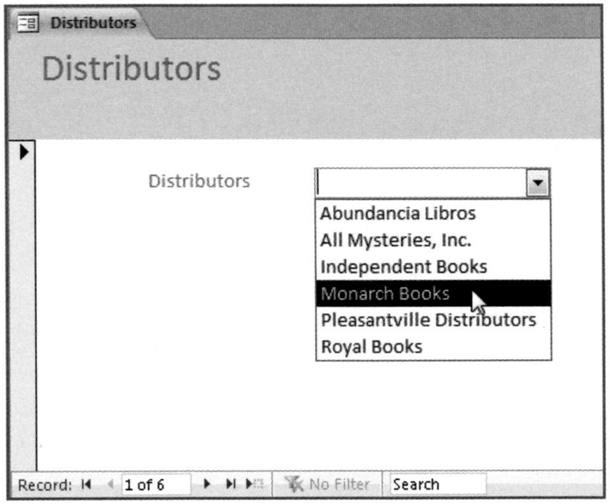

8. Choose whether to have Access remember the selected value for later use or store it in a field. If the latter, click the down arrow and select the field. Click **Next** when finished.

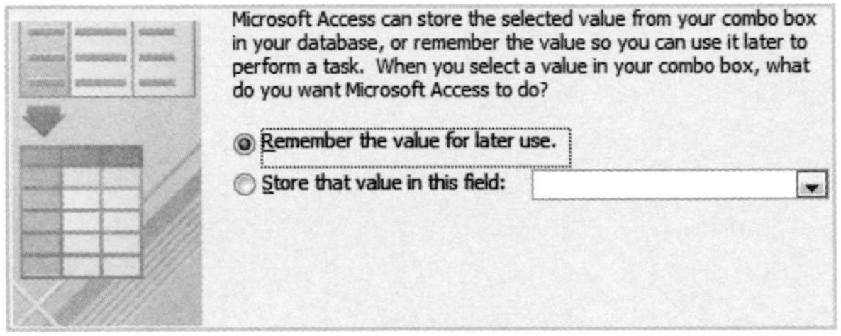

Microsoft Access can store the selected value from your combo box in your database, or remember the value so you can use it later to perform a task. When you select a value in your combo box, what do you want Microsoft Access to do?

⊙ Remember the value for later use.
○ Store that value in this field:

9. If desired, enter a label for the combo box control in the text box at the top of the page to replace the default label, and click **Finish**. Then switch to Form View to see the new combo box control, as shown in Figure 6-13.

ADD A CALCULATED CONTROL

Calculated controls combine values from several text, number, currency, or date fields that are included in the underlying table or query. A calculated control is a text box control whose control source property is set to an expression. Here are some examples:

- **=[price]*[onhand]** displays the total value of the inventory.
- **=[Expiration Date]-Date()** displays the number of days until the expiration date.
- **=[First Name] & " " &[Last Name]** displays both the first name and last name with a space between.

Depending on the data type of the calculated control, you may need to change some of its formatting properties. For example, if the result is a currency field, you may want to see a dollar sign. If you want to see the result in a different font or in bold, change those properties after creating the calculated control.

1. Open your form in Design View. In the Design tab (Form Design Tools) Controls group, click the **Text Box** tool. `ab|`

Distributors

Distributors

Distributors ▾

Abundancia Libros
All Mysteries, Inc.
Independent Books
Monarch Books
Pleasantville Distributors
Royal Books

Record: 1 of 6 ▶ ▶▶ No Filter Search

*Figure 6-13: **The Combo Box control allows you to create drop-down lists from which users can select values from a field or those you add.***

NOTE

You can use several formatting tools to change the appearance of a form. See Chapter 8 for more information.

NOTE

Controls are used in both forms and reports. Reports are discussed in Chapter 7.

LINKING A FORM TO A SUBFORM

A typical use for a subform is to allow users to select from values in one table that are related to those in another—for example, if you wanted to see only those books in a Books table that belong to each distributor in a Distributors table. The main form would allow the user to select which distributor's book to view, and the subform would display the books. Assuming the two tables are related, it's a simple matter to set up the main form and subform.

1. In Layout View or Design View, create a form containing the fields for the distributors' ID (the distributors' ID is the primary key in the Distributors table and also the foreign key in the Books table) and distributor names. This will be the main form.

2. Create a second form that contains the fields from the Book table that you want to be visible when a distributor is selected in the main form. Close the form when finished. This will be the subform.

3. Open the Navigation Pane, and drag the subform onto the main form.

4. Select the subform by clicking its select box in the upper-left corner, and open its property sheet if not already open.

5. Click the **Data** tab in the property sheet, click the **Link Master Fields** property, and click its Builder button .

Continued . . .

2. Click the form design area where you want the new control. The control and its label are displayed.

3. In the property sheet, click the **Data** tab. (If the property sheet is not displayed, double-click the control, not the label.)

4. Click **Control Source** and type the expression you want.

–Or–

Click the **Builder** button to use the Expression Builder to help you set up the expression (see Chapter 5 for more information on using the Expression Builder).

5. Click the **Format** tab to set the formatting properties that suit your needs, such as formatting currency or fonts. For example, to format for currency, in the Format tab, click the **Format** down arrow, and choose **Currency**. The data will appear in U.S. currency format.

6. Click the label of your new text box. On the property sheet, click the **Format** tab, and type the name for your label in the Caption property box.

7. Right-click the form's tab, and click **Save**. Right-click the form's tab again, and click **Form View** to see the results.

ADD A YES/NO CONTROL OR OPTION GROUP

Yes/No controls—such as toggle buttons , check boxes , and option buttons —can appear on a form as single controls or as part of an option group control . (An option group control combines a set of Yes/No controls in a group within a frame. When the user selects one of the options, that value is stored in the field associated with the option group control.) When you select or clear one of these buttons, the Yes or No value is displayed in the underlying table or query. The way it is displayed depends on the format property set in the table design.

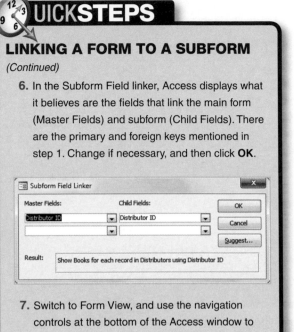

LINKING A FORM TO A SUBFORM

(Continued)

6. In the Subform Field linker, Access displays what it believes are the fields that link the main form (Master Fields) and subform (Child Fields). There are the primary and foreign keys mentioned in step 1. Change if necessary, and then click **OK**.

7. Switch to Form View, and use the navigation controls at the bottom of the Access window to move through the list of distributors. As you do, the subform will contain only those books that are identified as related to that distributor. You can move through the books in the subform by using its navigation controls, as shown in Figure 6-14.

1. In a form open in Design View, in the Design tab (Form Design Tools) Controls group, click the control you want to use.

2. Position your mouse pointer in the form design where you want the control to appear, and click. Check boxes and option buttons include a generic label, while the toggle buttons show no label or image. (Yes/No controls can be grouped within an option group control that offers a list of mutually exclusive alternatives. The control itself is the frame around the Yes/No controls. The Option Group Wizard is on hand to guide you through adding an option group, including labels, a default option, and button appearance, as seen in Figure 6-15.)

3. If you have chosen a control with a generic label, click the control label (not the Yes/No control itself).

4. On the property sheet, click the **Format** tab, and type the desired text in the Caption property text box.

5. Switch to Form View to see the results.

Add Unbound Controls

Unbound controls can be used to improve the appearance of the form and add some user-interfacing tools, such as command buttons. You can also add the current date, time (see "Include the Date and/or Time on a Form" earlier in the chapter), and images to the form.

ADD A COMMAND BUTTON

Command buttons are true user-interactive tools. For example, you can add a command button that opens or closes a form, moves to the next or to a new record, or deletes the current record. Through the Command Button Wizard, you can create more than 30 different types of command buttons. To add a command button that moves to the next record in Form View:

1. Open the form in Design View.

2. In the Design tab (Form Design Tools) Controls group, click the **More** button, and verify that **Use Control Wizards** is selected to ensure the wizards are active. Click the **Button** tool.

Figure 6-14: **The link between a main form and a subform is based on the relationship of their underlying data sources.**

Main form

Subform

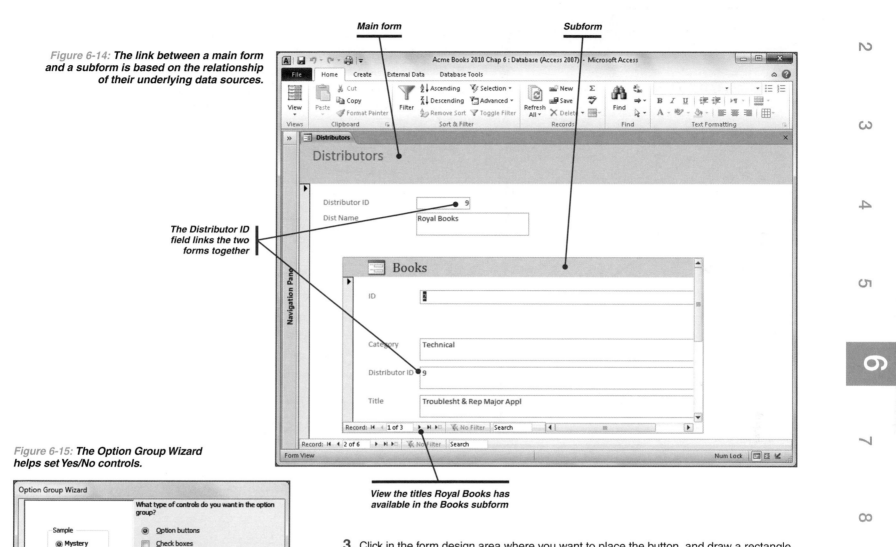

The Distributor ID field links the two forms together

View the titles Royal Books has available in the Books subform

Figure 6-15: **The Option Group Wizard helps set Yes/No controls.**

3. Click in the form design area where you want to place the button, and draw a rectangle. The Command Button Wizard opens. Figure 6-16 shows the first Command Button Wizard page, with the categories of actions and commands in the left list and groups of related individual actions and commands in the right list. The Sample pane displays the button's default image.

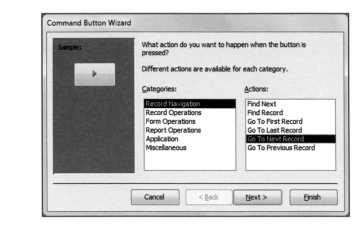

Figure 6-16: *Create interactive tools with command buttons.*

4. In the Categories list, click the **Record Navigation** category.

5. Select **Go To Next Record** in the Actions list. Click **Next**.

6. In the next page, the wizard lets you choose between text and a picture to show on the button. Accept the default text name, or type a different name in the text box.

–Or–

Choose **Picture** and accept the default picture, or click **Show All Pictures**, and choose another image from a list that includes all the Access icons.

In either case, click **Next**.

7. Type a name for your button, if you choose, and click **Finish**. In Form View, the button appears with the database's theme color and font (Chapter 8 describes how to apply a theme to a database).

INSERT IMAGE CONTROLS

You can add images that will remain constant on your form. To add an image from a file on your computer:

1. In an open form in Design View, in the Design tab (Form Design Tools) Controls group, click the **Image** tool, and draw a frame in the form design area.

2. In the Insert Picture dialog box, locate the picture you want on your form, as seen in Figure 6-17. Once you have located the file you want to use on your form, double-click the file.

3. Your image is displayed on the form. Use the sizing handles to adjust the frame, if necessary.

Figure 6-17: *You can add images to your form with the image control.*

4. Right-click the form's tab, and click **Save** to save your form.

Copy or Delete a Control

After you have built a control and set its special properties, you can create copies of it to add to the form design and remove controls you no longer need.

COPY A CONTROL

1. Click the control itself, not the label. An orange selection border surrounds the control.

2. Right-click the control and click **Copy**.

   –Or–

   In the Home tab Clipboard group, click **Copy**.

3. Position your mouse pointer where you want the copy to be on the form, right-click again, and click **Paste**.

   –Or–

   In the Home tab Clipboard group, click **Paste**.

4. Drag the copy to where you want it on your form.

DELETE A CONTROL

To remove a control from the form design:

1. Click the control.

2. Press **DELETE** on your keyboard.

   –Or–

   Right-click the control and click **Delete**.

If you change your mind, click the **Undo** down arrow on the Quick Access toolbar, and click the action you want reversed.

Select, Move, and Resize Controls

Even if you used wizards to create controls for your form (or report), you will probably want to make some changes. Before you can make any control changes, however, you will need to select the control.

When you select a control, you will see a border around it. In addition, there are sets of small darker squares in several locations on the border. These are

QUICKSTEPS

NAVIGATING IN A DATA ENTRY FORM *(Continued)*

5. Click **Auto Order** to build a path left to right, then top to bottom.

   –Or–

   Under Custom Order, click the field selection box (the square at the left of the field name), and drag it to a new position in the list, as seen in Figure 6-18. Repeat with other fields as necessary.

6. Click **OK** when the fields are in the order you want.

Figure 6-18: **You can arrange the order in which you move through the fields in a form.**

the *handles*. The larger square in the upper-left area of the control is the *move handle*; the smaller ones are *sizing handles*. Once one or more controls have been selected, you can move, resize, align, adjust spacing, and change their properties, either individually (if only one is selected) or as a group.

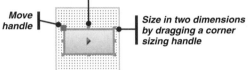

SELECT A SINGLE CONTROL

1. Open your form in either Design View or Layout View.

2. Click the control you want to select.

   –Or–

   Click the **Selection Type** down arrow on the property sheet, and click the control you want to select.

SELECT MULTIPLE CONTROLS

If you want to make the same changes to several controls, select them all before making the changes. You may use one of the following methods:

- In either Layout View or Design View, hold down **SHIFT** while you click each control that you want to change.

- Press **CTRL+A** to select all controls on a form.

- Click any control in a group of selected controls, and you will notice a small four-headed arrow inside a box at the upper-left area of the controls. Click it to select all the controls.

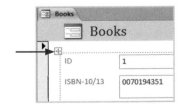

In Design View only, you may select controls using these methods:

- To select a column or row of controls, click the horizontal ruler above the controls or the vertical ruler left of the controls when your mouse pointer turns into a bold arrow.

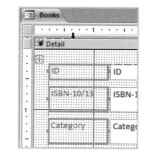

TIP

To display or hide the rulers, on the Arrange tab (Form Design Tools), Sizing & Ordering group, click **Size/Space**. Under the Grid section, click **Ruler** to show or hide both rulers.

- To select a block of controls, drag to draw a rectangle in the form design area around the controls. This selects all controls within or partially within the rectangle. (Make sure the Select tool is selected in the Design tab Controls group.)

- To retain a selected block of controls as one unit, you can *group* them. Select the controls you want in the group, and on the Arrange tab (Form Design Tools) Sizing & Ordering group, click **Size/Space**, and then click **Group**. Sizing and movement now affect all controls in the group. To revert to individual control behavior, click **Ungroup** from the Size/Space menu.

MOVE AND RESIZE CONTROLS

- To move a control, select the control and point the mouse pointer either on the upper-left move handle or anywhere on the border until it turns into a four-headed arrow. Drag the control to another location.

- To move a control with both an edit region and a label, drag any border to move them together.

- To move just the label by itself or the edit region by itself, drag either move handle to move just that part of the control, independent of the other.

- If you have grouped a set of controls, moving one control moves all the controls together.

- To resize a control, drag one of the sizing handles. Dragging a corner sizing handle can change both the height and width at once. If you have selected a group of controls, they are all resized at once.

- Anchoring options determine how controls automatically resize with the form; that is, the controls you specify will increase and decrease as the user resizes the form, in the direction(s) you select. By default, the controls on a form stay anchored to the upper-left corner of the form, and do not resize when you resize the form. To change this behavior:

In the Arrange tab (Form Design Tools) Position group, click **Anchoring**, and select anchor options, as shown in Figure 6-19.

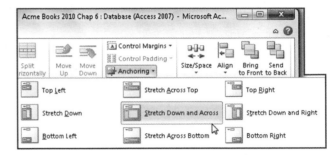

Figure 6-19: *You can arrange controls on your form to grow and shrink in several directions as the form is resized.*

ARRANGE CONTROLS

In Design View, in the Arrange tab (Form Design Tools) Sizing & Ordering group, you can adjust the position of one or more controls by clicking the **Size/Space** tool.

Size options include:

- **To Fit** resizes a control to fit its contents.
- **To Grid** resizes a control so that all four corners reach the nearest grid points. (To hide the grid and/or turn off the snapping feature, deselect their options from the Grid area of the Size/Space menu.)
- **To Tallest**, **To Shortest**, **To Widest**, and **To Narrowest** adjust the size of all other members of the group to fit one.

Spacing options allow you to provide equal, increased, or decreased horizontal or vertical spacing between selected controls.

QUICKFACTS

UNDERSTANDING LAYOUTS

Control layouts can be compared to a table that is aligned both vertically and horizontally so that your form will have a professional appearance. These layouts help you to present your information. There are two types of control layouts, each of which arranges your data differently. Also, you can modify a layout by adding, splitting, and moving rows and columns. These tools are available in Layout View or Design View on the Arrange tab (Form Design Tools) when one or more controls are selected, as shown in Figure 6-20.

USE A TABULAR CONTROL LAYOUT

In tabular layouts, your controls are organized like an Excel spreadsheet. Headers or labels are across the top. For example, if you created a text box control for a telephone number, in a tabular layout, the label for your text box would be in the form header, and the control would be beneath it in the detail section of your form.

USE A STACKED CONTROL LAYOUT

When you use a stacked control layout, each of the labels appears on the left of the form, with the control containing the information to its right.

Books	
Books	
ID	1
ISBN-10/13	0070194351
Category	Technical

ALIGN CONTROLS

The aligning and spacing options apply to groups of controls. Forms look more professional when the elements are lined up evenly and are equally spaced.

1. With a form open in Design View, select a group of controls using any of the methods described in "Select, Move, and Resize Controls" earlier in this chapter.

2. In the Arrange tab (Form Design Tools) Sizing & Ordering group, click **Align** to access the following alignment options:

   - Use **To Grid** to place the upper-left corner of all controls on a grid mark.
   - Use **Left** to place all controls in a column with the left sides lined up.
   - Use **Right** to place all controls in a column with the right sides lined up.
   - Use **Top** to place all controls in a row with the tops lined up.
   - Use **Bottom** to place all controls in a row with the bottoms lined up.

Bound	Hardcover	E-book	Audio Book
☑	☑	☐	☑

3. To move controls into a different order when they cover one another in an ungrouped stack, also in the Sizing & Ordering group, select the control you want to move, and click **Bring To Front** to move it from a covered position.

   –Or–

   Click **Send To Back** to place it behind other controls in the stack.

Layout selection options

Reposition controls within the layout

Figure 6-20: Access provides several tools to work within stacked and tabular layouts.

Change the layout of selected controls

Add rows and columns to place additional controls

Divide a control into segments

Chapter 7
Working with Reports

Access provides numerous ways to display your information in printed format (see Chapter 8 for information on printing). For the best physical display, however, using *reports* is the way to go. Within reports, you can determine the size and appearance of each item, allowing you complete control over the spotlight of each page. This chapter will take you through the basics of creating reports, starting with using the built-in tools and wizards, and ending with a "do-it-yourself" approach using Design View. Chapter 8 continues with ways to provide visual enhancements to your reports (and forms) through formatting, color- and font-coordinated themes, and by adding graphic elements.

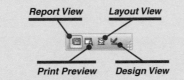
Create Reports

Reports provide a method for presenting information residing within tables and queries. This information may be presented in its current format or manipulated to display comparisons, subtotals, and totals. Although the latter can be accomplished by using queries, reports achieve this task with much less effort. The construction of reports is similar to building forms. Because of this, many of the detailed techniques used when working with the similar tools or objects are the same as those provided in Chapter 6.

Use the Report Tool to Create a Report

The quickest way to create a report is to use the Report tool. It creates a report that displays all fields and records in the underlying table or query. Using this tool necessitates that the report be based on a single table or query.

1. In the Navigation Pane, click the table or query on which you want your report based.
2. In the Create tab Reports group, click **Report**. The report is displayed in Layout View.

3. Press **CTRL+S** to save the report. The Save As dialog box appears.
4. Enter the name for your new report, and click **OK**. The saved report appears in the Navigation Pane in the Reports group and in other groups with its underlying data (tables or queries).

Use the Report Wizard to Create a Report

If you would like to include more than one table or query in one report and add some customization, the Report Wizard is your quickest way to achieve this.

1. In the Create tab Reports group, click **Report Wizard**.
2. The Report Wizard opens, asking which fields you want on your report.

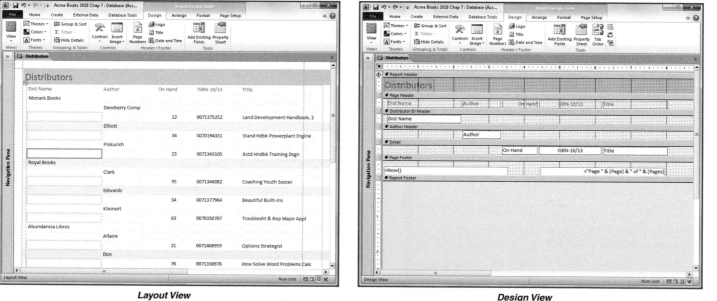

Report View

Print Preview

Layout View

Design View

Figure 7-1: **Each report view highlights a specific aspect of a report.**

QUICKFACTS

VIEWING REPORTS (Continued)

VIEW REPORTS IN LAYOUT VIEW

Layout View is a hybrid of the Report View and the Design View, providing a finished appearance with a subset of the design, arranging, and formatting tools that are available in Design View. Depending on the complexity of the report, Layout View may be all you need to make structural changes to the report, while at the same time allowing you to immediately view the results of those changes in a final appearance instead of in the blueprint-like matrix of Design View.

VIEW REPORTS IN PRINT PREVIEW

Print Preview shows an entire page of the document as it would look in printed form. You can use navigation and zoom controls on the status bar to view each page in the report as well as enlarge or reduce the page image as you want. Chapter 8 describes Print Preview and printing reports in detail.

NOTE

Forms and reports share many similarities in the way they are designed, arranged, and formatted, including the use of controls, field selection and placement, design grid layout, and others. Chapter 6 describes many of these techniques when using forms, and for the most part, the same techniques are not repeated in this chapter. Conversely, this chapter describes some attributes that also apply to forms. To gain a full understanding of using either forms or reports, it's recommended you review both Chapter 6 and this chapter for underlying information on the objects, and Chapter 8 for information on formatting and presentation.

SELECT FIELDS FOR YOUR REPORT

In the first page of the Report Wizard, shown in Figure 7-2, you will select the data source and the fields you want in your report.

1. Click the **Tables/Queries** down arrow, scroll through the list, and select a table or query.

2. Double-click a field (or select it and click the single right arrow) to choose individual fields from the Available Fields list, or click the double right arrow to choose all fields. The fields will be displayed in the Selected Fields box.

3. If you are unsatisfied with the chosen results, click the double left arrow to remove all the fields from the Selected Fields box. To remove individual fields, double-click the field, or select the field and click the single left arrow.

4. Repeat steps 1–3 if you want to include fields from other tables or queries. Click **Next** when finished adding fields.

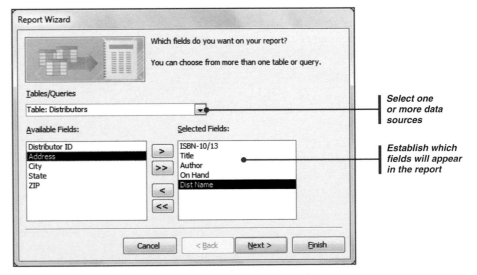

Select one or more data sources

Establish which fields will appear in the report

Figure 7-2: **You can add fields from several tables and queries when using the Report Wizard.**

NOTE

The fields appear in your report in the same order as in the table or query on which you based your report. You can modify this order in the Report Wizard as you move fields to the Selected Fields list (added fields are placed above the selected field), or you can change the order later in Layout View or Design View.

TIP

If you want to use all the fields but in a different order, choose the fields one at a time in the order you want them on your report.

QUICKFACTS

UNDERSTANDING GROUPING IN REPORTS

When you create a report, you often want to present your information in the most organized manner possible, such as sorting alphabetically or chronologically. Access allows another level of organization, called *groups*. A group is a set of records that can include a header, footer, and other such introductory information, as well as summary data. Grouping allows you to present your data in a way that separates records into classifications that you determine. For example, you could create a report that displays book metrics by author under each of your distributors (see Figure 7-3). By grouping your information, you can:

- Create separate sections for each of your classifications, including a separate header and footer.
- Show a total for each section.
- Choose up to four grouping levels
- Group on up to 10 fields. Access will nest each group according to its level.

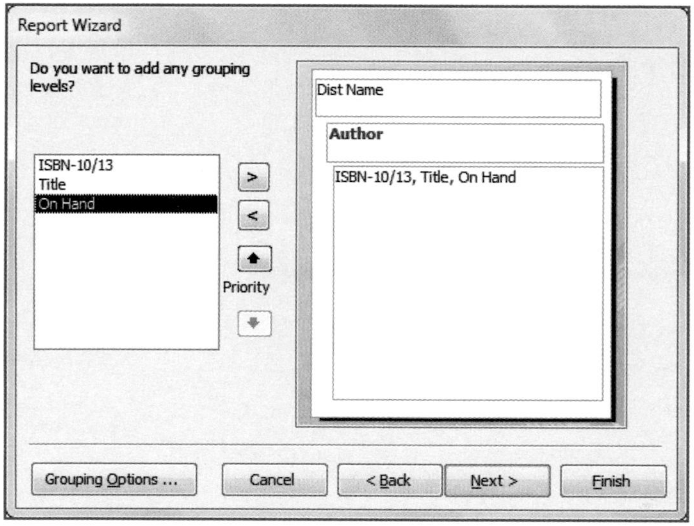

Figure 7-3: ***Grouping allows you to present the data in your report in several configurations.***

ADD GROUPING LEVELS AND INTERVALS

The second step allows you to add *grouping levels*. See the "Understanding Grouping in Reports" QuickFacts for more information. (If you derived fields from more than one table or query, you will first have the opportunity to view the data in terms of each of the data sources.)

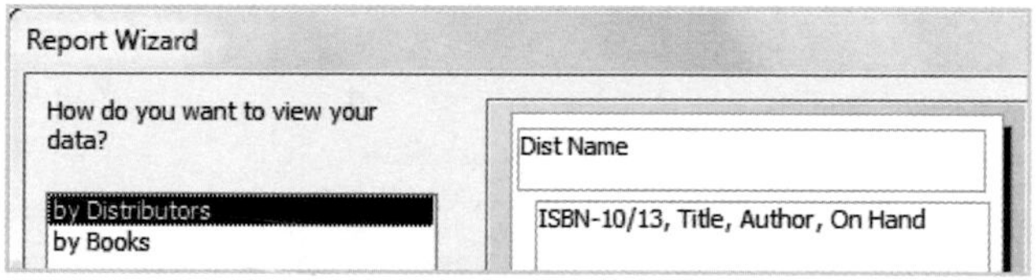

1. Select the item by which you want to group your data, if any. Click the single right arrow to set up the first level of grouping.

Grouping Intervals

What grouping intervals do you want for group-level fields?

OK

Cancel

Group-level fields: Grouping intervals:

On Hand   Normal

Normal
10s
50s
100s
500s
1000s
5000s
10000s

2. To create grouping intervals, click **Grouping Options**. You can customize how the detail for your report is grouped. Each type of field has different choices, appropriate for that field type. For example, if a group level is a number field, you are offered the option of grouping by 10s, 50s, and so forth.

3. Make any selections for each of your group levels. Click **OK** to close the Grouping Intervals dialog box.

4. Click **Next** to move to the next page of the wizard.

SET THE SORT ORDER AND SUMMARY INFORMATION

1. Select a field in the first sort order box. (Note that the choices do not include any of the fields by which you elected to group.)

You can sort records by up to four fields, in either ascending or descending order.

1   On Hand   Ascending

2   Ascending

2. If you would like to change the sort method from ascending to descending, click **Ascending** and it will toggle to Descending.

3. If you would like to add sort fields, repeat steps 1 and 2. You can choose up to four sort fields.

4. To create summary values in the group footers, click **Summary Options**. This opens a dialog box that makes it easy to calculate and display summary values for any grouped numeric fields that the wizard finds. Do one or more of the following:

- Click the calculation you would like for each detail field. You can select multiple options.

- If you only want to see the totals for each group, click **Summary Only** in the Show area. If individual detail amounts are preferred, click **Detail And Summary**.

- By clicking the **Calculate Percent Of Total For Sums** check box (when you have selected the Sum option), the wizard will display an additional field that shows the percent of the grand total this sum represents.

- Click **OK** to close the Summary Options dialog box.

5. Click **Next** to continue.

NOTE

The Summary Options button only appears if you have numeric data in at least one field in the report.

Summary Options

What summary values would you like calculated?

OK

Cancel

Field	Sum	Avg	Min	Max
On Hand	☐	☐	☐	☐

Show
- ◉ Detail and Summary
- ○ Summary Only

☐ Calculate percent of total for sums

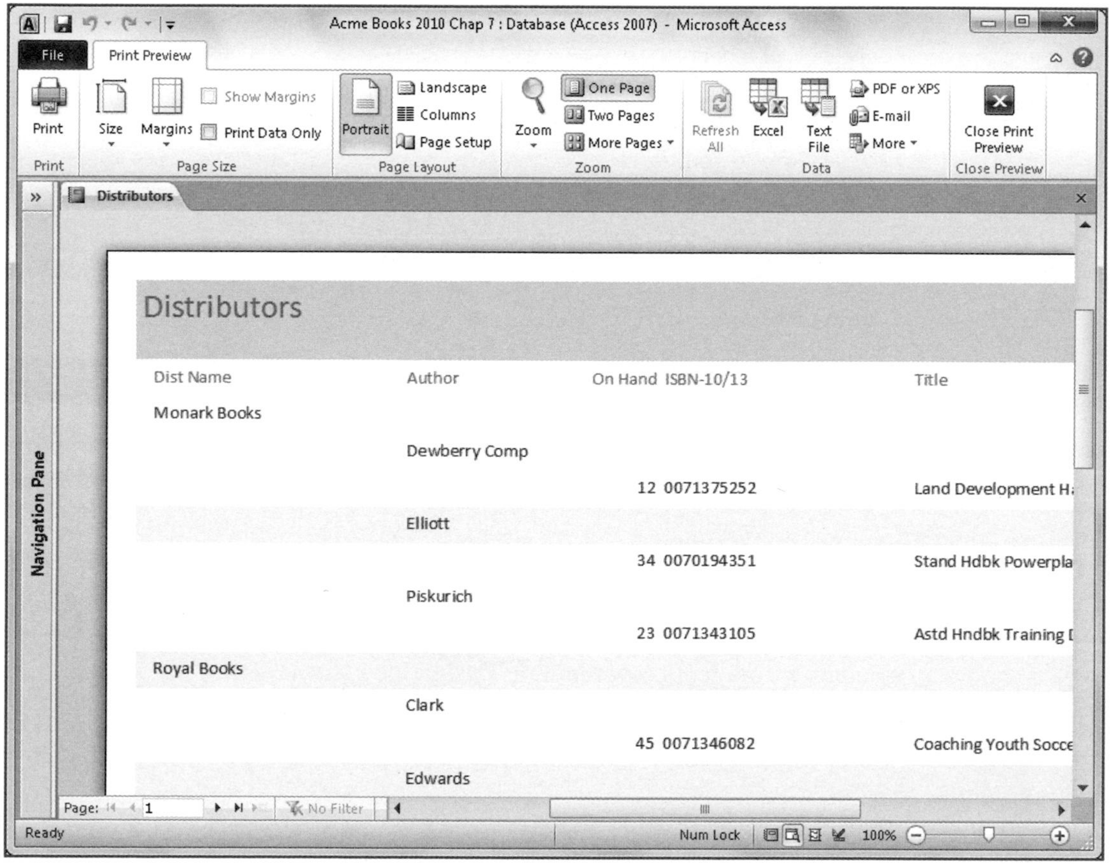

![Microsoft Access Print Preview window showing the Distributors report]

```
A | 🖫 | ↻ ▾ ↺ ▾ | ▾              Acme Books 2010 Chap 7 : Database (Access 2007) - Microsoft Access
File    Print Preview
```

Print	Size	Margins	☐ Show Margins ☐ Print Data Only	Portrait	🔲 Landscape 🗏 Columns 🗐 Page Setup	Zoom	🔲 One Page 🔲 Two Pages 🔲 More Pages ▾	Refresh All	Excel	Text File	🔲 PDF or XPS 🔲 E-mail 🔲 More ▾	☒ Close Print Preview
Print	Page Size			Page Layout		Zoom		Data				Close Preview

Distributors

Dist Name	Author	On Hand	ISBN-10/13	Title
Monark Books				
	Dewberry Comp			
		12	0071375252	Land Development Ha
	Elliott			
		34	0070194351	Stand Hdbk Powerpla
	Piskurich			
		23	0071343105	Astd Hndbk Training [
Royal Books				
	Clark			
		45	0071346082	Coaching Youth Socce
	Edwards			

Page: ◄ ◄ 1 ► ►► ⊠ No Filter ◄

Ready   Num Lock 🔲🔲🔲 100% ⊖ ──── ⊕

Figure 7-4: The initial Report Wizard report is close to being acceptable, but could use some minor adjustments in Layout View or Design View.

ESTABLISH THE REPORT'S LAYOUT AND ORIENTATION

The next page of the Report Wizard offers choices of layout and style. Select the layout descriptions to view the examples.

1. Select the layout that best fits your design needs. If you are not sure which one you want, click each option to see how your report would be presented.

2. Choose the page orientation, and determine whether to adjust the field widths so that all fields fit on a page. Click **Next**.

CREATE THE REPORT TITLE AND PREVIEW YOUR REPORT

1. Specify the report title by accepting the default title or typing a new one in the text box.

2. Choose to preview the report in Print Preview (see Figure 7-4) or to open it in Design View to make additional modifications.

3. Click **Finish**. Access creates your new report.

Use the Blank Report Tool

To quickly create a report from scratch, especially if you want only a few fields on your report, use the Blank Report tool.

1. In the Create tab Reports group, click **Blank Report**. A blank report is displayed in Layout View with the Field List pane visible on the right. You may see a link to Show All Tables. If so, click it to display the Field list.

TIP

To add multiple fields quickly from the Field list to the report pane, hold the **CTRL** key and click nonadjacent fields to select them. To select adjacent fields, click the first field in the group, hold the **SHIFT** key, and click the last field in the group. Drag any of the selections to the report pane to include all selected fields.

2. Click the plus sign (+) to the left of the table or query that has the fields you want to use on your report.

3. Double-click or drag each field you want to use in your report. They will appear in the order that you select.

–Or–

Select several fields and then drag them as a group onto your report (see the accompanying Tip). To select multiple fields, press and hold CTRL and click noncontiguous fields, or press and hold SHIFT and click the first and last field in a contiguous block.

4. Add a title, logo or other image, or page numbers, as described in the "Accomplishing Common Tasks in Reports" QuickSteps later in this chapter.

5. Press **CTRL+S** to save your new report. In the Save As dialog box that appears, type a name and click **OK**.

Create a Report in Design View

When creating a report in Design View, it is helpful to see the framework of the report. Figure 7-5 shows an example of Design View with the possible sections you may encounter (a new report in Design View displays the Page Header, Detail, and Page Footer sections). The seven sections to the report, each with its own purpose, are listed in Table 7-1.

SECTION	DESCRIPTION
Report Header	Contains information printed once at the beginning of the report. This includes such information as the report title, company logo, author, and so on.
Page Header	Contains information that is printed at the top of every page, such as the page number and dates.
Group Header	Contains information that is printed at the beginning of each new group of records, such as the group name.
Detail	Contains records from a table or results from a query.
Group Footer	Contains information that is printed at the end of each group of records, such as summary details for each group.
Page Footer	Contains information printed at the bottom of each page.
Report Footer	Contains information printed once at the bottom of the last page, such as report totals.

Table 7-1: Report Sections

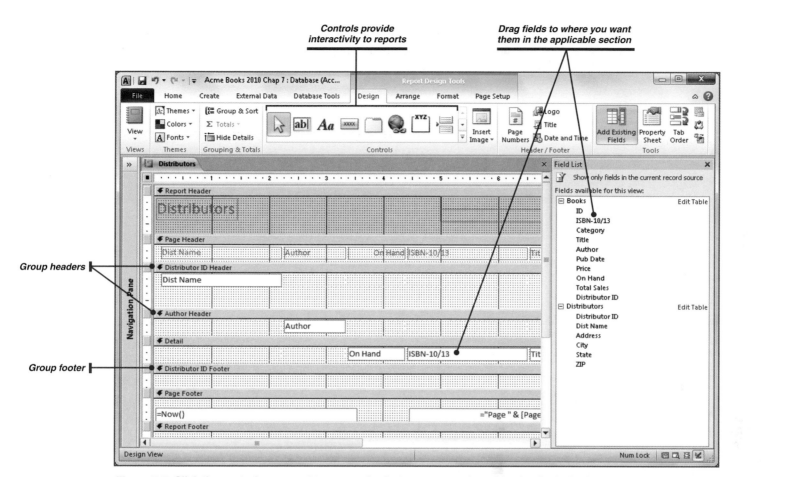

Controls provide interactivity to reports

Drag fields to where you want them in the applicable section

Group headers

Group footer

Figure 7-5: *Click the controls you want to use, and select a space on the grid to begin designing your report.*

The Design tab Controls group contains the report controls provided in Access. These controls can be selected and placed in the grid accordingly. The controls may be *bound* (linked directly to underlying data) or *unbound* (not connected to a record source). See Chapter 6 for more information about commonly used controls and their purpose. The Field list provides the names of fields from an underlying table or query. When creating a basic report, you can simply drag fields to the grid. Controls can then be added to enhance your basic report.

1. In the Create tab Reports group, click **Report Design**. A blank report design grid appears.

2. If the Field list is not already displayed, click **Add Existing Fields** in the Design tab (Report Design Tools) Tools group.

   –Or–

   Press **ALT+F8**.

3. Drag a field name from the Field list to the desired location within the report's design grid. Repeat this process until you are satisfied with the report contents.

4. Right-click the **Report** tab, and click **Save** to save your new report. If this is the first time that you have saved this report, the Save As dialog box will appear. Type a name for this report, and click **OK**.

Modify Reports

Many of the modifications made to a report (or form) revolve around controls and the customization of them. To view specific information on controls and making changes within the controls, see Chapter 6. Other modifications, such as grouping data, are only found in reports.

Work with Fields

There are several things you can do to the fields in a report to make the finished document more attractive to you and your users.

FORMAT TEXT

You can customize how the text looks in your report with a subset of common Office-wide text formatting tools. In Layout View or Design View, the text formatting tools are available in their respective contextual Format tab Font group.

1. Select the field where you want to apply the formatting.

2. Click the text formatting tool you want. See Table 7-2 for a review of the text formatting choices.

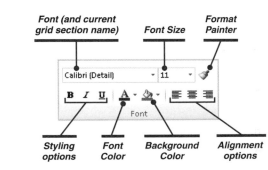

FORMATTING TOOL	DESCRIPTION
Font	Used to change the font that appears on your report. The default is Calibri.
Font Size	Used to change the size of your font. The default is 11 points.
Format Painter	Copies the format of a selected control to another control.
B	Used to display your font in **bold**.
I	Used to display your font in *italics*.
U	Used to display your font with an underline.
Font Color	Sets the color for your font.
Background Color	Fills in the background of a control or label.
Align Left	Aligns data to the left in a control or label.
Center	Aligns data in the center of a control or label.
Align Right	Aligns data to the right in a control or label.

Table 7-2: *Font Group Tools*

FORMAT NUMBERS

In Layout View or Design View, the number formatting tools are available in their respective contextual Format tab Number group. Number formatting tools are only available to fields that contain a numerical data type, such as Number, Date/Time, or Currency.

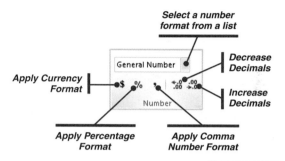

Select a number format from a list

Decrease Decimals

Apply Currency Format

General Number

Number

Increase Decimals

Apply Percentage Format

Apply Comma Number Format

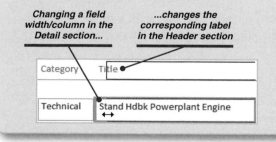

NOTE

When dragging the left side of a field to change its width within a row of fields, the adjacent field width is increased or decreased as you change the selected field. When dragging the right side of a field, the fields to the right are "pushed" or "pulled" by the width of the change. Similar behavior is exhibited in the page header for the associated label fields.

Changing a field width/column in the Detail section...

...changes the corresponding label in the Header section

Category | Title

Technical | Stand Hdbk Powerplant Engine

1. Select the field that contains a number data type where you want to apply the formatting.

2. In the Format tab Number group, click the **Format** down arrow, and select the number format you want.

–Or–

Click one of the number format tools below the Format text box.

General Number
General Number
Currency
Euro
Fixed
Standard
Percent
Scientific

CHANGE THE FIELD WIDTH

1. In either Design or Layout View, click the field you want to size. An orange border appears around either the detail information or the field name, whichever you have clicked.

2. Position your mouse pointer on either side of the border until you see a double-headed arrow.

$39.95

3. Drag until the field width is the way you want it.

SELECT AN ENTIRE ROW OR COLUMN

In Layout View or Design View, right-click a field in the row or column you want, and click Select Entire Row or Select Entire Column.

–Or–

QUICKSTEPS

WORKING WITH DATA IN REPORTS

One way that reports differ from forms is in their ability to display information in groups. You can quickly sort, group, or filter fields in your report.

SORT A SINGLE FIELD

1. In the Navigation Pane, right-click the report you want to work with, and click **Layout View**.

2. Right-click the field by which you want to sort.

3. Click **Sort A To Z** to create an ascending sort. (The sort label reflects the data type of the field. For more information, see Table 7-3.)

   –Or–

   Click **Sort Z To A** to create a descending sort. The report reflects your change.

GROUP BY A SINGLE FIELD

1. In Layout View, right-click the field you want to group by.

2. Click **Group On** *field name*.

FILTER A FIELD

1. In Layout View, right-click the field by which you want to filter, for example, an author's name.

2. Click *DataTypeName* **Filters**, where *DataTypeName* refers to the data type of the field you want to filter. Filter options are tuned to each data type, with several filtering options based on the value of the field selected, and other options available on a submenu from which you can choose other values in the field to filter from one of several custom filters, as shown in Figure 7-6. (For more information on applying filters, see Chapter 5.)

Select a field in the row or column you want, and in the Arrange tab (Report Layout/Report Design Tools) Rows & Columns group, click **Select Column** or **Select Row**.

–Or–

DATA TYPE	SORT OPTIONS
Text	With A on top With Z on top
Date	From oldest to newest From newest to oldest
Number	From smallest to largest From largest to smallest
Expression	Ascending Descending

*Table 7-3: **Sort Options in Group Levels***

Click at the left end of a row or the top of a column (Design View) when the pointer turns into a bolded arrow. In the case of selecting a column in Layout View, clicking a field in the column selects the column.

DELETE FIELDS

1. In either Layout View or Design View, select the field(s) you want to delete, right-click the selection, and click **Delete**, as shown in Figure 7-7.

   –Or–

   After selecting the fields, press **DELETE**.

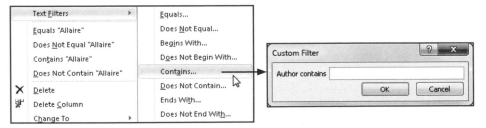

*Figure 7-6: **Filtering in reports is a powerful tool to view only the information you seek.***

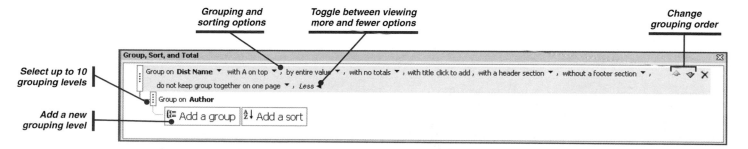

Figure 7-7: *Fields in a report are removed by standard object selection and deletion actions.*

Use the Group, Sort, And Total Pane

You can also add or modify groups, sorts, and totals on your report from the Group, Sort, And Total pane, as shown in Figure 7-8. An example of a grouping on two levels is shown in Figure 7-9.

Depending on the type of data in your underlying table, each grouping and sorting level has several options from which you can choose. To display all of the options, click **More** on the level you want to change. To hide these options, click **Less**.

OPEN THE GROUP, SORT, AND TOTAL PANE

1. Open a report in either Layout View or Design View.

2. In the Design tab (Report Layout/Design Tools) Grouping & Totals group, click **Group & Sort**. The Group, Sort, And Total pane will appear on the bottom of the report area.

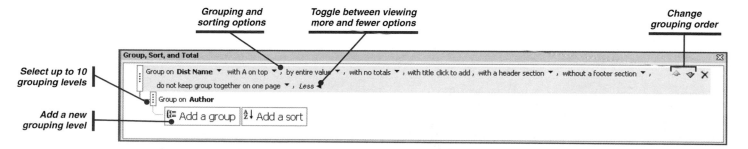

Figure 7-8: *The Group, Sort, And Total pane lets you group and sort by up to 10 levels.*

First group level   Second group level

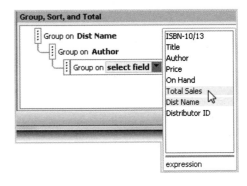

Figure 7-9: *This Report View shows the report grouped by two levels.*

NOTE

While you can add up to ten levels of groups in a report, if you have more than one or two, you may have to scroll down to see the Add A Group button.

ADD A NEW GROUP LEVEL

1. In the Group, Sort, And Total pane, click **Add A Group**.

2. A list of the available fields in your report is displayed, and a new line is added to the Group, Sort, And Total pane.

3. Click the field by which you want to group. The grouping level is added to your report, and, in Layout View, you can see the change to your report.

USE AN EXPRESSION TO GROUP BY

In addition to choosing grouping levels, you can create a group using an *expression*. An expression is a calculation. It is comparable to a formula in Microsoft Excel.

1. Click the down arrow next to the field name in the grouping level on which you want to build an expression.

2. From the drop-down list, click **Expression** at the bottom.

3. Complete your expression using the Expression Builder, as shown in Figure 7-10 (see Chapter 5 for information on using the Expression Builder).

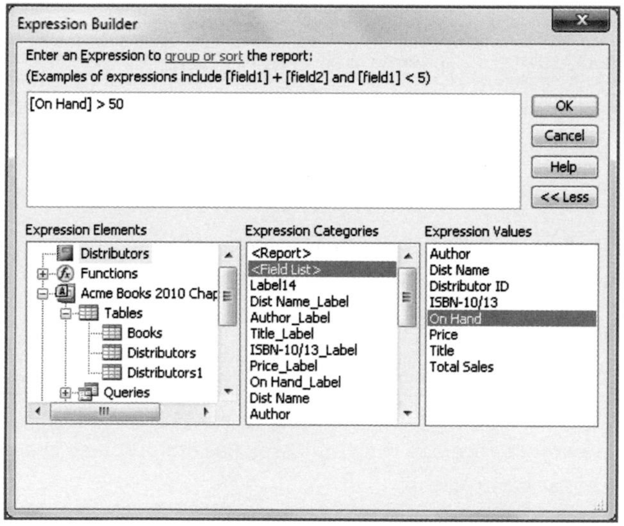

Expression Builder

Enter an Expression to group or sort the report:
(Examples of expressions include [field1] + [field2] and [field1] < 5)

[On Hand] > 50

OK

Cancel

Help

<< Less

Expression Elements	Expression Categories	Expression Values
Distributors	<Report>	Author
Functions	<Field List>	Dist Name
Acme Books 2010 Chap	Label14	Distributor ID
Tables	Dist Name_Label	ISBN-10/13
Books	Author_Label	On Hand
Distributors	Title_Label	Price
Distributors1	ISBN-10/13_Label	Title
Queries	Price_Label	Total Sales
	On Hand_Label	
	Dist Name	
	Author	

*Figure 7-10: **You can create an expression for your group.***

ADD A NEW SORT LEVEL

1. In the Group, Sort, And Total pane, click **Add A Sort**.

2. Select the field in your report that you would like to establish as the main group. The sort order field will automatically default to With A On Top in Text data type fields. To change this, click the **With A On Top** down arrow to display a drop-down list, from which you can choose **With Z On Top** to create a descending order. Options for other data types are shown in Table 7-3.

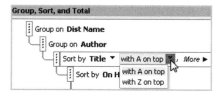

Group, Sort, and Total

Group on **Dist Name**

Group on **Author**

Sort by **Title** ▾ with A on top ▾ *More ▶*

with A on top

Sort by **On H** with Z on top

CHANGE A GROUP TITLE

1. In the Group, Sort, And Total pane, click the group level for which you want to change the title, and then click **More** to display the options.

2. Next to With Title, click **Click To Add**. (The default title of a grouping is the field name.) The Zoom dialog box appears, as shown in Figure 7-11. Type the title you want.

3. Click **Font** to display the Font dialog box. Make any changes and click **OK** to return to the Zoom dialog box.

4. Click **OK** when you are done.

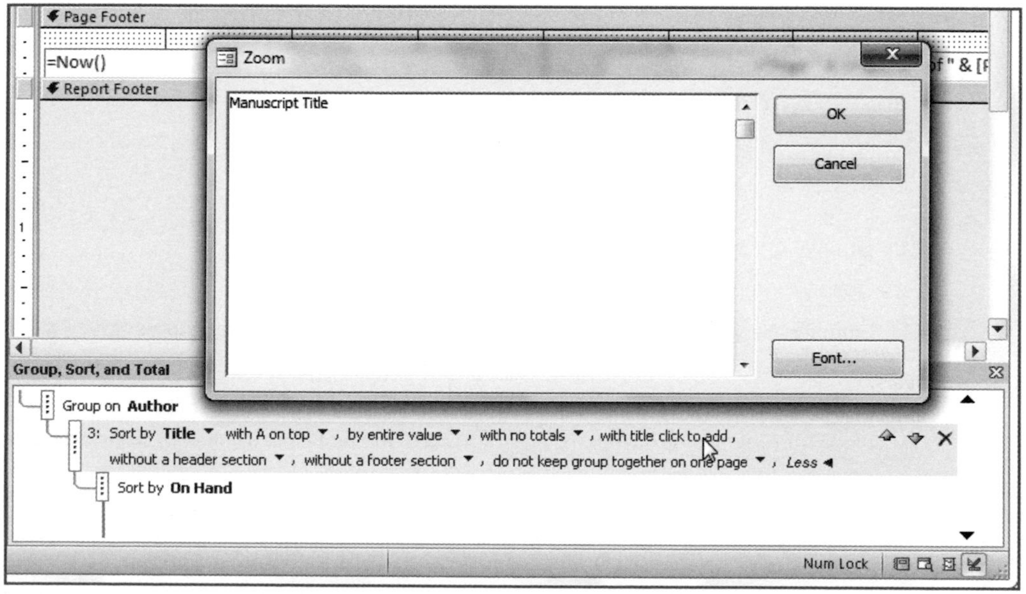

FINE-TUNE HOW DATA IS SORTED

1. Click the group level you want to change, and click **More**.

2. Click the **By Entire Value** down arrow to make the changes. The default is By Entire Value; however, you can choose to sort by using just the first one or two characters, or create a custom group of characters.

by entire value ▾ , with no

● by entire value
○ by first character
○ by first two characters
○ Custom:
   Characters: 1

3. If you are in Layout View, your changes will appear immediately on your report.

Page Footer

=Now()

Report Footer

Zoom

Manuscript Title

OK

Cancel

Font...

Group, Sort, and Total

Group on **Author**

3: Sort by **Title** ▾ with A on top ▾ , by entire value ▾ , with no totals ▾ , with title click to add ,
   without a header section ▾ , without a footer section ▾ , do not keep group together on one page ▾ , *Less ◀*

Sort by **On Hand**

Num Lock

*Figure 7-11: **You can change a group title to something different than its field name.***

Calculate a Value

Reports, like queries, have the ability to perform calculations of field values within their designs. The benefit of using a report is its further ability to display the information in a customized and formatted printable fashion (Chapter 8 provides information on formatting and printing options).

ADD CALCULATIONS TO A REPORT

1. Open a report in Layout View, as this view is the quickest way to add calculations.
2. Click the field to which you want the calculation applied.
3. In the Design tab (Report Layout Tools) Grouping & Totals group, click **Totals**.
4. Select one of the calculations from the menu.
5. A total appears in the group footer (an average is shown here). Its control source is an expression reflecting your chosen calculation.

Build An Ebay Business Quic	978007160145(	$19.99
Microsoft Office Access 2007	9780072263718	$16.99
Microsoft Office Excel 2007 (	9780072263725	$19.99
Ms Office Access 2003 Quick	9780072232295	$16.99
Ms Office Excel 2003 Quickst	9780072232288	$19.99
		$ 18.79

You can see this expression in Design View.

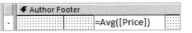

CALCULATE A GROUP TOTAL

1. Open your report in Layout View.
2. From the Design tab (Report Design Tools) Grouping & Totals group, click **Group & Sort** to open the Group, Sort, And Total pane.
3. Click the grouping or sort level where you want to create totals. Click **More** and click the **With *Field Name* Totals** (or With No Totals, the first time you see it) down arrow to open the Totals menu.
   - Click **Total On** to display the drop-down list of fields from which you can choose. Click the field you want to use for totals.

ACCOMPLISHING COMMON TASKS IN REPORTS

Open a report in Design View.

INSERT PAGE BREAKS

1. In the Design tab (Report Design Tools) Controls group, click the **Insert Page Break** icon.

2. Click where you want the page break on the report. You will see a yellow line with dots at the far left side of the report. Click elsewhere in the grid, and you will only see a series of small dots to indicate the page break in Design View.

3. Open the report in Print Preview to page through the new page layout.

ADD OR CHANGE THE REPORT TITLE

1. If a title is not already in the report header, in the Design tab (Report Design Tools) Header/Footer group, click **Title**. The default title name is highlighted. Type a new title. Press **ENTER** to save your new title.

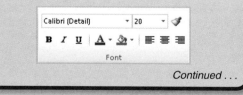

2. To change font characteristics of the title text, select the characters you want to format, and choose the applicable tool from the Format tab Font group (see Chapter 6 for descriptions for each tool).

Continued . . .

- Click **Type** to display the list of calculations you can perform. Click the type of calculation you want Access 2007 to perform.

- Click **Show Grand Total** to add a grand total in the report footer at the end of the report.

- Click **Show Group Totals As % Of Grand Total** to add a calculated percentage of the grand total for each group.

- Click **Show In Group Header** or **Show In Group Footer** if you want this total displayed in each group.

4. Click outside the Totals menu to close it. Your report reflects your changes at once.

Set Group Headers and Footers in a Report

You can create headers and footers within groups.

1. In Design View or Layout View, open the Group, Sort, And Total pane, and select the group level with which you want to work.

2. Click **More**.

ADD OR REMOVE A GROUP-LEVEL HEADER OR FOOTER

By default, groups include a header section but not a footer section. You can easily change this behavior.

- To remove a header section, click the **With A Header Section** down arrow to open a drop-down list, and click **Without A Header Section** to remove the default header. If the header section contains controls other than the grouping field, a dialog box appears, warning you that these controls will be removed. Click **Yes** if that is all right. Click **No** to retain the controls.

- To include a footer, click the **Without A Footer Section** down arrow to open a drop-down list, and click **With A Footer Section** to add the section.

ACCOMPLISHING COMMON TASKS IN REPORTS *(Continued)*

ADD PAGE NUMBERS AND THE DATA AND TIME

Both tools are located in the Design tab (Report Design Tools) Header/Footer group.

1. Click **Page Numbers**. Select how you want page numbers to display from the Page Numbers dialog box that appears. Click **OK**.

2. Click **Date And Time**, choose the format you want from the Date And Time dialog box, and click **OK**.

LOCATE ERRORS

If Access finds something not quite right with your design, it will indicate this to you by placing a green triangle in the upper-left corner of the report selector. To see the problem:

1. Click the selector to display an informational tooltip.

2. Point to the tooltip to see an explanation of the error.

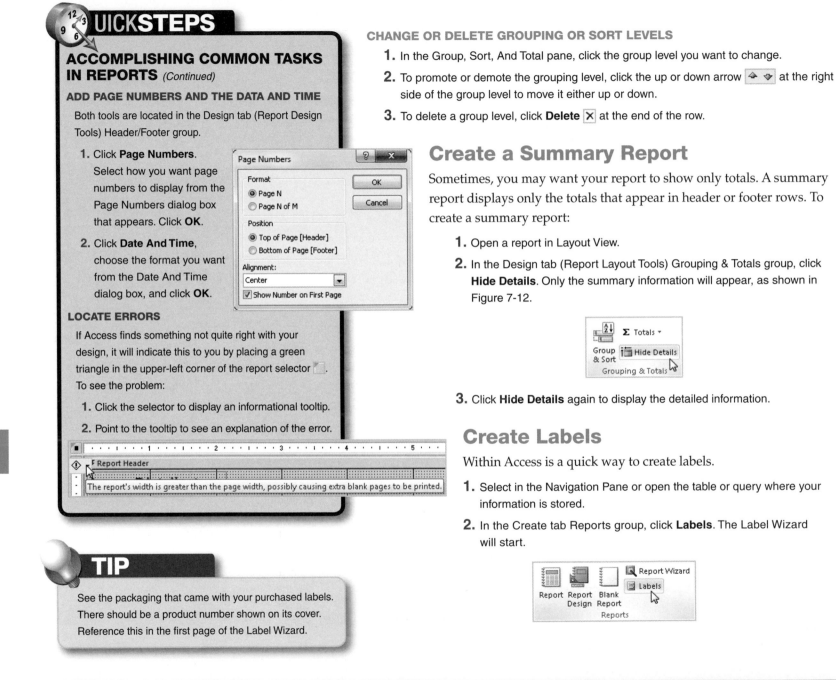

The report's width is greater than the page width, possibly causing extra blank pages to be printed.

TIP

See the packaging that came with your purchased labels. There should be a product number shown on its cover. Reference this in the first page of the Label Wizard.

CHANGE OR DELETE GROUPING OR SORT LEVELS

1. In the Group, Sort, And Total pane, click the group level you want to change.

2. To promote or demote the grouping level, click the up or down arrow at the right side of the group level to move it either up or down.

3. To delete a group level, click **Delete** ☒ at the end of the row.

Create a Summary Report

Sometimes, you may want your report to show only totals. A summary report displays only the totals that appear in header or footer rows. To create a summary report:

1. Open a report in Layout View.

2. In the Design tab (Report Layout Tools) Grouping & Totals group, click **Hide Details**. Only the summary information will appear, as shown in Figure 7-12.

3. Click **Hide Details** again to display the detailed information.

Create Labels

Within Access is a quick way to create labels.

1. Select in the Navigation Pane or open the table or query where your information is stored.

2. In the Create tab Reports group, click **Labels**. The Label Wizard will start.

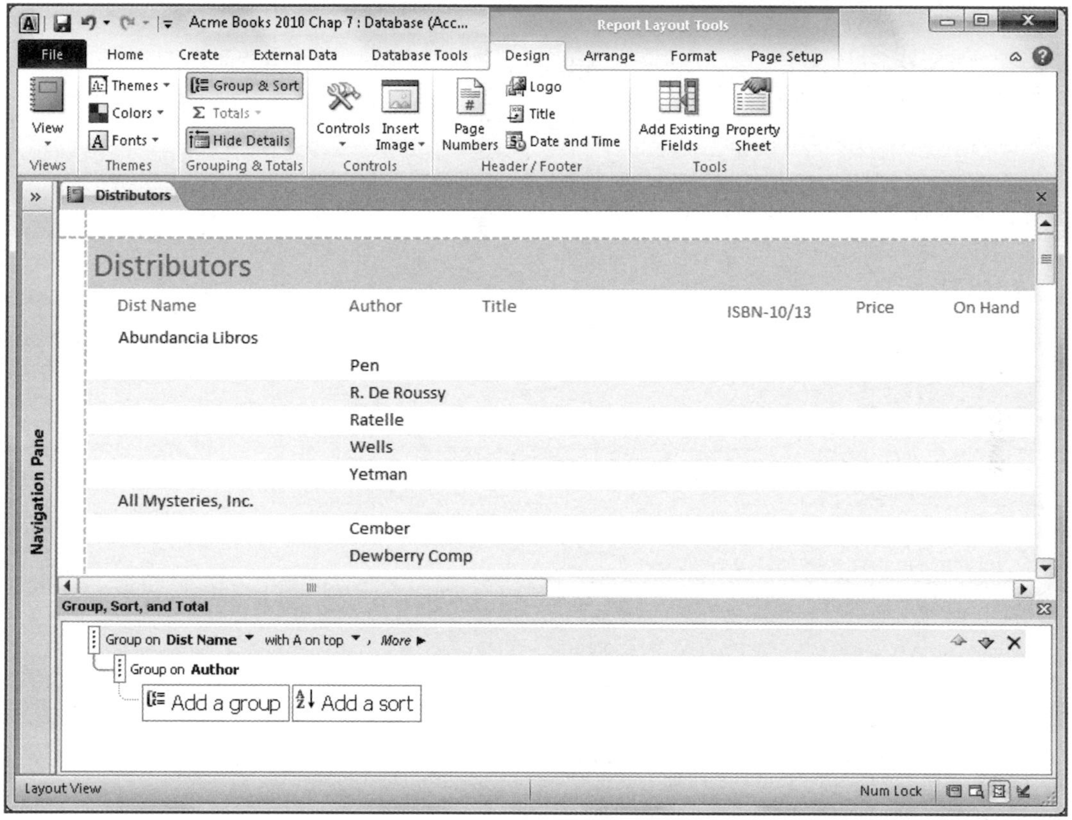
Acme Books 2010 Chap 7 : Database (Acc...
Report Layout Tools
File
Home
Create
External Data
Database Tools
Design
Arrange
Format
Page Setup
View
Themes
Colors
Fonts
Group & Sort
Totals
Hide Details
Controls
Insert Image
Page Numbers
Logo
Title
Date and Time
Add Existing Fields
Property Sheet
Views
Themes
Grouping & Totals
Controls
Header / Footer
Tools
Distributors
Navigation Pane
Distributors
Dist Name
Author
Title
ISBN-10/13
Price
On Hand
Abundancia Libros
Pen
R. De Roussy
Ratelle
Wells
Yetman
All Mysteries, Inc.
Cember
Dewberry Comp
Group, Sort, and Total
Group on Dist Name with A on top , More
Group on Author
Add a group
Add a sort
Layout View
Num Lock

Figure 7-12: ***Information can be hidden except for the grouping fields.***

3. Select the size and type of label you would like to print, as seen in Figure 7-13. If you can't find the right size in the preset label sizes, click **Customize** and set your own parameters by creating a new label definition. Click **Close** to return to the Label Wizard, and then click **Next**.
4. Choose the font and color you would like applied to your text, as shown in Figure 7-14. To see the available color choices, click the **Builder** button to the right of the Text Color text box. Click a basic color, or click the **Define Custom Colors** button to select a custom hue. Click **OK** to return to the Label Wizard. Click **Next**.

NOTE

Refer to Chapters 6 and 8 for additional information about other formatting features for your reports and forms.

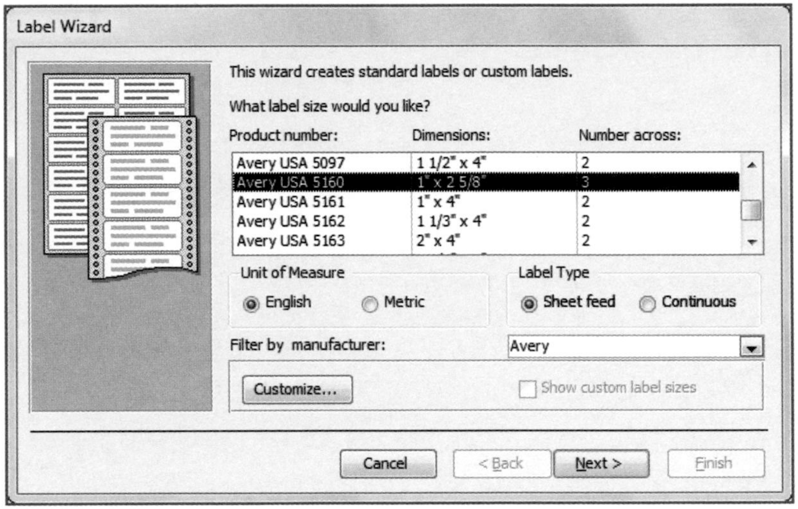

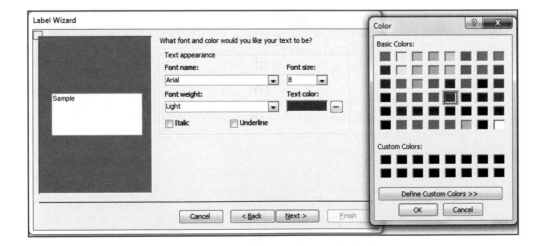

Figure 7-13: *With the Label Wizard, creating new mailing labels is accomplished in just a few mouse clicks.*

5. Select a field you want on the label, and click the right arrow to move it to the Prototype Label list box. If you are creating a mailing label or a label containing more than one line of text, press **ENTER** to move to the next line of the Prototype Label box. Type commas and spaces as needed. Continue selecting and moving fields until the label is designed to your liking. Click **Next**.

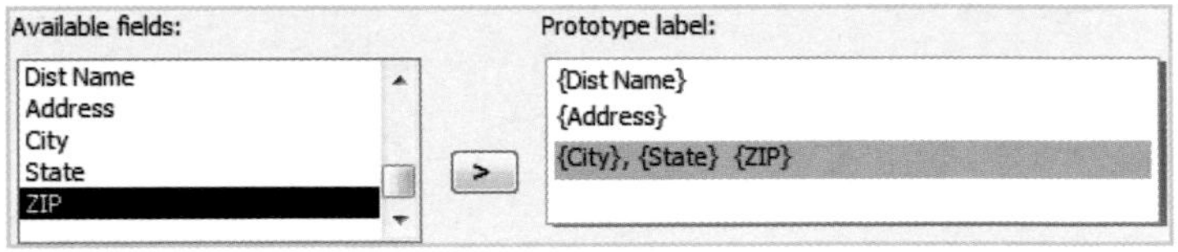

6. Select the fields you would like to sort by, and click the right arrow to move it to the Sort By box. Use the direction arrows to move or remove fields from the Sort By box.

   –Or–

   Double-click a field to move it from one list to the other.

   Click **Next** to move to the final page.

7. Type a report name in the text box, or accept the default name. Select whether to view the labels in Print Preview as they will be printed or to continue modifying the label design in Design View. Click **Finish**.

Figure 7-14: *Preview your font and font color in the sample window.*

Chapter 8
Preparing Your Data for Presentation

You can make several visual enhancements to your forms and reports before you release them to be used (in the case of forms) or printed (in the case, typically, of reports). The first part of this chapter describes many of these features in addition to how you can format forms and reports in Design View (and at times, Layout View) and apply Office-wide themes to provide a consistent color and font scheme throughout your documents. The latter part of the chapter describes further options you have for printing your data.

Improve the Data's Appearance

The judicious use of color, graphics, and lines can transform a drab collection of data into an appealing presentation for people who enter or analyze your data. The features and techniques described in this section apply to forms and reports in both Layout View and Design View, unless otherwise noted. A majority of the tools are found on the Format and Design tabs of the two objects, within their respective Layout and Report Tools collections.

Modify Images

Chapter 6 describes how to insert images by use of the Image control in Design View (you can also use the Image control in Layout View). This section describes changes you can make to the image after it has been placed in a form or report in Design View or Layout View.

Begin by selecting the image control.

CHOOSE AN IMAGE FORMAT

Image controls support many graphic formats. The common graphic types supported are listed in Table 8-1.

CHANGE IMAGE PROPERTIES

There are a number of properties specifically associated with images that you can use to change the characteristics of images you add to a form or report, as shown in Figure 8-1. To change a property's setting, do one of the following:

- Type a value. For example, to precisely change the location of an image in the form or report section that it is in, type units of measurement in the Top and Left property text boxes. The intersection of these two numbers defines the location of the upper-left corner of the image.

Width	8.2917"
Height	5.6667"
Top	0.375"
Left	6.5833"

- Click the property's down arrow, and select a setting from the drop-down list. For example, to decrease the size of your database, you could change each image file picture type from being *embedded* (each file becomes part of the .accdb file) to being *linked* (a pointer is placed in the database to the actual location of the image file outside the database). See Chapter 10 for more information on linking.

Visible	Yes
Picture Type	Embedded
Picture	Embedded
Size Mode	Linked
Picture Alignment	Shared
Width	8.2917"

TIP

While you cannot change the format of an image that is applied to an image control within Access, you can open the source image in a graphics program (for example, Microsoft Paint or Adobe Photoshop Elements) and save the image in a different format. Then in Access, click the **Builder** button ... in the image's Picture property and re-insert the image with the new format.

FILE TYPE	EXTENSION
Bitmap/Device Independent Bitmap	.bmp/.dib
Graphics Interchange Format	.gif
Icon	.ico
Joint Photographic Experts Group	.jpg
Portable Network Graphic	.png
Windows Metafile/Enhanced Metafile	.wmf/.emf

*Table 8-1: **Graphic File Types Used in Forms or Reports***

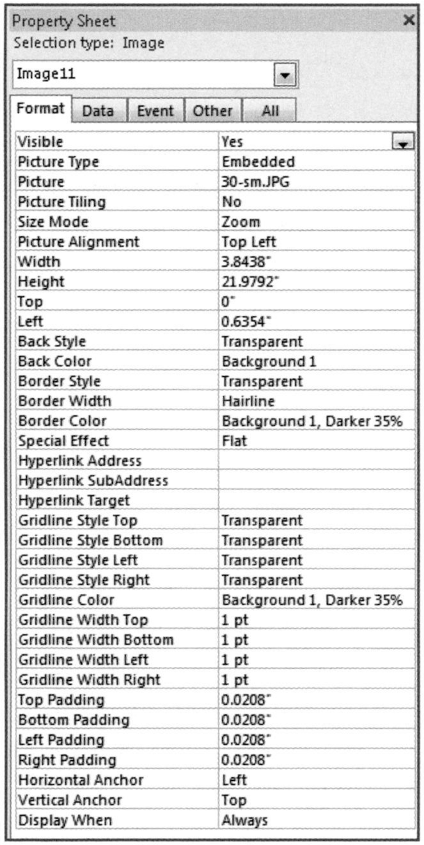

Property Sheet				
Selection type: Image				

Image11 ▼

Format	Data	Event	Other	All

Visible	Yes
Picture Type	Embedded
Picture	30-sm.JPG
Picture Tiling	No
Size Mode	Zoom
Picture Alignment	Top Left
Width	3.8438"
Height	21.9792"
Top	0"
Left	0.6354"
Back Style	Transparent
Back Color	Background 1
Border Style	Transparent
Border Width	Hairline
Border Color	Background 1, Darker 35%
Special Effect	Flat
Hyperlink Address	
Hyperlink SubAddress	
Hyperlink Target	
Gridline Style Top	Transparent
Gridline Style Bottom	Transparent
Gridline Style Left	Transparent
Gridline Style Right	Transparent
Gridline Color	Background 1, Darker 35%
Gridline Width Top	1 pt
Gridline Width Bottom	1 pt
Gridline Width Left	1 pt
Gridline Width Right	1 pt
Top Padding	0.0208"
Bottom Padding	0.0208"
Left Padding	0.0208"
Right Padding	0.0208"
Horizontal Anchor	Left
Vertical Anchor	Top
Display When	Always

*Figure 8-1: **Many properties are available when working with images.***

NOTE

The pictures (or *images*) and graphics that are described in this chapter are *unbound* objects, meaning they are stored in the design of the form or report and do not change when you move from record to record or from page to page. *Bound* pictures, such as photos that identify each item in your antique collection, are bound to the underlying data.

- Click the **Builder** button [...] to open a dialog box for supplementary information. For example, clicking the Picture property Builder button opens the Insert Picture dialog box, where you can change the location of the present image or browse to a new image (see Chapter 6).

- Click **Insert Image** in the Design tab (Form/Report Design Tools) Controls group. A gallery of the images previously inserted in the database is displayed so you can easily re-insert an image.

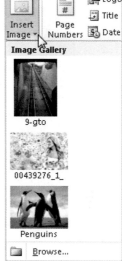

Use Conditional Formatting in Reports and Forms

You can use *conditional formatting* to change how your controls look in a form or report by applying formatting to data that satisfies a set of criteria you select. For example, you can have each value over $50.00 be on a yellow background, as seen in Figure 8-2.

SET CONDITIONAL FORMATTING

You can set conditional formatting in both reports and forms. The following instructions refer to a report. To set a conditional format:

1. In the Navigation Pane, right-click the report you want to change, and click **Design View** or **Layout View**.

2. Click the control on which you want conditional formatting applied. In the Format tab (Report Layout/Design Tools) Control Formatting group, click **Conditional Formatting**. The Conditional Formatting Rules Manager dialog box appears, as seen in Figure 8-3.

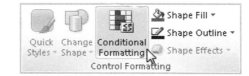

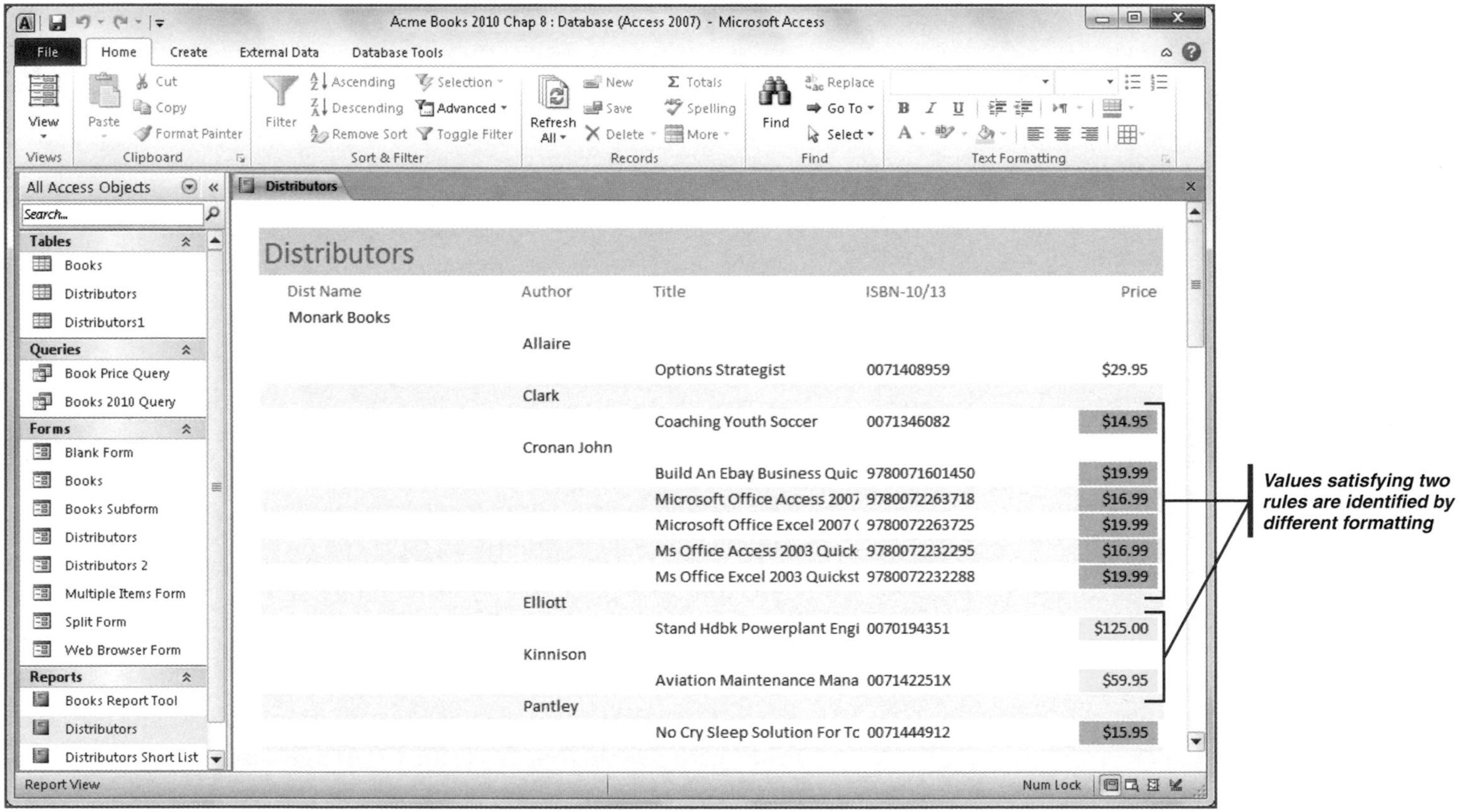

Values satisfying two
rules are identified by
different formatting

Figure 8-2: *Conditional formatting draws attention to data on your form or report.*

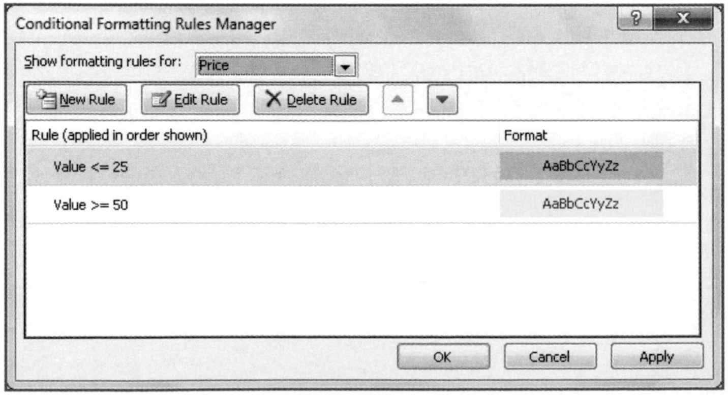

Figure 8-3: *The Conditional
Formatting Rules Manager
displays the rules you create
to apply conditional formats.*

3. Click **New Rule** to open the New Formatting
Rule dialog box shown in Figure 8-4. Under
Select A Rule Type, accept the default Check
Values In The Current Record Or Use An
Expression.

4. Under Format Only Cells Where The, click
the first down arrow, and select whether the
control contains a value or expression.

QUICKSTEPS

FORMATTING VALUES WITH DATA BARS

Data bars provide a visual clue to the relative comparison of numerical data in a report or form. As a data bar grows in width from the left edge of the field with ever-increasing values, its color gradually fades—that is, the lowest values have a solid color and the higher values gradually fade to white. Data bars are easily created using the Conditional Formatting Rules Manager (see "Use Conditional Formatting in Reports and Forms").

1. Open a report or form in Layout View or Design View (the fields in the report should be using data from only one data source, i.e., one table or query), and click the control on which you want conditional formatting applied.

2. In the Format tab (Report Layout/Design Tools) Control Formatting group, click **Conditional Formatting**. In the Conditional Formatting Rules Manager, click **New Rule**.

3. In the New Formatting Rule dialog box, under Select A Rule Type, click **Compare To Other Records**. The lower half of the dialog box shows data bar settings.

4. Select whether to show only the data bar (the field values will be hidden), which values to compare, and the bar color. Click **OK** when finished, and then close the Conditional Formatting Rules Manager.

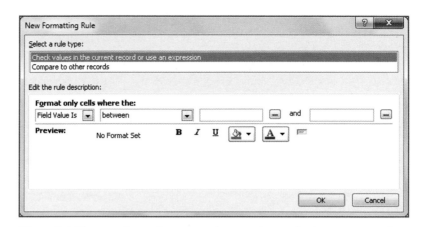

Figure 8-4: **You can choose from several comparisons of values or expressions and set up the formatting you want applied to those values that meet the criteria.**

5. If the control contains a value, click the second comparison down arrow (the default is Between) to choose from a list of comparison operators. Type a constant value in the text box (the third box) or use the Builder and, depending on what you chose as your comparison operator, type another constant value or use its Builder in the fourth box.

–Or–

If the control contains an expression (as selected in step 3), type the expression in the single text box.

6. Click the formatting you want to appear for values (or expressions) that are true for the condition you set.

- Click **B** to make the font bold.
- Click **I** to set the font in italics.
- Click **U** to underline the text.
- Click the **Background Color** down arrow [🎨 ▾] to display a gallery of background colors (clicking the tool itself applies the color displayed under the icon).
- Click the **Font Color** down arrow [**A** ▾] to choose the font color (clicking the tool itself applies the color displayed under the icon).

7. Click **OK** to complete the rule and return to the Conditional Formatting Rules Manager dialog box. Click **New Rule** to set additional conditions for the same field.

–Or–

Click the **Show Formatting Rules For** down arrow, and select a different field on which to apply rules. Click **OK** when finished.

8. Right-click the report tab, and click **Report View** to see how your report looks with the conditional formatting applied (see Figure 8-2).

DISPLAY HIDDEN BACKGROUND COLORS

If you have set a background color and cannot see it, you may have to change the field property for the control where you have applied a condition format.

1. In the Design tab (Report Design/Layout Tools) Tools group, ensure the control that has the conditional format is selected, and click **Property Sheet**.

Left	7.25"
Back Style	Transparent ▾
Back Color	Transparent
Border Style	Normal
Border Width	Hairline

2. Click the **Format** tab, click the **Back Style** down arrow, and change the setting from Transparent to **Normal**.

3. Switch to Report View. You should see the background color.

Add a Chart

You can add *charts* by copying them from other programs, such as Microsoft Excel; by creating your own using the Excel menus and tools within Access; or by using the Access Chart Wizard.

INSERT AN EXCEL CHART

1. Open Microsoft Excel and locate the chart you want to insert.

2. Right-click the chart and click **Copy**.

CAUTION

Excel charts cannot be linked or imported. They must be copied manually into your form or report.

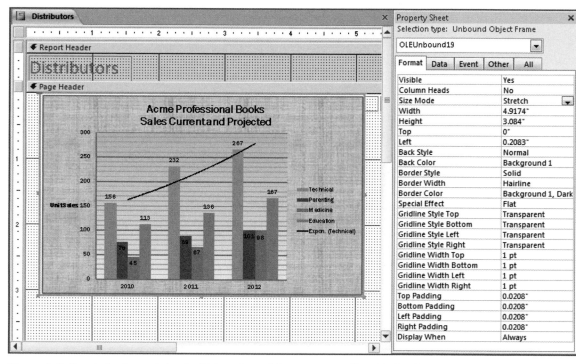

Figure 8-5: **Excel charts contained within unbound frames are easily added to forms and reports by copying and pasting.**

3. Open the report or form in Design View, and right-click where you want to place the chart. (See "Select Design View Components," later in the chapter.)

4. Click **Paste**. The chart is placed in an Unbound Object Frame box, which you can resize and move as necessary, as shown in Figure 8-5.

CREATE A CHART USING EXCEL FEATURES

1. Open the report or form in Design View.

2. In the Design tab (Report Design Tools) Controls group, open the gallery of controls, and click the **Unbound Object Frame** icon . The Unbound Object Frame mouse pointer will appear.

3. Drag a rectangle on your form or report where you want to place the chart. The Microsoft Access dialog box appears.

4. Click **Create New**. In the Object Type list box, click **Microsoft Excel Chart**, and then click **OK**. A sample chart opens and the Access ribbon is replaced with the ribbon from Microsoft Excel 2010, containing charting tools and features, as shown in Figure 8-6.

TIP

By default, the Size Mode property for unbound object frames has its attribute set to Clip, which removes portions of the chart as you decrease its size. Select the Stretch attribute to provide standard sizing capabilities associated with dragging the sizing handles surrounding the frame.

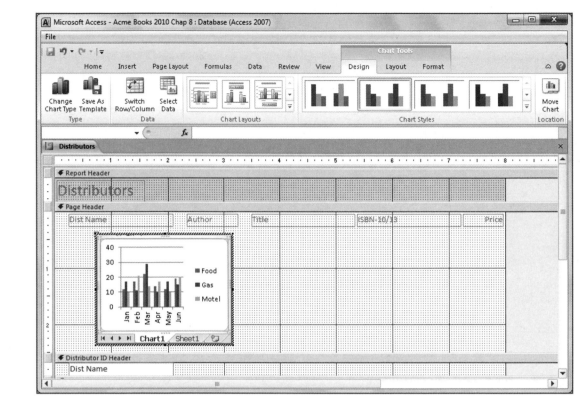

Figure 8-6: *You can modify a sample chart within Access 2010 using Excel 2010 tools.*

5. Click **Change Chart Type** in the Design tab (Chart Tools) Type group to choose a different chart (see the next section for more information on chart types), or use the other tools to build the chart.

6. Click outside the chart to return to full Access functionality. To edit the chart with Excel features, double-click it.

CREATE A CHART USING A WIZARD

1. Open the report or form in Design View.

2. In the Design tab (Report Design Tools) Controls group, click the **Chart** icon 📊.

3. Drag a rectangle in the location where you want the chart.

4. The Chart Wizard appears. Choose the table or query whose data you want to use. Click **Next**.

5. Select the fields from the table or query that contain the data you want to see charted by moving fields from the Available Fields list to the Fields For Chart list (see Chapters 6 and 7 for information on how to move fields between the lists). Click **Next**.

NOTE

To learn more about using Excel and charting, see *Microsoft Office Excel 2010 QuickSteps,* also published by McGraw-Hill/Professional.

6. Choose a chart type. Click a chart type to see its description displayed in the wizard, as shown in Figure 8-7. Click **Next**.

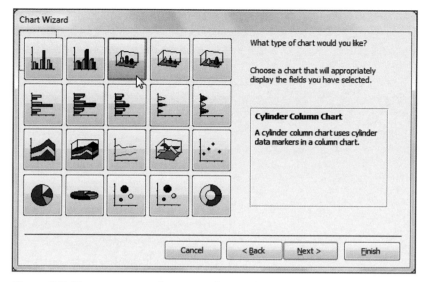

Figure 8-7: *There are many chart types from which to choose.*

7. To lay out your chart, drag the field buttons into the field boxes on the sample chart, as seen in Figure 8-8. Click **Preview Chart** to see how you're doing. If you don't like the layout of the chart, change the location of the fields, and click **Preview Chart** again. When you are satisfied with your chart, click **Next**.

8. To have the chart reflect changes record by record, link the fields in the form or report to the fields on the chart. Click **Next**.

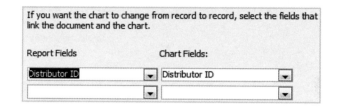

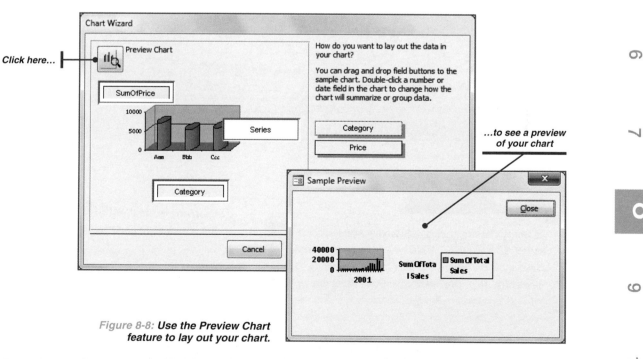

Figure 8-8: *Use the Preview Chart feature to lay out your chart.*

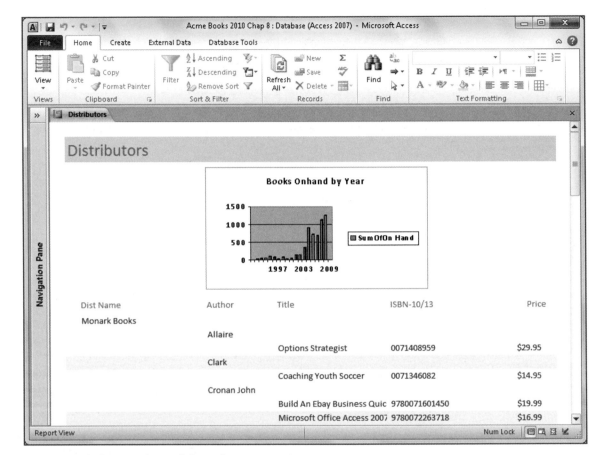

Figure 8-9: *A chart can be useful on a form or report.*

9. Type a title for the chart, and choose whether to display a legend for the data series. Click **Finish**. Figure 8-9 shows the results of a chart created using the Chart Wizard.

Use Graphics

Though Access doesn't provide the full breadth of drawing tools available in other Office programs, you can still be quite creative by using lines and rectangles to separate, encompass, or emphasize areas in your forms and reports. An example of how lines and rectangles can enhance a form is shown in Figure 8-10.

ADD LINES AND RECTANGLES

1. Open the report or form in Design View.

2. In the Design tab (Report/Form Design Tools) Controls group, click the **Line** ╲ or **Rectangle** ▢ tool, and drag in the Design View section to the approximate size and location to more precisely modify the graphic.

3. Drag one of the three sizing handles on the border of the line or eight handles on the rectangle to resize it.

4. Point to the border of the graphic, and when the mouse pointer changes into a cross, drag the graphic to reposition it.

–Or–

Use the applicable property in the property sheet to set width, height, and location (see the next section, "Modify Graphics Properties").

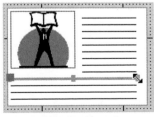

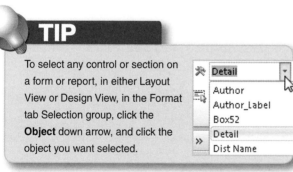

Figure 8-10: *Rectangles and lines can be combined with other graphics to embellish your forms and reports.*

TIP

To select any control or section on a form or report, in either Layout View or Design View, in the Format tab Selection group, click the **Object** down arrow, and click the object you want selected.

TIP

See Chapters 6 and 7 for more information on working with controls, such as how to move, resize, and arrange them.

MODIFY GRAPHICS PROPERTIES

1. In Design View, click the graphic to select it.

2. In the Design tab (Report Design Tools) Tools group, click **Property Sheet**.

   –Or–

   Right-click the graphic and select **Properties**.

3. Change the settings for the property you want (see "Change Image Properties" earlier in the chapter for ways to change property settings).

Modify the Form or Report Design

Forms and reports have several properties that determine their appearance and behavior.

SELECT DESIGN VIEW COMPONENTS

Before you can work on a particular section of a form or report, you need to select it. In the Navigation Pane, drag the form or report to the Access work area to open it. Right-click the object and click **Design View**.

- To select the object itself (form or report), click the object selector (the box at the intersection of the rulers) ▪, or click anywhere in the background outside the form/report design area.

- To select a form or report section, click the form/report section selector—the small square in the vertical ruler next to the section divider. (If the ruler is not displayed, right-click in an empty area of the grid, and click **Ruler**.)

- To select controls, click a single control; to select multiple controls, hold down SHIFT while clicking each control, or drag a selection rectangle around the controls you want.

- To select all components on the report or form, press CTRL+A; or in the Format tab Selection group, click **Select All**.

CHANGE FORM AND REPORT PROPERTIES

1. Open the form or report in Design View or Layout View.

2. In Design View, click the form/report selector at the intersection of the horizontal and vertical rulers. In Layout View, click the section you want to select.

3. In the Design tab (Form/Report Tools) Tools group, click **Property Sheet**, if it is not selected, to display the property sheet.

QUICKFACTS

UNDERSTANDING FORMATTING RULES

There are several rules you need to remember regarding formatting:

- The format that is applied to a field in your table is applied to all form and report controls that you link or bind to that field. It also will apply to any query you create with the Query Designer.

- The display format you set affects the appearance of your data, not how someone enters it. For example, if you set a field to display a number in a currency format, the user need not enter the dollar sign.

- When you set an input mask for a field as well as a display format, Access applies the display format only after that record is saved.

- To enable rich text formatting in a Memo field, the Text Format property must be set to Rich Text (see "Enable Rich Text Formatting" later in the chapter).

TIP

You can quickly determine the theme currently in effect in a report or form. In Layout View or Design View, in the Design tab (Layout/Design Tools) Themes group, point to **Themes** (or **Colors**). The tooltip displays the current theme (similarly, point to the **Fonts** button to see the current theme fonts in use, as well as the current theme).

> Themes | Group & Sort
> Colors | Σ Totals
> Fonts | Hide Details
> Themes | Grouping & Totals
>
> **Themes**
>
> Current: Hardcover
>
> Change the overall design for your database, including colors and fonts.
>
> Press F1 for more help.

4. In the property sheet, click the **Format** tab, which lists the format properties you can set for a report or form. (Other tabs in the property sheet offer data, event, and other properties.)

5. Click the text box next to a property, and click the down arrow or the **Builder** button to see a list, gallery, or dialog box of choices, as shown in Figure 8-11.

–Or–

Type a value.

6. When finished, close the property sheet, and in the Design tab Views group, click **View** and change to Report View or Form View to see your changes.

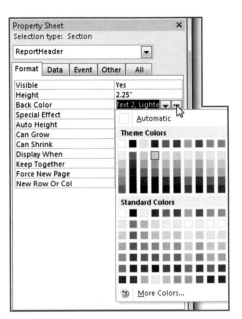

Figure 8-11: Formatting properties can be selected from a list, menu, or dialog box, or the value typed.

Apply Themes

Themes are the most hands-off way to add a coordinated look and feel to a database. Built-in themes control the formatting of themed elements within reports and forms, such as the color of report and form headers, and the font used in reports and forms. In addition, you can change themes and modify themed elements (colors and fonts).

CHANGE THE CURRENT THEME

By default, Access applies the Office theme to new forms and reports (see the "Locating and Selectively Applying Themes" QuickSteps for ways to selectively apply themes). You can easily view the effects from the other built-in themes and change to the one you prefer.

1. Open a form or report in Layout View or Design View.

2. In the Design tab (Layout/Design Tools) Themes group, click **Themes**. A gallery of the available themes (in current use, custom, and built-in) is displayed, as shown in Figure 8-12.

NOTE

If you used the AutoFormat feature in Access 2007 to format your objects, they will look the same in Access 2010; however, AutoFormat is not available in Access 2010. In order to achieve consistent formatting throughout your database/application, you should change to an appropriate theme.

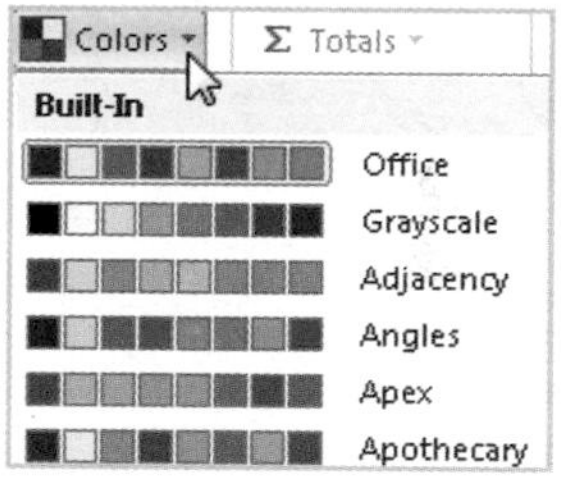

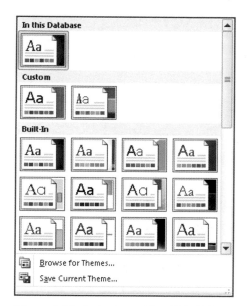

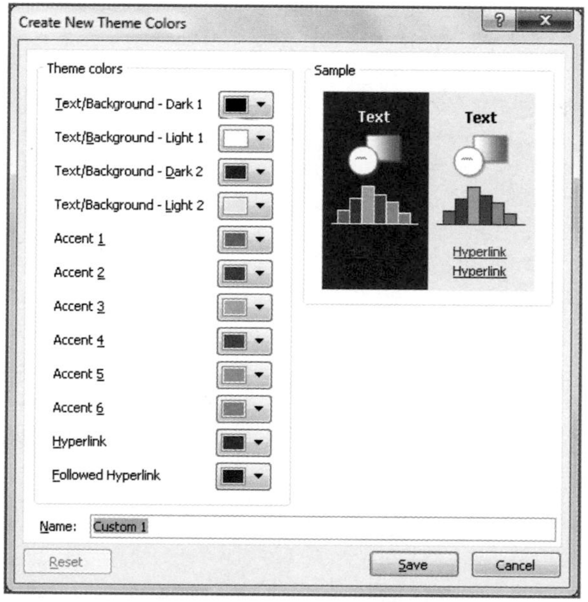

Figure 8-12: ***Access provides 40 built-in professionally designed themes.***

3. Point to each theme and see how colors and fonts change in themed elements. (See "Create Custom Themes" later in the chapter to design your own color and font combinations.)
4. Click the theme you want, and save your report.

CHANGE THEMED COLORS

Each theme comes with 12 primary colors affecting text, accents, and hyperlinks. You can choose a theme with different colors or modify each constituent color.

1. In the Design tab (Layout/Design Tools) Themes group, click **Colors**. The drop-down list displays the built-in and online themes and 8 of the 12 colors associated with each theme.
2. At the bottom of the list, click **Create New Theme Colors**. The Create New Theme Colors dialog box displays each constituent theme color and a sample displaying the current selections (see Figure 8-13).

Figure 8-13: ***Each theme color can be modified from an essentially infinite number of choices.***

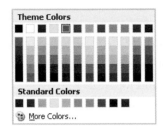

3. Click the theme color you want to change. A gallery of colors displays and provides the following three options from which you select a new color:

- **Theme Colors** displays a matrix of the 12 primary colors in the current theme and 6 shades associated with each. Click a color and see the change in the Sample area of the Create New Theme Colors dialog box.

- **Standard Colors** displays the 10 standard colors in the color spectrum (red through violet). Click the color you want.

- **More Colors** opens the Colors dialog box, shown in Figure 8-14, from where you can select a custom color by clicking a color and using a slider to change its shading, or by selecting a color model and entering specific color values. In addition, you can click the **Standard** tab and select from a hexagonal array of Web-friendly colors (the Web-friendly colors should appear the same irrespective of the browser used to display the Web page).

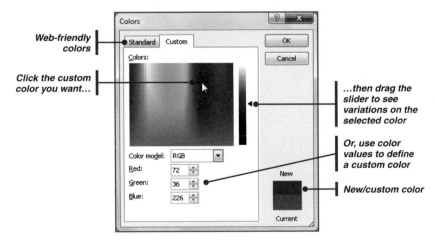

Figure 8-14: The Colors dialog box offers the greatest control of custom color selection, as well as a collection of standard Web-friendly colors.

4. Repeat step 3 for any other theme color you want to change. If you get a bit far afield in your color changes, don't panic. Click **Reset** at the bottom of the Create New Theme Colors dialog box to return to the default theme colors.

5. Type a new name for the color combination you've selected, and click **Save**. Custom colors are available for selection at the top of the theme Colors drop-down list.

Create New Theme Fonts

Heading font:
Cambria

Body font:
Calibri

Name: Custom 1

Sample
Heading
Body text body text body text.
Body text body text.

Save   Cancel

CHANGE THEMED FONTS

Each theme includes two fonts. The *body* font is used for general text entry (the Calibri font in the default Office theme is the body font). A *heading* font is also included and used in report and form headers.

1. In the Design tab (Layout/Design Tools) Themes group, click **Fonts**. The drop-down list displays a list of theme font combinations (heading and body). The current theme font combination is highlighted.

2. Point to each combination to see how the fonts will appear in your report or form.

3. Click the combination you want, or click **Create New Theme Fonts** at the bottom of the drop-down list.

A Fonts ▾   Hide Details

Built-In

Office
Cambria
Calibri
A a

Office 2
Calibri
Cambria
A a

4. In the Create New Theme Fonts dialog box, click either or both the **Heading Font** and **Body Font** down arrows to select new fonts. View the new combination in the Sample area.

5. Type a new name for the font combination you've selected, and click **Save**. Custom fonts are available for selection at the top of the theme Fonts drop-down list.

Create Custom Themes

Changes you make to a built-in theme (or to a previously created custom theme) can be saved as a custom theme and reused in other Office 2010 documents.

1. Make color, font, and effects changes to the current theme (see "Apply Themes" earlier in this chapter).

2. In the Design tab (Layout/Design Tools) Themes group, click **Themes** and click **Save Current Theme**. The Save Current Theme dialog box appears with the custom Office themes folder displayed.

3. Name the file and click **Save** to store the theme in the Document Themes folder (only themes stored here will appear in the Custom area of the Themes menu).

   –Or–

   Name the file and browse to the folder where you want to store it. Click **Save** when finished.

LOCATING AND SELECTIVELY APPLYING THEMES

You can quickly find individual theme files and themed documents, and apply them to your database. In addition, you can choose how to apply themes selectively.

LOCATE THEMES

You can apply themes from other files to your databases, either as individual theme files or from other Office 2010 files that have themes applied to them.

1. In the Design tab (Layout/Design Tools) Themes group, click **Themes** and click **Browse For Themes** at the bottom of the gallery.

2. In the Choose Theme Or Themed Document dialog box, browse to the folder where the themes or themed documents are located. Only those documents will display. (*Themed documents* are Office 2010 files that contain a theme, such as Word files, Excel workbooks, PowerPoint presentations, Access databases, and their respective templates.)

3. If you are only looking for theme files (.thmx), click the files of type drop-down list box, and click **Office Themes (.thmx)**.

> Office Themes and Themed Do ▼
> Office Themes and Themed Documents
> Office Themes (*.thmx)
> All Files (*.*)

4. Select the Office document whose theme you want to apply or the theme file you want to apply, and click **Open**.

Continued . . .

Work with Rich Text Formatting

Access has several types of formatting you can use to display your data. You can set how your data appears on-screen and when printed. As discussed in Chapter 3, you can set input masks to force database users to enter information in a preset manner, such as (***) ***-**** in a telephone number. Both of these format options affect only the appearance of the data, not how it is stored in Access 2010. You can apply rich text formatting to text blocks in much the same way that you apply formatting in Microsoft Word, Excel, and PowerPoint.

The type of formatting available depends on the data type you set in your database. If you have set a field's data type as Date/Time, you may choose from predefined formats or customize a setting based on the predefinitions. Memo and Text fields have no predefined formats. For an explanation of some formatting rules, see the "Understanding Formatting Rules" QuickFacts elsewhere in this chapter.

You can turn on rich text formatting on any Memo field in your table. Some text can be bold or italicized, and you can change the text colors (unlike in standard plain text fields where formatting applies to all text in the table). In the background, Access uses *HTML* (HyperText Markup Language) to make this happen.

ENABLE RICH TEXT FORMATTING

1. Open the table in Datasheet View.

2. Add a new field with the Rich Text data type (skip to step 5).

   –Or–

   Add a new field with the Memo data type.

   –Or–

   Click an existing **Memo** field.

   In the case of the latter two options, switch to Design View.

3. In the Field Properties section of the Design View grid, click the **General** tab.

	Click to Add ▼
AB	Text
12	Number
	Currency
	Date & Time
☑	Yes/No
	Lookup & Relationship
Aa	Rich Text
AB	Memo

QUICKSTEPS

LOCATING AND SELECTIVELY APPLYING THEMES *(Continued)*

SELECTIVELY APPLY THEMES

When you select a new theme, that theme applies to all current forms and reports in the database and to any new reports or forms you create. You can also choose to apply the new theme to only the open object (form or report), or to all forms or to all reports in the database (that is, all objects that match the open object).

1. Open the form or report whose theme you want to apply to other objects in the database.

2. In the Design tab (Layout/Design Tools) Themes group, click **Themes**, and right-click the theme you want to apply.

3. From the context menu, choose which objects you want the theme applied to.

> Apply Theme to All Matching Objects
> Apply Theme to This Object Only
> Make This Theme the Database Default
> Add Gallery to Quick Access Toolbar

---

4. Click the **Text Format** down arrow, and click **Rich Text**. A message box appears. If you want to convert the column to rich text, click **Yes**.

5. Save your table.

APPLY RICH TEXT

When a Memo data type field with rich text formatting is highlighted on a datasheet, additional tools become available within the Text Formatting group on the Home tab or from the mini-toolbar that appears above selected text (you may need to move your mouse pointer above the selected text to better see the mini-toolbar).

1. Open a form in Form View or a table/datasheet in Datasheet View.

2. Select text in a Memo field that has been enabled for rich text. See "Enable Rich Text Formatting."

3. Select the word(s) you want to format. In the Home tab Text Formatting group or mini-toolbar, apply one of the rich text tools such as numbered or bulleted lists. Figure 8-15 shows some examples of how rich text can spice up your data.

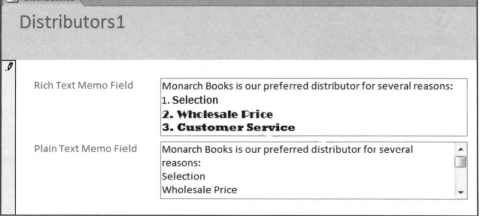

Figure 8-15: **Rich text formatting allows you to create colorful forms and reports.**

Print Your Data

Access provides a broad array of printing options, many tailored to the object you are interested in printing.

Print

Quick Print
Send the object directly to the default printer without making changes.

Set Up the Print Job

You can print an object directly, modify several printing features in the Print dialog box that affect the printed page, and review and make changes to the page in Print Preview prior to printing. Some features are not available for all objects you want to print (for example, tables/datasheets and queries don't let you change columnar settings) and only affect printing of the current object (although the settings are retained for the next time you print the same object).

USE QUICK PRINT

If you want to print an Access object without making any changes, you can send it directly to the default printer.

1. Ensure that the object you want to print is the active object in your database.
2. Click the **File** tab in the upper-left corner of the Access window, click **Print** on the File menu, and then click **Quick Print**. You may see a message that the object is printing to the default printer.

CHANGE PAPER LAYOUT, SIZE, AND SOURCE

1. Click the **File** tab, click **Print** on the File menu, and click **Print**. The Print dialog box appears, as shown in Figure 8-16.
2. Click **Properties**. The Document Properties dialog box for your printer appears. (The available options vary according to each printer/printer manufacturer.)

3. Click **OK** twice to return to the Print dialog box.

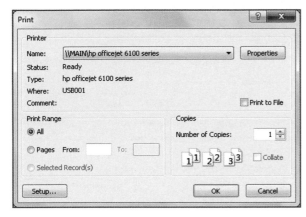

Figure 8-16: ***The Print dialog box lets you set many printing options.***

ADJUST MARGINS AND SET OTHER PRINT OPTIONS

You can adjust the distance between edges of the printed page and where text and pictures are printed for the current object.

1. Click the **File** tab, click **Print**, and then click **Print** to open the Print dialog box (see Figure 8-16).
2. Click **Setup** to open the Page Setup dialog box, shown in Figure 8-17.

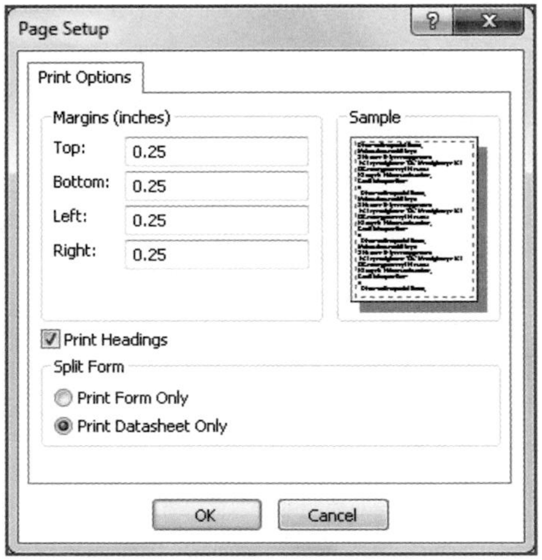

Figure 8-17: ***Print options include margin adjustments, table headings, and split form choices.***

3. Adjust the settings in the Top, Bottom, Left, and Right text boxes to the respective margins you want by typing new values. As you make changes, the Sample area shows the new location of the margins.
4. Click **Print Data Only** if you want to print just the information from a form or report. (If printing a datasheet, you can select whether to print headings. When printing a table, this option is "Print Heading.") In the case of *split forms* (a form in which you see both the Datasheet and Form Views at the same time):

   Click **Print Form Only** to print just the form.

   –Or–

   Click **Print Datasheet Only** to print just the datasheet.

   If neither option is selected, both will print.
5. Click **OK** when finished making all changes in the Page Setup dialog box.

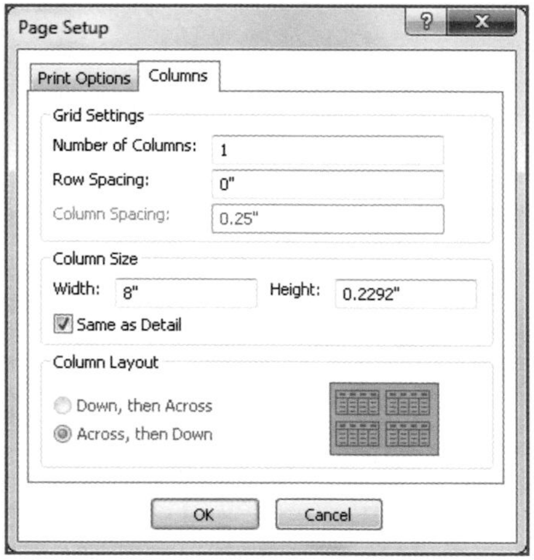

Figure 8-18: *The Columns tab lets you determine how your object will print.*

![Clock icon] **QUICKSTEPS**

OUTPUTTING THE PRINT JOB

You can print to printers attached to your computer or to printers on your network. You can also print to a file instead of a printer and choose features provided by your printer manufacturer. All this is accomplished from the Print dialog box (see Figure 8-16).

To open the Print dialog box, press **CTRL+P**.

–Or–

Click the **File** tab, click **Print** on the File menu, and then click **Print**.

CHOOSE A PRINTER

In the Printer dialog box, click the **Name** down arrow, and select a printer that is installed on your computer from the drop-down list.

Continued . . .

CHANGE COLUMNAR PRINT SETTINGS

The output from a report, or the labels and fields in Form View, are printed together as a column. You can make more efficient use of paper by aligning the printed data into more than one column.

1. In the Page Setup dialog box, click the **Columns** tab, shown in Figure 8-18.

  ● In the Grid Setting area, type how many columns you want (your paper width and column width will be determining factors), and determine the sizing between rows and columns.

  ● In the Column Size area, click the **Same As Detail** check box to print the column the same size as you set up in the form or report in Design View. To adjust the column width and row height, clear the check box, and type new values.

  ● In the Column Layout area (multiple columns only), select the direction in which you want the columns printed.

2. Click **OK** when finished making all changes in the Page Setup dialog box.

Review Data Before Printing

Print Preview, whose window is shown in Figure 8-19, provides an accurate picture of your data and layout so that you can make changes before committing to expending ink/toner and paper.

Print Preview's main features are available from the Print Preview tab on the ribbon.

1. To open Print Preview, click the **File** tab, click **Print**, and then click **Print Preview**.

  –Or–

  For forms and reports, switch to Print Preview from the Views area on the status bar, the Views group on the Home tab, or by right-clicking the open object.

2. In the Print Preview tab Print group, click **Print** to open the Print dialog box.

3. In the Print Preview tab Page Size group:

  ● Click **Size** to set the paper size on which to print.

OUTPUTTING THE PRINT JOB
(Continued)

The printer name is displayed in the Name drop-down list box, and information about the printer is listed below the printer name.

PRINT MULTIPLE COPIES

1. In the Copies area, click the **Number Of Copies** spinner to the number of copies you want.

2. Click the **Collate** check box to print each copy from start to finish before starting to print the next copy.

   –Or–

   Clear the **Collate** check box to print each page the number of times set in the Number Of Copies spinner before printing the next page.

PRINT TO A FILE

You can print your printer information to a file instead of directly to a physical device.

1. Click the **Print To File** check box.

2. Select any other print options you want, and click **OK**.

3. In the Print To File dialog box, type the path and file name of where you want the print file located.

4. Click **OK**.

PRINT ALL PAGES

● Open the object (or run the object, in the case of queries) that you want to print. In the Print dialog box, under Print Range, click **All**. Click **OK**.

   –Or–

● Use a Quick Print technique described earlier in the chapter.

Continued . . .

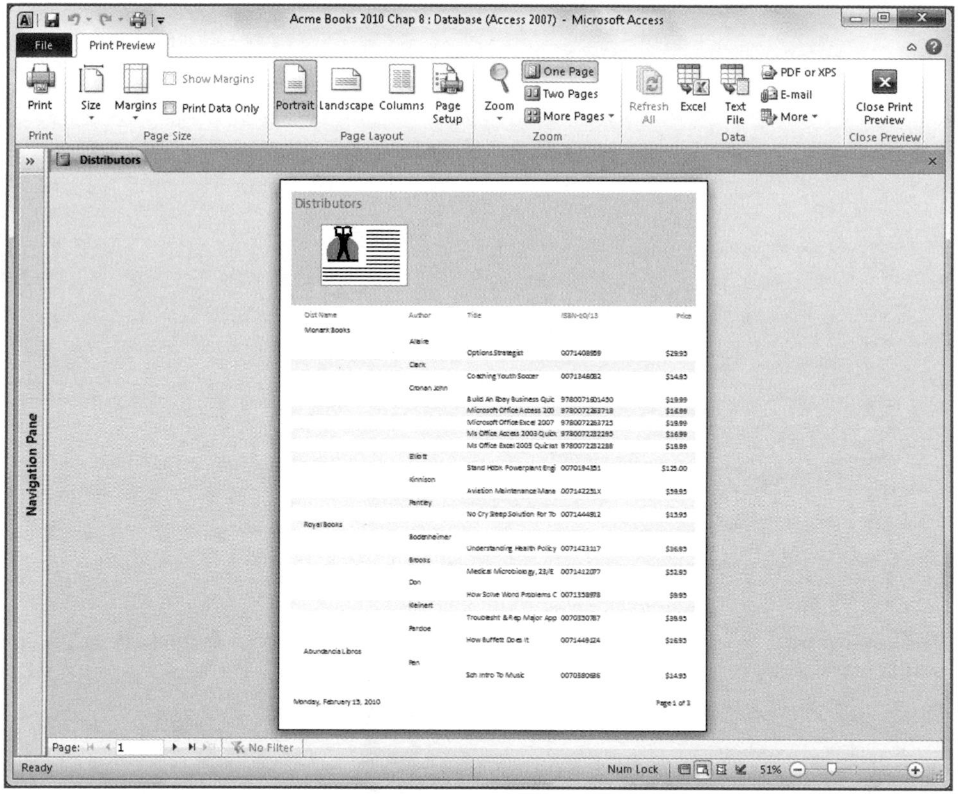

*Figure 8-19: **Print Preview allows you to see your object and make changes before you print.***

● Click **Margins** to choose from three predefined settings or to choose the last custom setting.

● Click **Print Data Only** to print the data without the form labels.

4. In the Print Preview tab Page Layout group:

   ● Click **Portrait** or **Landscape** to set the orientation of your printed object.

   ● Click **Columns** to open the Page Setup dialog box for the Columns tab.

   ● Click **Page Setup** to open the Page Setup dialog box and change the margins, orientation, and set columns.

UICK**STEPS**

OUTPUTTING THE PRINT JOB

(Continued)

PRINT SPECIFIC PAGES

1. In the Print dialog box, under Print Range, click **Pages**, and do one of the following:

   - To print a range of pages, use the From and To fields to set starting and ending pages.

   - To print one page, set both the From and To fields to the same page number.

   - To print from a page to the last page, set only the From field.

2. Click **OK**.

PRINT SPECIFIC RECORDS

1. Select the records in Datasheet View that you want to print.

2. In the Print dialog box, under Print Range, click **Selected Record(s)**.

3. Click **OK**.

NOTE

When you use the Navigation Pane to select the object you want to print and then click **Print** on the Quick Access toolbar, some objects might behave differently from what you'd expect. For example, when you print a query, the query is run first, then printed.

TIP

You can also use the Zoom tools in the Access window status bar to change the magnification in Print Preview.

5. In the Print Preview tab Zoom group:

   - Click **Zoom** to choose from several magnifications.

   - Click **One Page**, **Two Pages**, or **More Pages** to see pages in those respective configurations.

```
»   [ ]  Distributors
```

6. In the Print Preview tab Data group, you may export Access data to other Office programs and formats. For more information on exporting Access data, see Chapters 9 and 10.

7. Click **Close Print Preview** to return to your object.

Chapter 9
Securing, Sharing, and Administrating Access

This chapter addresses the issue of database security. The overriding purpose of database security is to prevent both inadvertent and intentional damage to the data and the database objects. Proper security measures prevent anyone who might view or edit the information from gaining unauthorized access. They also prevent anyone from making design changes without express permission to do so. You can protect both the data and the design elements with a variety of approaches. Security measures are particularly important to protect shared data, which is also covered in this chapter. In addition, there are administrative measures you can take, such as creating database backups that supplement the security precautions you have in place.

9

UNDERSTANDING ACCESS 2010 SECURITY

Access borrows from former President Reagan's philosophy of détente, that is, "trust but verify," in its pursuit to simplify database security and avoid most of the repetitious and annoying dialog boxes you had to deal with in earlier versions of Access to open a database.

Access believes that it's better to let you open a database and view its data and disable any potential malicious code or actions that could cause security risks, unless it's verified that:

Security Warning

Active content might contain viruses and other security hazards. The following content has been disabled:

Enable Content ▾

■ VBA Macros

You should enable content only if you trust the contents of the file.

Trust Center Settings

Learn more about Active Content

● The database is stored in a trusted location.

−Or−

● The database is digitally signed and you trust the originator of the certificate.

Chapter 1 described the security warning that appears in the message bar below the ribbon and the steps to take to enable content or not.

Users familiar with earlier versions of Access are probably wondering what happened to user-level security, where you could grant access to various components of the database based on the permissions you granted to others. Good news and bad news. For databases saved in the earlier Access file formats, such as .mdb, user-level security is supported within Access 2010. If you open

Continued . . .

Apply Security to an Access Database

Access offers several comprehensive methods of securing a database and its objects, including digitally signing databases, encrypting database files, and applying user-level security. Several security measures are unique to Access 2007 and Access 2010 files, although provisions are made for security models in earlier Access versions. In addition, there are less comprehensive actions you can take to prevent users from inadvertently making changes to data.

Create a Trusted Location

The easiest way to let Access know that you trust the content in a database is to store the database file in a folder that you let Access know you trust. Your local computer is the recommended place to locate a trusted folder, although you can use a folder on your network. When you open a database stored in a trusted location, content will be enabled and you will no longer see the security warning advising you of that.

⚠ **Security Warning**   Some active content has been disabled. Click for more details. | Enable Content | ×

1. Click the **File** tab, click **Options**, and click the **Trust Center** option. Under Microsoft Office Access Trust Center, click **Trust Center Settings**.

2. In the Trust Center, click the **Trusted Locations** option. The Trusted Locations page appears, with at least one default secure location for databases created by Access wizards, as shown in Figure 9-1.

Trust Center

Trusted Publishers

Trusted Locations

Trusted Documents

Add-ins

3. To add a secure location on your network, first click the **Allow Trusted Location On My Network** check box. Then, to add a secure location on your local computer or on the network, click **Add New Location**.

QUICKFACTS

UNDERSTANDING ACCESS 2010 SECURITY *(Continued)*

a database in Access's .accdb format, user-level security will not be available. (See the "Understanding the User-Level Security Model" QuickFacts later in the chapter.)

Another layer of database protection Access provides is the file encryption feature common to other Office 2010 programs. By password-protecting a database, you can sleep well at night, knowing that if your data falls into nefarious hands, the database cannot be opened and your private information will appear as gobbledygook if attempts are made to use it.

Finally, for a more casual sense of security, you can keep others from viewing certain aspects of the database by simply removing those objects from view.

All of these security precautions are described in this chapter.

4. In the Microsoft Office Trust Location dialog box, click **Browse** and navigate to the folder you want to secure. Click **OK**.

5. Click the **Subfolders Of This Location Are Also Trusted** check box if you want to include them. Add a description if you want to provide amplifying information in addition to the time and date the folder is secured that Access provides. Click **OK** and the location will be added to the User Locations list under Trusted Locations.

You can include or exclude subfolders in a trusted location

Default location for trusted documents

Select if you want trusted folders on other computers on your network

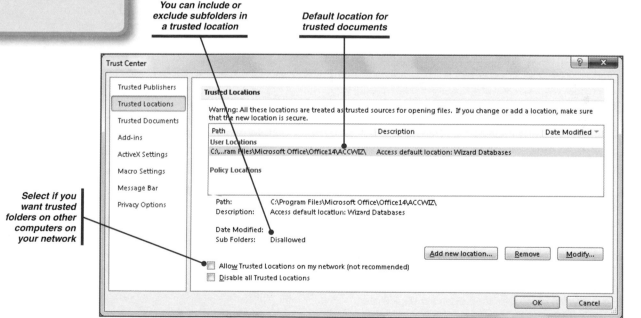

*Figure 9-1: **Access will not disable content for databases stored in trusted locations.***

6. To remove or change an existing trusted location, select the location and click **Remove** or **Modify**, respectively (see Figure 9-1).

7. Click **OK** twice when finished to close the Trust Center and Access Options windows.

Create and Use Certificates to Trust Databases

A certificate provides a digital signature to a file and lets others know that a database came from a trusted source (if you trust the certificate originator, you trust the files that are digitally signed by the originator and are assured the files have not been altered). You can create your own certificate and apply it to Access 2010 databases you provide to others as part of a *package*. Packaging encapsulates the database in an Access Deployment file (.accdc) and signs the package with a certificate. For databases you receive from others, Access will alert you to the presence of an untrusted certificate, and you can decide whether or not to trust the content.

CREATE A CERTIFICATE

You need a certificate before you can digitally sign a database and publish it to others.

1. Click the Windows **Start** menu button.

2. Click **All Programs**, click **Microsoft Office**, click **Microsoft Office 2010 Tools**, and click **Digital Certificate For VBA Projects**. The Create Digital Certificate dialog box appears, shown in Figure 9-2.

3. Type a name for the certificate (this is the name others will see when they open a signed database from you), and click **OK**. You are notified that your self-certificate is created. Click **OK**.

NOTE

You can create a *self-signed* certificate, which provides a limited measure of confidence to recipients of your databases that the data really came from a trusted source. To be fully confident that a database containing executable code (that is, code that can perform actions on your system or data) is from a trusted source, you can provide a certificate from a commercial certificate authority that attests you are who you profess to be. VeriSign (www.verisign.com) is an example of one of the larger certificate authorities.

Create Digital Certificate

This program creates a self-signed digital certificate that bears the name you type below. This type of certificate does not verify your identity.

Since a self-signed digital certificate might be a forgery, users will receive a security warning when they open a file that contains a macro project with a self-signed signature.

Office will only allow you to trust a self-signed certificate on the machine on which it was created.

A self-signed certificate is only for personal use. If you need an authenticated code signing certificate for signing commercial or broadly distributed macros, you will need to contact a certification authority.

Click here for a list of commercial certificate authorities

Your certificate's name:

CBTS

OK   Cancel

Figure 9-2: You can provide some assurance to others that databases they receive from you are really from you and have not been changed.

SelfCert Success

Successfully created a new certificate for CBTS.

OK

PUBLISH A DIGITALLY SIGNED DATABASE

1. Open an Access database using the Access 2007 file format (.accdb).

2. Click the **File** tab, click **Save & Publish** on the File menu to open its view, and then under File Types, click **Save Database As**. In the Save As Database right pane, under Advanced, select **Package And Sign**, and then click **Save As** at the bottom of the right pane.

3. In the Select A Certificate dialog box, select the certificate you want to use to sign the database, and click **OK**.

4. In the Create Microsoft Office Access Signed Package dialog box, navigate to the folder where you want the database/package located. Name the package and click **Create**. (Note that the package is saved in the .accdc file format.)

You cannot digitally sign a database in a pre-Access 2007 file format (.mdb) using the Save & Publish view. However, you can use a technique from earlier versions to digitally sign a database. Open the pre-Access 2007 database, and, in the Database Tools tab Macro group, click **Visual Basic**. In the Visual Basic window, select the database in the Project Explorer in the left pane, click the **Tools** menu, and click **Digital Signature**. In the Digital Signature dialog box, click **Choose** (see Figure 9-3), select the certificate you want to assign to the database (see step 3 in "Publish a Digitally Signed Database"), and click **OK** twice. Close the Visual Basic window.

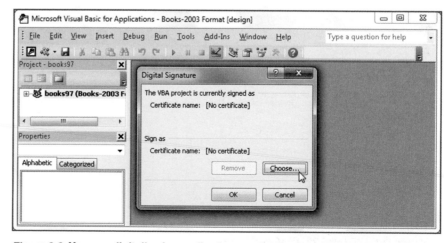

Figure 9-3: You can digitally sign earlier Access databases using the Visual Basic window.

TIP

You can only add one database (the one you open) to a trusted package.

USE A DIGITALLY SIGNED PRE-ACCESS 2007 DATABASE

1. Open the database.

2. If the certificate is validated and trusted by Access (typically, this is a certificate issued by a commercial certificate authority), there is no action needed on your part. The database will open with enabled content, and the security warning in the message bar will be omitted.

3. If the signed database is from a self-certificate, Access will not typically trust it. Click the security warning **Options** button in the message bar below the ribbon. You should see the Microsoft Office Security Options dialog box, similar to that shown in Figure 9-4. Access will display the particulars of the certificate. Review them and when satisfied they are trusted, click **OK** to enable the content.

Figure 9-4: *Access will notify you of self-certificates, but will not enable content without your approval.*

EXTRACT AN ACCESS 2007 DATABASE FROM A PACKAGE

When you open a package sent to you by another Access user, you open it as you would any other database file.

1. If the publisher is trusted (that is, you've previously trusted content from them and they are listed in the Trusted Publishers list of your Trust Center), the database file can be extracted from the package.

   –Or–

   If the package comes from an untrusted publisher (even if the digital signature is valid), a Security Notice dialog box appears, where you can both choose to open the database and add the publisher to your Trusted Publishers list.

2. In either case, in the Extract Database To dialog box that appears, select where you want the extracted database file stored, and rename it if desired. Click **OK**.

CREATING PASSWORDS

Some basic guidelines for creating a password include the following:

- Create a strong password that combines uppercase and lowercase letters with numbers and symbols. For example, "67TrCg!89sdJ" is a strong password, while "MyFavoriteCat" is not.
- Passwords should be eight or more characters.
- Never use a word that appears in the dictionary.
- Do not use characters that have a special meaning in Access: "\ [ ] : | < > + = ; , . ? *.

TIP

When you encrypt a database in the .accdb format, you are using one of the Microsoft Office 2010 128-bit encryption algorithms. These provide greater security than the encryption algorithms used in earlier versions of Access that used the .mdb database format. (You can still protect older databases; however, Access uses security features from Access 2003.)

NOTE

By default, databases are opened in *shared* open mode, which allows others to concurrently open the database and access the data. You can change this behavior so that only one user has exclusive use of the data. To change the default open mode behavior, click the **File** tab, click **Options**, and click the **Client Settings** option. Under Advanced, click the behavior you want, and click **OK** when finished. (To open a particular database exclusively without changing the default behavior, see Figure 9-5.)

Encrypt a Database

Encrypting a database provides a high degree of confidence that only those users you want to be able to access your data will be able to. You maintain control over whether a database is available to someone by creating and distributing a password. Without the password, your data is merely gobbledygook, even to you, so don't forget or lose the password! But also understand that anyone who has possession of the password can open the database and do anything with it, unless you apply other security measures (see the "Keeping Data Safe" QuickSteps).

ASSIGN A PASSWORD

You must have exclusive use of the database to assign a password.

1. Make sure all users have closed the database.

2. Click the **File** tab, and click **Open**. In the Open dialog box, select the database you want to protect with a password, click the **Open** down arrow, and click **Open Exclusive**, shown in Figure 9-5.

3. Click the **File** tab, and click **Info**. In the Info view, click **Encrypt With Password**.

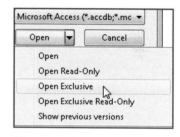

Figure 9-5: **You can select how to share a database using options in the Open dialog box.**

Encrypt with Password
Use a password to restrict access to your database. Files that use the 2007 Microsoft Access file format or later are encrypted.

4. In the Set Database Password dialog box, type the password (see the "Creating Passwords" QuickFacts). Repeat the password in the Verify text box, and then click **OK**.

Advanced

☐ Open last used database when Access starts
Default open mode
◉ Shared
○ Exclusive

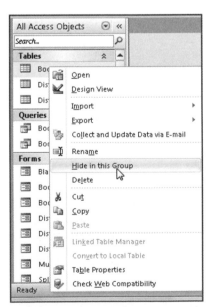

CAUTION

Don't forget your password. You won't be able to open the database without it. Write it down and store it in a safe place.

QUICKSTEPS

KEEPING DATA SAFE

There are several actions you can take to keep data safe from unintended changes that supplement any security measures you are implementing.

PREVENT EDITING TO RECORDS

You can lock all records, or just the record you are editing, from changes in the open form or datasheet (and also lock records in underlying tables). This feature is useful when a database is shared (see "Share Data" later in this chapter).

1. Open the database whose records you want to protect against editing.

2. Click the **File** tab, click **Options**, and click the **Client Settings** option.

3. Under Advanced, click the default record-locking behavior you want.

Default record locking
- ◉ No locks
- ○ All records
- ○ Edited record
- ☑ Open databases by using record-level locking

4. Click **OK** when finished.

LIMIT VALUES IN A LOOKUP FIELD

A lookup field can appear in a form as a combo box or as a list box from which the user chooses a value (Chapter 3 describes how to set up a lookup field).

Continued . . .

5. The next time you try to open the database, you will be asked for the password.

Password Required

Enter database password:

[   ]

[OK] [Cancel]

REMOVE A PASSWORD

1. Open the database in Exclusive mode using the encryption password.

2. Click the **File** tab, and click **Info**. In the Info view, click **Decrypt Database**.

Decrypt Database
Removes the password from this database.

Decrypt Database

3. In the Unset Database dialog box, type the encryption password, and click **OK**.

Remove Database Objects from View

Hiding database objects does not really tighten security, per se; although it does keep certain objects from appearing in the Navigation Pane and out of sight/out of harm's way to casual users.

HIDE DATABASE OBJECTS

- To hide a group of objects in the Navigation Pane, right-click the group title bar, and click **Hide**.

- To hide an object within a group in the Navigation Pane, right-click the object and click **Hide In This Group**, as shown in Figure 9-6.

Figure 9-6: Individual objects, as well as groups of objects, can be removed from the Navigation Pane.

KEEPING DATA SAFE *(Continued)*

Users may also enter a value not already on the list. If you don't want other values in the field:

1. Open the table in Design View.

2. Select the lookup field in the upper pane.

3. Click the **Lookup** tab in the lower Field Properties pane.

4. Click the **Limit To List** property text box, click its down arrow, and click **Yes**.

5. Save the table design.

REQUIRE VALID DATA

To make sure that newly entered data is correct, include data validation rules in a table or form design. See Chapter 3 for more information on using data validation.

PREVENT DATA CHANGES IN A FORM

To keep a user from entering, deleting, or editing data in a form:

1. Open the form in Design View, and double-click the form selector to open the property sheet.

2. In the property sheet, click the **Data** tab.

3. Click the **Allow Edits** property text box, click its down arrow, and click **No**.

4. Repeat step 3 to also set the Allow Deletions and Allow Additions properties to No.

5. Save the form design.

General	Lookup	
Display Control	Combo Box
Row Source Type	Value List
Row Source	"Technical";"Business";"Computer";"Medical"
Bound Column	1
Column Count	1
Column Heads	No
Column Widths	1"
List Rows	16
List Width	1"
Limit To List	Yes
Allow Multiple Values	Yes
Allow Value List Edits	No
List Items Edit Form	
Show Only Row Source V	No

VIEW HIDDEN DATABASE OBJECTS

In order to view objects or groups that are hidden, you will need to see them in order to change their status.

1. Right-click the Navigation Pane header, and click **Navigation Options**.

2. In the Navigation Options dialog box, under Display Options, click the **Show Hidden Objects** check box, and click **OK**. Any hidden objects or groups appear dimmed in the Navigation Pane.

Tables	⌃
Books	
Distributors	
Distributors1	

3. Right-click the hidden object or group you want to return to full view, and click **Unhide In This Group** or **Unhide**, respectively.

4. To return any remaining hidden objects back to a fully hidden status, right-click the Navigation Pane header, click **Navigation Options**, and clear the **Show Hidden Objects** check box. Click **OK**.

Share Data

Sharing data is an essential element of any workplace environment. This section will take you through exporting and linking Access data to a variety of applications. In addition, the Internet has done a great job of connecting people and information. Access taps into Web technology in a variety of ways.

You can create a *hyperlink*, a direct link providing access from one object to another, within an Access table to connect users to information on the World Wide Web or elsewhere. Existing database objects can be saved as static Web pages that provide access to data from a variety of locations and using different tools.

CAUTION

Applying user-level security to a database can prevent opening the file if you lose or forget required information to access the database, or if you are otherwise unfamiliar with working with users, groups, and setting permissions. It's recommended that you use this feature only to change existing settings to a workgroup information file, unless you are comfortable working in a multiuser environment.

NOTE

Moving data from Access to a Microsoft SQL Server database is covered in Chapter 10.

QUICKFACTS

UNDERSTANDING THE USER-LEVEL SECURITY MODEL

Pre-Access 2007 versions used a different security scheme than the encryption provided in the two most recent versions. The *user-level security* model is based on the idea of workgroups whose members share the data and privileges. The group and user accounts list the members of the workgroup. A *group account* is a collection of user accounts. Each member of the group is permitted some degree of freedom in dealing with data and objects. A *user account* belongs to a single user and includes the user name and personal ID (PID).

The four pieces of a user-level security model are:

- A **user** is a person who uses the database.
- A **group** is a set of users, all of whom operate at the same security level and need access to the same parts of the database.

Continued . . .

Export Access Data

Just as you can import data from other programs (see Chapter 4), you can export Access objects to a variety of other data formats.

1. Open the Navigation Pane in the database whose objects you would like to export.
2. Click the table, query, form, or report you would like to export. If you want to export specific records, open the object and select the records you want to export.
3. In the External Data tab Export group, the export options that are available for the object you selected will be available. Click the **More** button to see additional options. Figure 9-7 shows the export formats that are available for tables, forms, and reports.

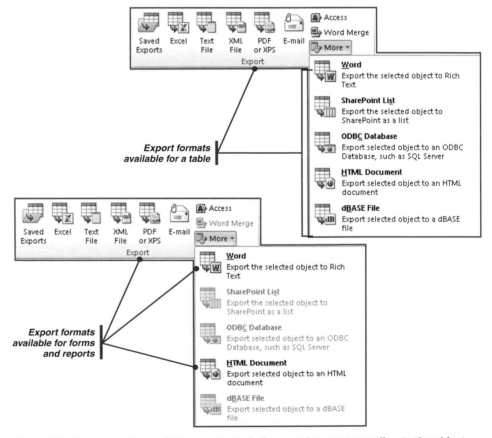

Figure 9-7: *Access makes available a subset of all export formats according to the object that is selected or opened.*

UNDERSTANDING THE USER-LEVEL SECURITY MODEL *(Continued)*

- A **permission** gives a user or group the right to carry out a specific action. For example, Read Data permission allows opening a table or query for viewing but not for entering new data or editing existing data.

- An **object** refers to any of the Access tables, queries, forms, reports, macros, or modules—as well as to the database itself.

Depending on what the user needs to do with the database, you can assign her to any of the groups provided by the User-Level Security Wizard. To give a user more permissions than one group has, you can assign that user to more than one group; for example:

- **Backup Operators** can open the database exclusively for backup and compacting, but are not permitted to see any of the database objects.

- **Full Data Users** have full permission to edit data, but are not allowed to make any design changes.

- **Full Permission Users** have full permissions on all database objects, but are not allowed to assign permissions to others.

- **New Data Users** can read and insert data, but are not allowed to delete or update existing data. They are also not allowed to alter any object designs.

- **Project Designers** have full permission to edit data and all objects, but are not allowed to alter any tables or relationships.

- **Read-Only Users** can read all the data, but are not allowed to change data or any design object.

- **Update Data Users** can read and update all data, but are not allowed to insert or delete data. They are also not allowed to make any design changes.

Continued . . .

4. Click the export format you want. An Export dialog box appears, similar to that shown in Figure 9-8, that's tuned to the particular export format you have selected. Locate and name the files, and select any of the available options. Click **OK**.

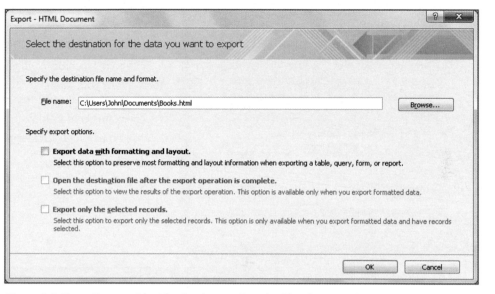

Figure 9-8: Exporting an object is simply a matter of telling Access where you want the new file located and then selecting options specific to the export format.

5. When the export is finished, you can save the steps you used for a quick way to repeat the export and create an Outlook task to remind you to repeat the export. Click the **Save Export Steps** check box, name the export, and click **Create Outlook Task**. Click **Save Export** when finished. If you chose to create a task, a new task is created, as shown in Figure 9-9.

6. To view the exported file, in the External Data tab Export group, click **Saved Exports** to open the Manage Data Tasks window, select the export you want to reuse in the Saved Exports tab, and click **Run** at the bottom of the window.

QUICK**FACTS**

UNDERSTANDING THE USER-LEVEL SECURITY MODEL *(Continued)*

To start the User-Level Security Wizard:

1. Open a database in the pre-Access 2007 .mdb file format.

2. Click the **File** tab, and click **Info**. In the Manage Users & Permissions area, click **Users And Permissions**, and click **User-Level Security Wizard**.

Manage Users & Permissions

Use passwords and permissions to allow or restrict the access of individuals, or groups of individuals, to the objects in your database.

Users and Permissions ▾

- User and Group *P*ermissions...
- User and Group *A*ccounts...
- User-Level Security *W*izard...
- *E*ncode/Decode Database...

*P*assword
...o restrict access to your database.
...2007 Microsoft Access file format

Link Tables

Access can *link*, or connect, data in multiple Access databases, as well as between Access databases and other applications. Linking maintains a connection between the source data, for example, an Excel spreadsheet, and a table created in Access. When changes are made to the source data, they are reflected in the new linked table (whether changes made in the linked table are reflected in the source data depends on the data format used). It doesn't matter whether the source data resides on your computer or on a network. (See Chapter 10 for an example of linking tables in a *split database*, where the data is separated and linked between back-end and front-end database systems.)

1. Open the database in which you would like to import one or more linked tables.

Figure 9-9: An Outlook task is created to remind you of the particulars of a saved export.

Export-Books - Task

File Task Insert Format Text Review

Save & Close | Delete | Forward | OneNote | Task | Details | Mark Complete | Assign Task | Send Status Report | Recurrence | Categorize | Follow Up | Private | High Importance | Low Importance | Zoom | Run Export

Actions | Show | Manage Task | Recurrence | Tags | Zoom | Microsoft Access

Subject: Export-Books

Start date: Mon 8/2/2010   Status: Not Started
Due date: Mon 8/2/2010   Priority: Normal   % Complete: 0%

☐ Reminder: None   None   Owner: John Cronan

Click the Run Export command in the Microsoft Access group to perform the saved export operation Export-Books to export data from the database \\Main\c\Matthews\QuickSteps\Access 2010\Chap9\Acme Books 2010 Chap 9.accdb.

Security warning: Performing this operation will export data using your identity based on details specified in the previously mentioned database. Click the Run Export button only if you trust the following:

- The source of the task, including the users who created and modified this task and the user who assigned it to you.
- The location of the database.

QUICKSTEPS

MERGING DATA WITH MICROSOFT WORD

You can link to a Microsoft Word document and use Access data as fields in a form letter and/or address envelopes. For example, in a Customers table, you already have fields for a customer's name and address, so a form letter could easily incorporate these fields. In addition, a Memo field from a table that contains the boilerplate contents of several letter types, such as Response To Inquiry, Acknowledgement Of Receipt Of Payment, and other typical uses, could be incorporated into the mail merge.

1. Open the Navigation Pane in the database whose table or query you would like to use.

2. Click a table or query (for example, an address table).

3. In the External Data tab Export group, click **Word Merge**. This starts the Microsoft Word Mail Merge Wizard.

Continued . . .

2. In the External Data tab Import & Link group, click the database format that contains the source data you want to link to.

3. In the Get External Data dialog box, browse to the location of the database file, and click **Link To The Data Source By Creating A Linked Table**, as shown in Figure 9-10. Click **OK**. (Some database formats require slightly different means to access their source data; for example, Open Database Connectivity—ODBC— databases use a Select Data Source dialog box to connect to data source drivers.)

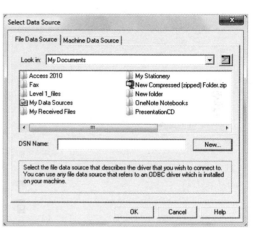

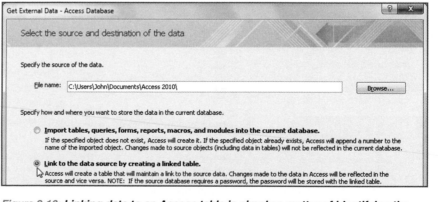

*Figure 9-10: **Linking data to an Access table is simply a matter of identifying the data source.***

QUICKSTEPS

MERGING DATA WITH MICROSOFT WORD *(Continued)*

4. Choose whether you want to merge to an existing or new Word document, and click **OK**. If you chose an existing document, the Select Microsoft Word Document dialog box appears, where you can browse to the document. In either case, Word opens with the existing document or a blank document and the Mail Merge pane on the right of the window.

5. Select your document type in the first step of the mail merge process, and click the next step link at the bottom of the pane. (Depending on the document chosen, the subsequent steps can be very different. Browse Word Help if you need assistance setting up the mail merge document.)

6. Continue through the mail merge process by clicking the subsequent steps in the pages in the Mail Merge Wizard to create your merged document using Access data (step 3, shown here, shows the data source you had selected in Access).

NOTE

Data access pages (or just *pages*) were created within Access 2003 to allow Internet and intranet users to view and work with data that is stored in an Access database. Pages are not available in Access 2010, and have been replaced by the functionality provided by SharePoint.

4. In the Link Tables dialog box, select the table(s) you want to link to, and click **OK**. Each linked table is listed in the Navigation Pane and identified with a right-pointing arrow icon.

Add a Hyperlink Field to an Existing Table

To create a hyperlink within a table, you need to establish the field data type as a hyperlink. A hyperlink data type lets you store simple or complex links to files or documents outside your database. The "pointer" can contain a Uniform Resource Locator (URL) that points to a location on the World Wide Web or to a place on a local intranet. It can also use a file address to provide access to a file on your computer or on a server in your network.

1. In the database that will hold your newly created hyperlink(s), open the table in Datasheet View.

2. Click **Click To Add** column header at the rightmost end of the table, and click **Hyperlink**.

3. Type over the highlighted Field*x* name with a name for your new hyperlink field, and press **ENTER**.

4. Right-click the table name tab, and click **Save**. Data typed into the new field will be underlined and ready to search for the hyperlinked location. (To edit the hyperlink, right-click it and click **Hyperlink**. See the "Creating a Hyperlink to a File or Web Page" QuickSteps, later in the chapter, for information on using the Edit (Insert) Hyperlink dialog box).

Distributor ID ▾	Web_Sites ▾
1	www.monarchbooks.com
2	www.royalbooks.com
3	www.abundancia-libros.es

UNDERSTANDING SHAREPOINT

Access 2010 integrates tightly with Microsoft SharePoint Server 2010 (the server-based product on which the latest version of SharePoint sites are created) to promote data sharing and linking. SharePoint sites, in combination with Access Services (a feature of Microsoft SharePoint Server 2010 Enterprise Edition), provide an interactive way for users to use Access data and objects using a Web browser, as well as to connect through Access 2010.

While setting up a SharePoint site is beyond the scope of this book (for more information on using SharePoint, see *Microsoft SharePoint 2010 QuickSteps*, (McGraw-Hill/ Professional, 2010), if you have access to such a site, you can use Access 2010 to great advantage, as the following sections explain.

MOVE DATABASES

- **Create a Web database** from the Available Template area in the File menu New view (see Chapter 2).

- **Save a database to SharePoint**, creating lists from your tables where users can work with the lists on SharePoint or create linked tables on their local version of Access. Click **SharePoint** under the Save As Database pane in the File menu Save & Publish view, and then click **Save As** to locate your SharePoint server.

- **Publish to Access Services** to provide a means to distribute and display Access database objects in a browser. Click **Publish To Access Services** in the File menu Save & Publish view,

Continued . . .

SharePoint
Share the database by saving it to a document management server.

Save As

Save a Database as a Template

You can use a database as a model from which to create other databases by saving the database as a template (with or without data), similar to those templates that appear in the File tab's New view (see Chapter 2).

1. Open the database that will serve as the basis for the template.

2. Click the **File** tab, and click **Save & Publish**. Under File Types, click **Save Database As**. Under the Save Database As pane, select **Template** and then click **Save As** at the bottom of the pane.

3. In the Create New Template From This Database dialog box, shown in Figure 9-11, provide a name, description, icon, and preview graphic (these help users identify the template).

Create New Template from This Database

Name:
Acme Book Inventory

Description:
Boilerplate database to contain yearly inventory

Category:
User Templates

Icon: Displayed as 64x32 pixels
C:\Users\John\Pictures\Microsoft Clip Organizer\MC900252

Preview:
C:\Users\John\Documents\Books_Page_01.jpg

Primary Table:
Books

Instantiation Form:
Books

☑ Application Part
☑ Include Data in Template

Learn more about advanced template properties.
Share your template with the community.

OK   Cancel

*Figure 9-11: **You can replicate and share your databases by creating templates.***

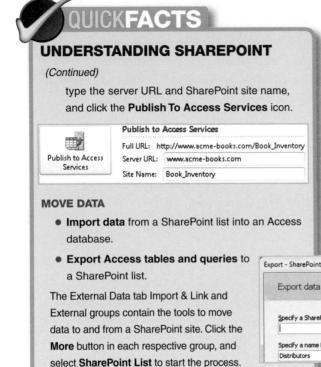

type the server URL and SharePoint site name, and click the **Publish To Access Services** icon.

Publish to Access Services

Publish to Access Services

Full URL: http://www.acme-books.com/Book_Inventory

Server URL: www.acme-books.com

Site Name: Book_Inventory

MOVE DATA

- **Import data** from a SharePoint list into an Access database.

- **Export Access tables and queries** to a SharePoint list.

The External Data tab Import & Link and External groups contain the tools to move data to and from a SharePoint site. Click the **More** button in each respective group, and select **SharePoint List** to start the process.

Export - SharePoint Site

Export data to SharePoint list

Specify a SharePoint site:

Specify a name for the new list. (Note:

Distributors

4. Select a primary table (the table most likely to be used in a relationship), whether to open with a form, whether to add the template to the Application Parts group on the Create tab of the ribbon (shown here), and whether to include data in the template.

5. Click **OK**. The template will appear under My Templates in the File tab New view.

Administer a Database

Access provides tools to assist you in managing the size of your database, as well as to repair a database that may have become corrupted. You can also create a printout of your database relationships, database properties, and definitions of your database objects.

Document a Database

If you are working alone on your own database, you probably don't need extensive documentation of the database objects. In a group setting, however, where there is a large information management team, documentation is extremely important. With up-to-date object definitions, errors can be quickly isolated and fixed.

A great compromise of true representation and broad sharing of data is to save the content as a PDF (Portable Document Format) or XPS (XML Paper Specification) file. Anyone with a free reader program can view the files in whatever venue it is delivered to them. You can save tables, forms, and reports. Select the object you want to capture in the Navigation Pane, and click **PDF Or XPS** in the External Data tab Export group. In the Publish As PDF Or XPS dialog box, select the format you want (PDF or XPS), browse to the folder where you want the file stored, select any options, and then click **Publish**.

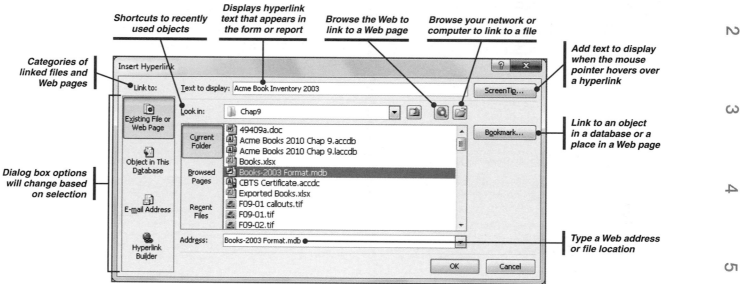

Shortcuts to recently used objects

Displays hyperlink text that appears in the form or report

Browse the Web to link to a Web page

Browse your network or computer to link to a file

Categories of linked files and Web pages

Add text to display when the mouse pointer hovers over a hyperlink

Dialog box options will change based on selection

Link to an object in a database or a place in a Web page

Type a Web address or file location

Figure 9-12: *The Insert Hyperlink dialog box provides a means to link to data residing at various locations.*

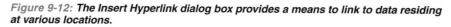

Continued . . .

CREATING A HYPERLINK TO A FILE OR WEB PAGE

Placing a hyperlink in a form or report is a great way to connect data from files or the Internet to the information displayed in your form or report.

1. Open your form or report in Design View.

2. In the Design tab (Report/Form Design Tools) Controls group, click **Hyperlink** , and click the form or report. The Insert Hyperlink dialog box appears, as shown in Figure 9-12.

3. In the Link To column, click one of the sources of the linked objects (**Existing File Or Web Page** in this example).

The documentation can include all or a select group of objects in the database.

1. Open the database you want to document.

2. In the Database Tools tab Analyze group, click **Database Documenter**. The Documenter opens, as shown in Figure 9-13.

Figure 9-13: *You can select just those objects you want documented.*

QUICKSTEPS

CREATING A HYPERLINK TO A FILE OR WEB PAGE *(Continued)*

4. Under Look In, click one of the location categories (only applicable to Existing File Or Web Page links). Click either the **Browse Web** or the **Browse File** button to find the Web page or file, respectively, to which you would like to link.

5. Type the text you would like displayed to represent the hyperlink in the Text To Display text box. Click **OK**. You will return to your previous view. Drag your new hyperlink control to the appropriate location within the form or report.

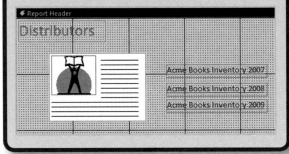

NOTE

You can export the Documenter's report as a Snapshot, as a Word RTF file, or in another format, such as HTML or PDF. Select the relevant option in the Print Preview tab Data group.

TIP

Some definitions can cover many pages. Be sure to check the count before you start to print.

3. Click each object tab, and click the objects you want documented; or click **Select All**.

    –Or–

    Click the **All Objects Types** tab, and click **Select All**. This includes relationships and the database properties, as well as the definitions of all the database objects.

4. If you don't need all the information about an object, you can click **Options** and choose how much you want to see. Figure 9-14 shows the choices you have with table documentation. Click **OK**.

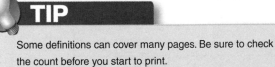

Figure 9-14: *Choose the table definition items to include in the Documenter's data.*

5. Click **OK** in the Documenter when you have finished making your selections. The results appear in Print Preview, as shown in Figure 9-15.

6. In the Print Preview tab, click **Print**, or press **CTRL+P**, to open the Print dialog box.

    –Or–

    Click **Print** on the Quick Access toolbar to print all pages to your default printer.

    See Chapter 8 for more information on printing database objects.

Compact and Repair a Database

As you improve and modify your database, the file can become scattered on your hard disk, with empty blocks of space in between. The *Compact And Repair Database* utility removes the empty spaces and rearranges the file more efficiently to improve performance. If there has been some damage, this utility can find the problems and offer to repair them.

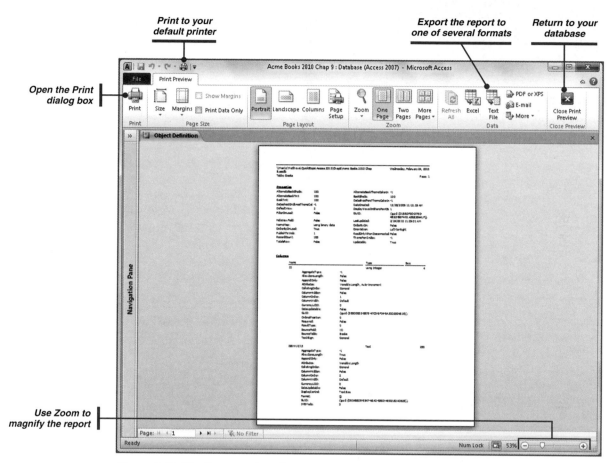

Print to your
default printer

Export the report to
one of several formats

Return to your
database

Open the Print
dialog box

Use Zoom to
magnify the report

*Figure 9-15: **The Documenter allows you to preview the documentation report before you print pages.***

You can start the compact and repair process with the database open or closed.

REPAIR AND COMPACT AN OPEN DATABASE

Open the database you want to compact and/or repair. Click the **File** tab, and in the Info view, click **Compact & Repair Database**.

–Or–

In the Database Tools tab Tools group, click **Compact & Repair Database**.

No other actions are required.

Information about Acme Books 2010 Chap 9
\\Main\c\Matthews\QuickSteps\Access 2010\Chap9\Acme Books 2010 Chap 9.ac...

Compact & Repair
Help prevent and correct database file problems by using Compact and Repair.

Compact &
Repair Database

REPAIR AND COMPACT A CLOSED DATABASE

If the database is closed, you can compact and repair it to the same file or with a different name in another location.

1. In the Database Tools tab Tools group, click **Compact And Repair Database** to open the Database To Compact From dialog box.

2. Locate the database file using the dialog box, and click **Compact**.

Back Up a Database

When working with an important database, it is a good idea to have a backup copy on hand. Creating a backup database on a regular basis can help reduce the risk of losing important data.

Before making a backup copy, make sure that all users have closed their databases so that all changes in the data have been saved.

BACK UP A DATABASE FROM ACCESS

You can use Access to create a regular copy to keep as a backup copy. No compression or other reformatting takes place—you just create a regular database file.

1. Open the database you want to back up.

2. Click the **File** tab, and click **Save & Publish** to open its view.

3. Under File Types, click **Save Database As**. In the right pane under Save Database As, click **Back Up Database**, and then click **Save As** at the bottom of the pane.

4. In the Save As dialog box, if desired, choose the location for the copy, and type a name for it. Click **Save**.

BACK UP INDIVIDUAL DATABASE OBJECTS

If you want to back up only a few objects instead of the whole database:

1. Create a new, blank database (see Chapter 2).

2. In the External Data tab Import & Link group, click **Access**.

3. Locate and select the database from which you want to back up objects in the Get External Data – Access Database dialog box. Accept the first option, and click **OK**.

4. Click each tab in the Import Objects dialog box, and select the objects you want. See Chapter 4 for more information about importing. Click **OK** to import the objects.

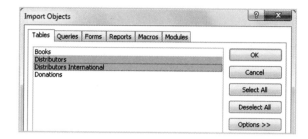

5. Save the new database.

Chapter 10
Extending Access

The final chapter of this book will take you one step deeper into some of the more advanced features of Access. You will analyze data using a Crosstab query, PivotTables, and by letting Access provide a second opinion on your database and table design. In addition, you will learn how to create a custom Navigation Pane to guide users when they first open a database you provide to them, and how to use Access as a more user-friendly means of interacting with the industrial-grade database program, Microsoft SQL Server.

Use Advanced Data Analysis Tools

Access provides both basic and advanced tools for use when analyzing and presenting data. This chapter will take you through a few of the advanced features, from using a Crosstab query, to creating PivotTables, and how to run analysis tools.

Create a Crosstab Query with a Wizard

A Crosstab query presents information in a slightly different way than do the other queries. (See Chapter 5 for more information on queries.) Rather than displaying the information in a standard datasheet format, the Crosstab query looks more like a spreadsheet, as shown in Figure 10-1. Calculated data and the fields from a table or query that supply the values that, in turn, make up the calculation reside in the grid of the query.

1. Open the Navigation Pane in the database in which you want to create the query.

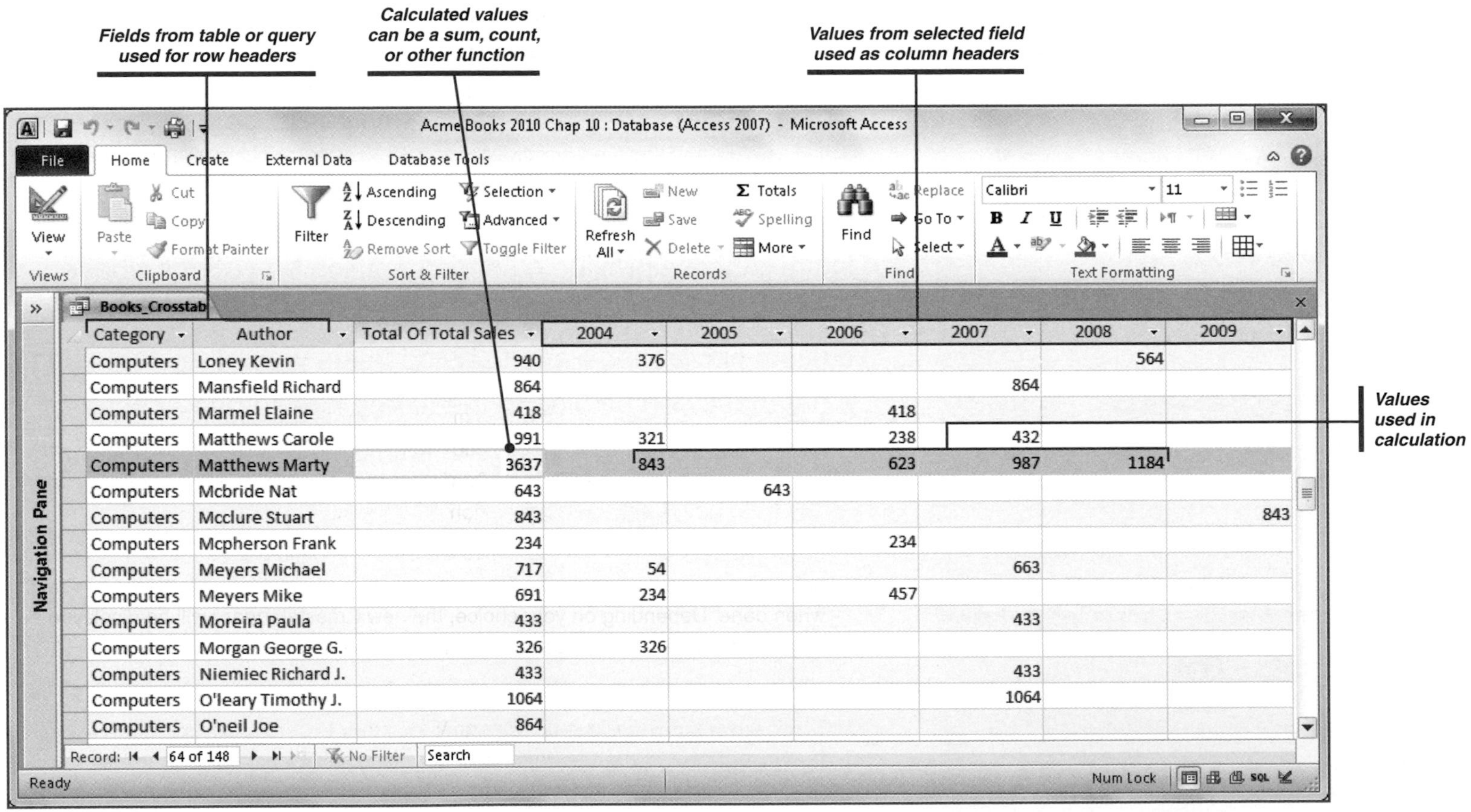

Figure 10-1: *The Crosstab query displays data based on the calculation of values at intersections of rows and fields you select.*

Fields selected for row headers...will be grouped and sorted in the PivotTable

Crosstab Query Wizard

Which fields' values do you want as row headings?

You can select up to three fields.

Select fields in the order you want information sorted. For example, you could sort and group values by Country and then Region.

Available Fields:

ID
ISBN-10/13
Title
Pub Date
Price
On Hand
Total Sales
Distributor ID

Selected Fields:

Category
Author

> | >> | < | <<

Sample:

Category	Author	Header1	Header2	Header3
Category1	Author1	TOTAL		
Category2	Author2			
Category3	Author3			
Category4	Author4			

Cancel | < Back | Next > | Finish

Figure 10-2: You can add up to three fields that are used as row headers.

TIP

If you use more than one field as a row header, add them to the Selected Fields list in the order you want the data sorted. For example, in Figure 10-1, first the Category field was added and then the Author field to see a breakdown of sales by author within each category.

NOTE

To include field names from more than one table in a Crosstab query, create a query combining all the field names you need, and then use that query to create a Crosstab query.

2. In the Create tab Queries group, click **Query Wizard**. In the New Query dialog box, click **Crosstab Query Wizard**, and click **OK**.

3. In the first page of the Crosstab Query Wizard, click **Tables**, **Queries**, or **Both** to display the tables and/or queries in the database. Click the table or query where you first want to select the fields that will appear in your query results, and click **Next**.

4. In the next page, shown in Figure 10-2, choose the field(s) you want as row headings (maximum of three fields). Move the field(s) from the Available Fields list to the Selected Fields list. Double-click the fields you want, or use the select/remove buttons between the two list boxes to add or remove fields. Click **Next**.

5. On the third page in the Crosstab Query Wizard, you select the field whose values you would like displayed as column headers (see Figure 10-1). Click the field you want, and it's added across the three rightmost columns in the Sample area. Click **Next**.

Sample:

Category	Author	Pub Date1	Pub Date2	Pub Date3
Category1	Author1	TOTAL		
Category2	Author2			
Category3	Author3			
Category4	Author4			

6. Click the field that you would like to make a calculated value. (In Figure 10-1, this would be Total Sales.) Click the function with which you would like to calculate the value. Click the **Yes, Include Row Sums** check box to display the row calculations. The Sample area shows your selections. Click **Next**.

7. In the final page of the wizard, accept the default query name or type a title/name for the query. Choose whether to view (run) the query as is or to modify its design. Click **Finish** when done. Depending on your choice, the new Crosstab query will be displayed as a datasheet with the fields you selected earlier in the wizard, shown in Figure 10-1.

–Or–

The Crosstab query will open in Design View, ready for adding criteria and other changes, shown in Figure 10-3 (see the "Sorting and Filtering a Crosstab Query" QuickSteps later in the chapter.)

In either case, the new query will be listed under Queries in the Navigation Pane.

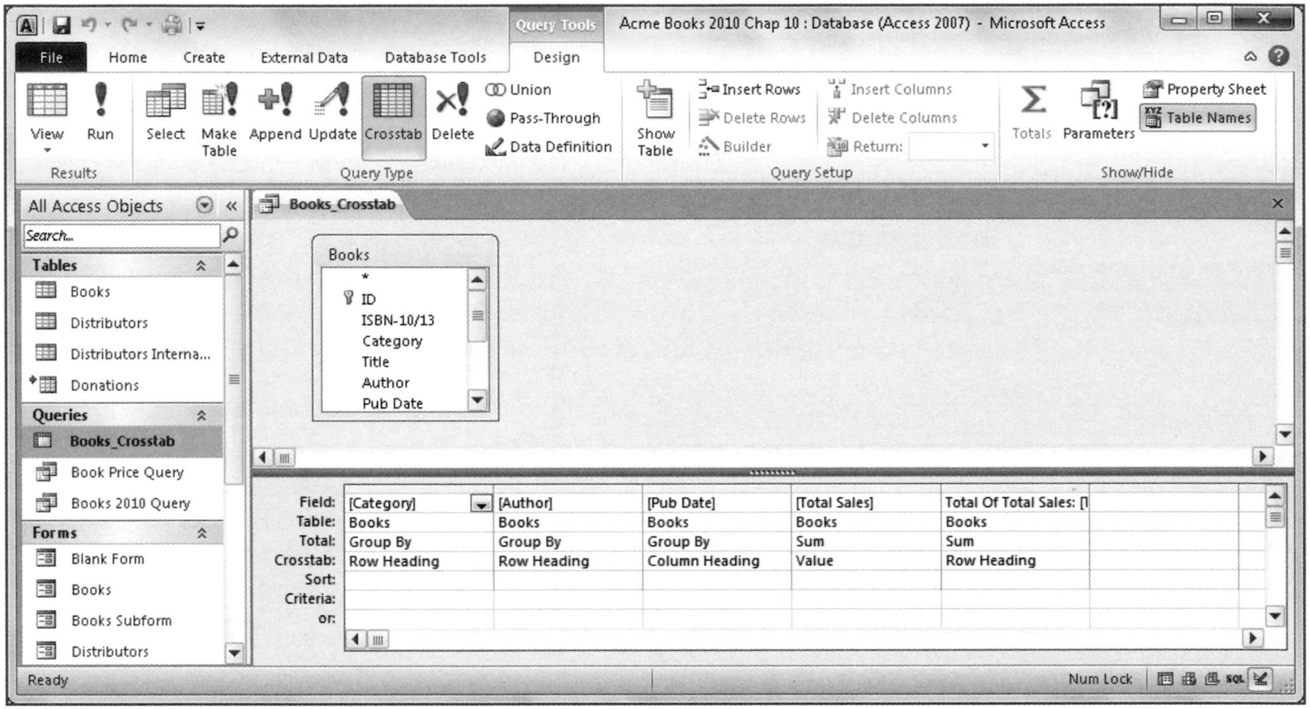

Figure 10-3: ***Design View of a Crosstab query looks and behaves similar to the queries described in earlier chapters.***

Create a PivotTable

PivotTables allow you to present your data in an easily understood format. You can dynamically "pivot" the layout of a PivotTable to analyze data in different ways. You can interchange row headings, column headings, and data fields until you achieve the desired layout. Each time you change the layout, the PivotTable immediately recalculates the data based on the new design. (See also the "Understanding Drop Zones in PivotTables" QuickFacts for more information on how a PivotTable works.)

1. Open the database that contains the table or query for which you want to create the PivotTable.
2. In the Navigation Pane, open the table or query you want to use as the basis for the PivotTable.

NOTE

Even though the table or query on which the data is based can be changed, you cannot update any of the field values using the PivotTable or PivotChart.

3. In the Home tab Views group, click the **View** down arrow, and click **PivotTable View**; or click the **PivotTable View** icon 📧 in the Views area on the status bar.

–Or–

To save the PivotTable as a form, in the Create tab Forms group, click **More Forms** and click **PivotTable**.

In either case, a new object is created and displays a PivotTable layout area with *drop zones* and a supporting Design tab (PivotTable Tools), as shown in Figure 10-4.

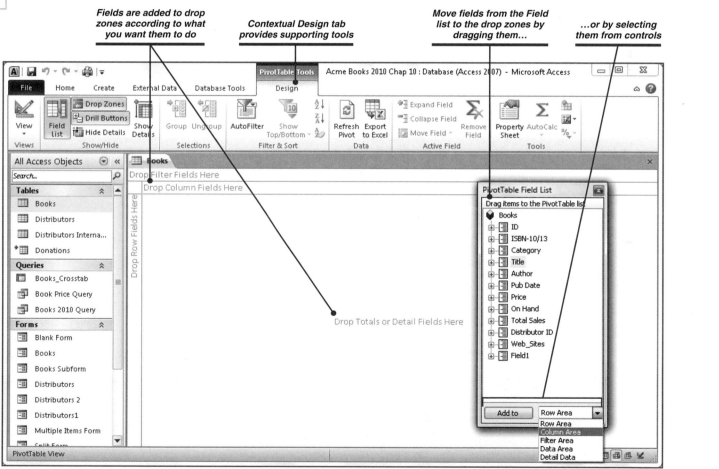

Fields are added to drop zones according to what you want them to do

Contextual Design tab provides supporting tools

Move fields from the Field list to the drop zones by dragging them…

…or by selecting them from controls

Figure 10-4: Fields are "dropped" within the PivotTable to act as row/column headers, filters, and data.

NOTE

More information on PivotCharts and on charting in general is offered in *Microsoft Office Excel 2010 QuickSteps* (McGraw-Hill/Professional, 2010).

TIP

You can tell if a field has filtered data by the color of the AutoFilter down arrow in the field header. A blue arrow indicates the field is filtered. To remove filters, click **AutoFilter** in the Filter & Sort group to turn them off.

Filtered field

| Category ▾ | Author ▾ |

4. Display the PivotTable Field list, if it is not shown (in the Design tab Show/Hide group, click **Field List**).

5. Drag a field from the PivotTable Field list to one of the drop zones (see the "Understanding Drop Zones in PivotTables" QuickFacts).

   –Or–

   Select the field in the Field list, click the down arrow in the lower-right corner of the Field list, click where you want the field added, and click **Add To** (see Figure 10-4).

6. To move a field from one drop zone to another, drag its header into the new drop zone.

   –Or–

   Select the new drop zone in the Field list, and click **Add To**.

7. Repeat steps 5 and 6 to create the layout that displays the information you want. You can drop more than one field in a drop zone and easily reverse any action you take. Figure 10-5 shows an example of how you can quickly view several key aspects of data (in this case, sales by year at each book price, by category and author).

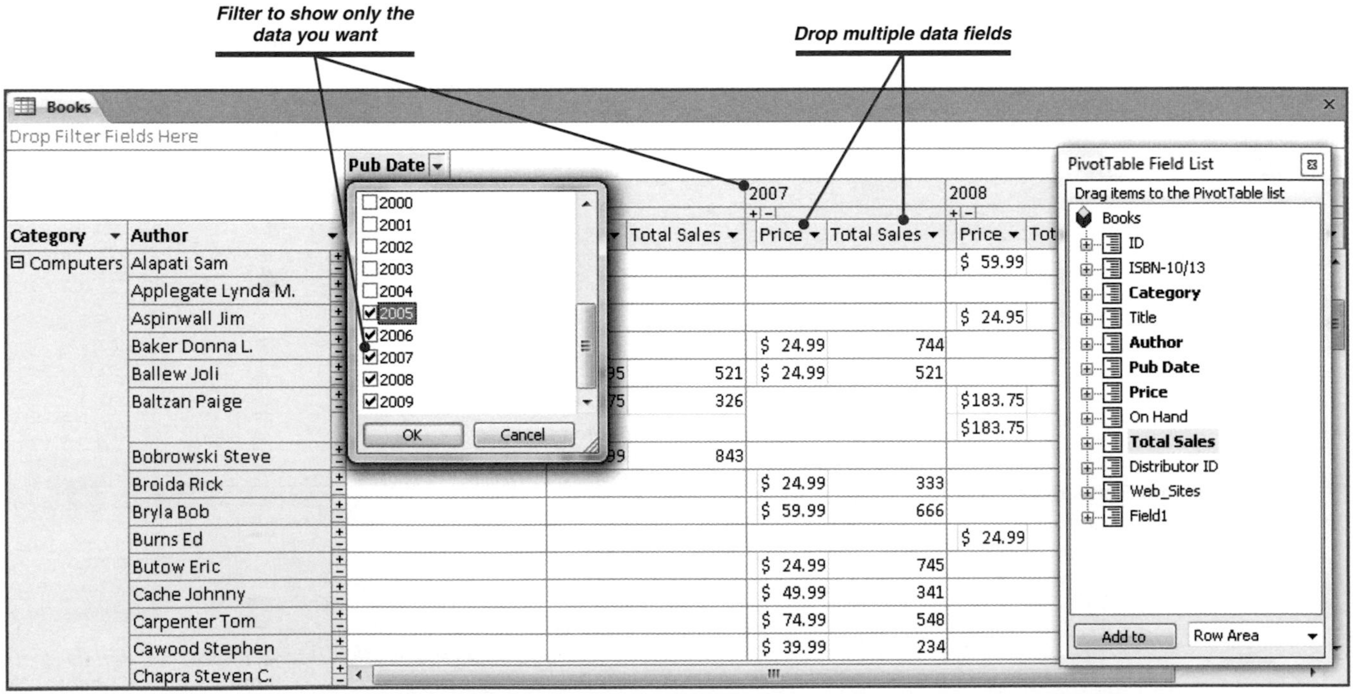

Filter to show only the data you want

Drop multiple data fields

Figure 10-5: You can quickly glean information from your data by pivoting fields and sorting and filtering the results.

To change and format individual chart elements, such as to format the axes, right-click the element and click **Properties** to open a dialog box with the options that are available to you. Once the Properties dialog box is open, you can click other chart elements to see their options displayed in the dialog box without having to reopen the dialog box for each element.

UNDERSTANDING DROP ZONES IN PIVOTTABLES

A PivotTable layout consists of several drop zones, where you place fields to give alternate views of your data. You "pivot" the data by moving fields from one zone to another.

- **Drop Row Fields Here** allows you to display each category of that item in its own row. Typically, these items are descriptive and identifying, not numerical—for example, Country, Salesperson, and Title.

- **Drop Column Fields Here** allows you to display each category of the item in its own column. Typically, these items are descriptive and identifying, not numerical—for example, Category or Product Name.

Continued . . .

Create a PivotChart

PivotCharts provide the same ability to dynamically change data as do PivotTables, but in a chart format. The creation method is just as simple as for PivotTables, though the drop zones and tools are tuned to construct a chart instead of a table.

1. Open the table or query in the database for which you want to create the PivotChart.

2. In the Home tab Views group, click the **View** down arrow, and click **PivotChart View**.

–Or–

Click **PivotChart View** in the Views area of the status bar.

In either case, the PivotChart layout area will be displayed, as shown in the top portion of Figure 10-6, with a Field list containing all the fields from the chosen table or query (if you saved the table or query after creating a PivotTable, the PivotChart will reflect those changes).

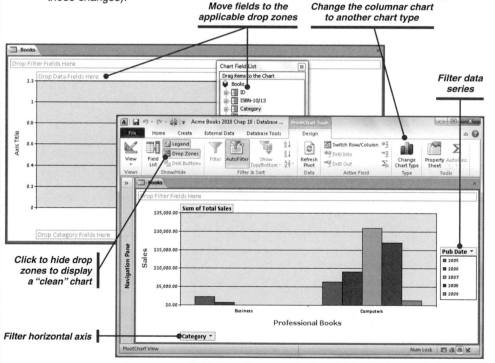

Figure 10-6: PivotCharts, similar to PivotTables, utilize a Design tab to provide associated tools and a methodology to move fields from the Chart Field list to drop zones on the chart-centric layout.

UNDERSTANDING DROP ZONES IN PIVOTTABLES (Continued)

- **Drop Totals Or Detail Fields Here** allows you to sum or otherwise perform calculations and display the results. Typically, these items are numerical and capable of being counted, summed, and calculated.

- **Drop Filter Fields Here** allows you to filter the view to a particular part of the data. For example, if your PivotTable displays information regarding your product line, you can place the field named Categories in the Drop Filter Fields Here area to display only the product line within selected categories.

QUICK**STEPS**

SORTING AND FILTERING A CROSSTAB QUERY

Setting up the Crosstab query (see Create a Crosstab Query with a Wizard earlier in the chapter) is only the beginning of what you can do to retrieve information from the query. You can apply filters and sort columns by using the AutoFilter down arrows in column headers and/or a column's context menu (see Chapter 5 for more information on retrieving information from a datasheet by sorting and filtering).

SORT CROSSTAB QUERY COLUMNS

1. Click the **AutoFilter** down arrow ▾ in the column header whose column contains the values by which you want to sort the query.

Continued . . .

---

3. Drag items from the Chart Field list to the applicable chart areas on the PivotChart layout to build the chart. Use the chart tools to filter data, add a legend, remove PivotChart elements, and add titles, as shown in the bottom half of Figure 10-6. Pivot the different values to analyze your data from a visual standpoint.

4. Right-click the **PivotTable** tab, and click **Close**. In the dialog box, click **Yes** to save the layout. To view the PivotChart again, select the table or query it's based on, and switch to PivotChart View.

Analyze Database Performance and Design

After you create a database and set up tables and other objects, you're probably wondering if there weren't things you could have done differently to be more efficient. One solution is to hire a database administrator to look over your design. A faster and cheaper method is to let Access take a crack at it. There are two tools you can use: one will take a look at any objects in your database that you select; the other is specific to tables.

USE THE PERFORMANCE ANALYZER

1. Open the database whose performance you want Access to check (close any open objects).

2. In the Database Tools tab Analyze group, click **Analyze Performance**.

> 🗐 Database Documenter
> 🗐 Analyze Performance
> 🗐 Analyze Table
> Analyze

3. In the Performance Analyzer, use the object tabs to select the objects you want Access to check.

SORTING AND FILTERING A CROSSTAB QUERY *(Continued)*

–Or–

Right-click a cell in the column that contains the values by which you want to sort the query.

2. Click the ascending or descending sort options at the top of the menu. The sort options are tuned to the data type of the column. For example, Number data type columns are sorted between smallest and largest. Text data type columns are sorted alphabetically between A and Z.

FILTER A CROSSTAB QUERY USING AUTOFILTER

Filters allow you to temporarily display only records that contain one or more values you select in a column.

1. Click the **AutoFilter** down arrow in the column header whose column contains the values by which you want to filter the query.

2. Click the check boxes for the values that are contained in the records you want to display, and click **OK**.

–Or–

Click *Data Type* **Filters** (where *Data Type* is the data type of the column), click prebuilt criteria, type the value(s) and any operators (such as AND or OR) you want, and click **OK**.

FILTER A CROSSTAB QUERY USING A CONTEXT MENU

● Right-click a value in the column you want to filter by, and click one of the criteria listed at the bottom of the menu.

–Or–

Continued . . .

–Or–

Click **Select All** to check all objects in the database.

In either case, click **OK** when finished. If Access detects any issues, it returns a report, similar to that shown in Figure 10-7, with varying degrees of recommendations.

4. If the recommendations won't affect underlying data, select the ones you want to change, and click **Optimize**. If the recommendations might cause potential loss of data, you will have to manually employ them. Click **Close** when finished.

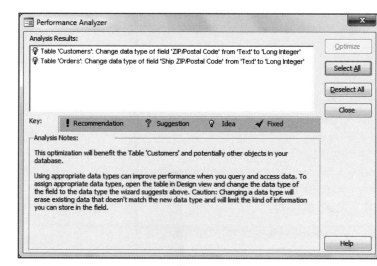

Figure 10-7: Access provides a "second opinion" on your design for the database objects you select.

CHECK TABLES FOR DUPLICATE DATA

The Table Analyzer Wizard looks at a table and determines whether your table can be divided into two or more related tables and your data parsed to avoid repeating data (and thereby making searches and other database actions more efficient). For example, if you have a table that stores ordering

SORTING AND FILTERING A CROSSTAB QUERY *(Continued)*

- Click *Data Type* **Filters** (where *Data Type* is the data type of the column), click prebuilt criteria, type the value(s) and any operators (such as AND or OR) you want, and click **OK**.

REMOVE AND REAPPLY FILTERS

Filtered Crosstab queries are identified by a filtering icon ▼ in the column header and on the navigation bar.

- To temporarily remove a filter, click the **Filtered** button ▼ Filtered on the navigation bar. The button is renamed "Unfiltered."

- To reapply the filter, click the **Unfiltered** button on the navigation bar (the button is renamed "Filtered")," or click **Toggle Filter** in the Home tab Sort & Filter group.

- To permanently remove a filter, click the **AutoFilter** down arrow of the filtered column, and click **Clear Filter From** *Field Name*.

CAUTION

Before you, or you let Access, make any changes to the design of your database, be sure to create a backup copy. See Chapter 9 for information on backing up a database.

and customer information, you wind up repeating information for each customer, such as name, address, and phone numbers, in repeat orders. The Table Analyzer Wizard might recommend that you create a Customer table and an Order table and then relate the two based on a generated unique primary key (and assist you along the way to perform the actions).

1. Open the database whose data you want Access to check.

2. In the Database Tools tab Analyze group, click **Analyze Table**. The first two pages in the wizard explain the problem created by duplicated data and provide examples (Figure 10-8 shows the first one). Click **Next** after reading through each page.

3. In the third page, click the table you want to Access to split into additional tables, and click **Next**.

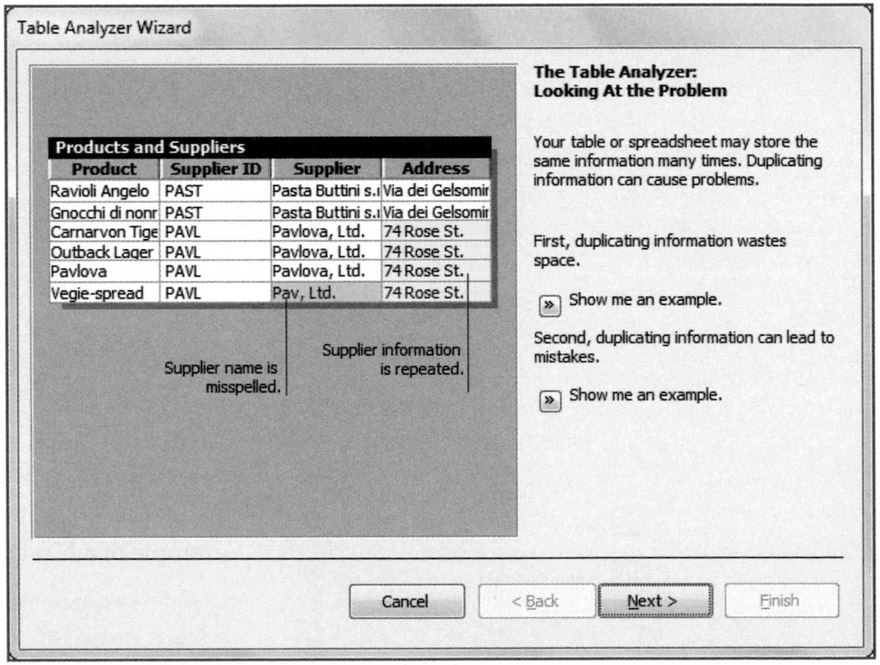

Figure 10-8: The Table Analyzer Wizard starts by informing you of the problem duplicate data creates and lets you know how it will try and fix your table.

Table Analyzer Wizard

Is the wizard grouping information correctly?
If not, you can drag and drop fields to form groups that make sense.

What name do you want for each table?
It's a good idea for the name to identify the kind of information the table contains.

Table1

ID
ISBN-10/13
Title
Author
Pub Date

Table2

Generated Uniqu

Cancel   < Back   Next >   Finish

Figure 10-9: Access proposes related tables and the relationships between them.

4. In the fourth, and subsequent, pages, let Access decide how to split the table (you will have final decision-making authority). You will have the opportunity to rename proposed tables (see Figure 10-9), select primary keys, correct any errors Access finds, and have Access create a query for you based on the new related tables.

Enhance Database Functionality

After a database is designed, structured, and populated with data, there are several things you can do to improve its usability. Three areas discussed in this section include adding a navigation form to the database to provide direction to users, splitting a database into back-end and front-end components, and interacting with SQL (Structured Query Language), the behind-the-scenes workhorse of many Access applications.

Create a Navigation Form

When you create a database, or *application*, intended to be used by other users, you can create a Navigation form (known as a *switchboard* in earlier editions of Access) that opens when the database is opened and offers a choice of activities and the ability to move around in your application. The user can click a button to open a form, preview a report, or perform nearly any action; and you can use standard form-building tools to create the look you want. Figure 10-10 shows an example of a Navigation form.

SET UP THE NAVIGATION FORM

1. Open the database in which you want a Navigation form.

2. In the Create tab Forms group, click **Navigation** and then select the layout for how the tabs will be placed on the Navigation form.

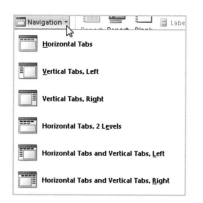

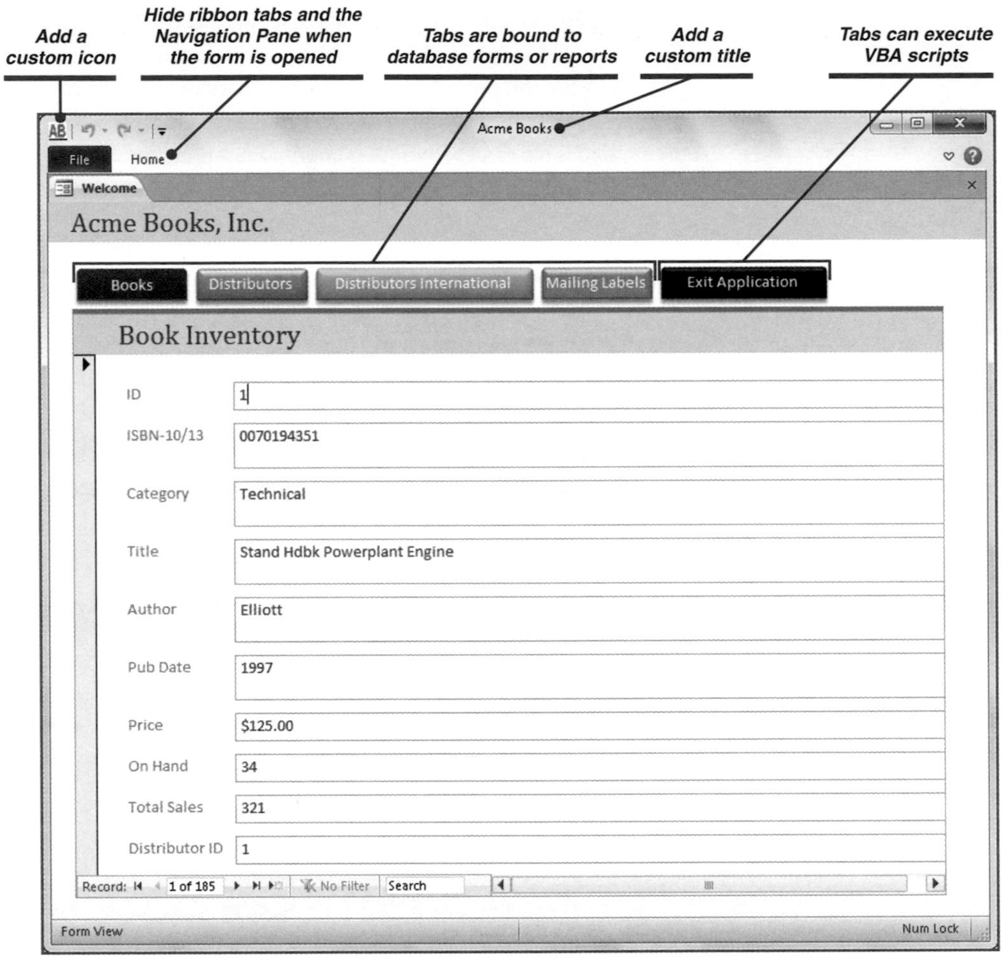

Add a custom icon

Hide ribbon tabs and the Navigation Pane when the form is opened

Tabs are bound to database forms or reports

Add a custom title

Tabs can execute VBA scripts

Figure 10-10: The Navigation form, with the help of a few property and settings changes, lets you easily create a custom greeting to users.

A new form, titled "Navigation Form," opens in Layout View. The form consists of one or more tabs with rows or columns where navigation buttons will be added (their location is dependent on your choice of layout) and an initially unbound subform that displays the target or contents of the chosen button (see Figure 10-10).

3. Click the **Add New** tab, and type the name of the form or report in your database that you want to be bound to the tab and that will display in the content area when clicked by a user (you can edit the tab name later). Press ENTER.

   –Or–

   Type a name for an action you want to be performed, for example, closing the form, and then switch to Design View. In the button's property sheet, click the **Event** tab, and click the **Builder** button [⋯] for the event (for example, when the user clicks the button) you want to initiate an action. In the Choose Builder dialog box, double-click **Code Builder** to open the Microsoft Visual Basic For Applications window, where you can add scripting programming to perform the action (see Figure 10-11).

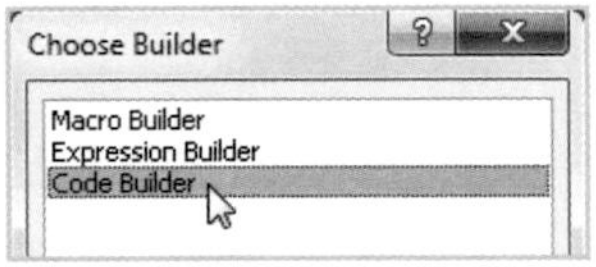

4. Continue to add buttons in sequence by using the **Add New** button that's displayed after the previous button is titled.

   –Or–

   Right-click in the row or column where you want a new button, and then click **Insert Navigation Button** at the top of the context menu.

TIP

Besides bounding forms and reports to navigation buttons by typing their names, you can choose them from the button's properties. Open the tab's property sheet (click **Property Sheet** in the Design tab (Form Layout Tools) Tools group), click the **Data** tab, click the **Navigation Target Name** property down arrow, and click the form or report you want associated with the button.

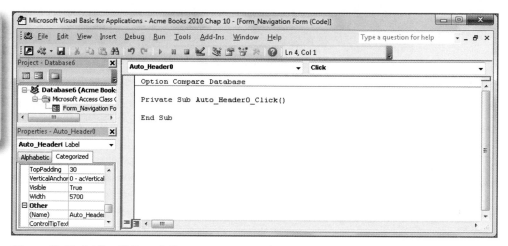

Figure 10-11: *Adding VBA scripting to your repertoire of skills will vastly increase the things you can accomplish in Access.*

NOTE

Scripting and working with macros and modules are beyond the scope of this book. See *Microsoft Access 2010 VBA Macro Programming* (McGraw-Hill/ Professional, 2010) for more information on scripting with VBA.

5. Double-click the default form title (Navigation Form), and type a name for the form title.

6. When finished, right-click the form tab, and click **Save**. Open the form in Form View to see how it will appear to users.

CHANGE THE APPEARANCE OF THE FORM BUTTONS

You can easily change the formatting and shape of the default buttons that appear in the Navigation form.

1. In Layout View or Design View, select one or more buttons whose characteristics you want to change.

2. In the respective Format tab (Form Layout/Design Tools), use the tools in the Font group to change the formatting of the button text.

3. In the Control Formatting group, use Shape Fill, Shape Outline, and Shape Effects tools to select combinations of fill, border color, and appearance, respectively.

–Or–

Use the Quick Styles and Change Shape tools to select from menus of options to apply button color, shading, and effects, as well as to change the actual shape of the button.

4. Press **CTRL+S** when finished to save your changes.

TIP

To add a custom name and look to your database other than the file name that appears in the title bar of Access, click the **File** tab, click **Options**, and click the **Current Database** option. Under Application Options, type a name in the Application Title text box, and browse for an icon or bitmap to be used in place of the Access icon in the upper-left corner of the database window. Click **OK** and reopen the database to see the changes. (See Figure 10-10 for examples.)

TIP

Prior to splitting a database, be sure to create a backup copy and, depending on the size of the database, you might want to inform users that the database may not be available for some time. Also, all users need to have a version of Access that is compatible with the file format being used. For example, if using the default Access 2010 .accdb format, users need to be using Access 2007 or Access 2010 (and be using Access 2010 to utilize its specific features).

DISPLAY THE NAVIGATION FORM

You will want your Navigation form to display when the database/application is first opened by a user.

1. Click the **File** tab, click **Options**, and click the **Current Database** option.

2. Under Application Options, click the **Display Form** down arrow, and select your Navigation form.

3. You may want to limit navigation to those choices in your Navigation form. Under Navigation, clear the **Navigation Pane** check box. The Navigation Pane will not appear in the database window so that it doesn't detract users from your Navigation form. Also, you can limit the appearance of the ribbon by minimizing it so it opens hidden and hiding all ribbon tabs except a limited File tab and the Home tab. Under Ribbon And Toolbar Options, clear the **Allow Full Menus** check box. (These actions can be easily reversed unless you choose other security measures to prevent changes.)

4. Click **OK**. The next time your database is opened, it reflects your changes.

Split a Database

When working with larger databases in a shared environment, database performance can be adversely affected because each user is not only transferring data, but all the objects of databases such as forms and reports also have to be transmitted to each user. In addition, the editing of data is slowed when several people are doing that task simultaneously. To counter these problems and to help prevent file corruption problems, a database can be divided into two components: a back end of data stored in tables and a front end of other Access objects, such as reports, forms, and queries. In this manner, only data is transferred from one data location to users, cutting down on the network traffic and isolating many problems to individual users so that others can continue working.

1. Open the database that you want to split.

2. In the Database Tools tab Move Data group, click **Access Database**. The Database Splitter dialog box appears, informing you of several of the benefits and considerations of splitting a database, as shown in Figure 10-12.

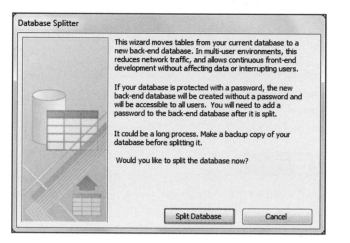

Figure 10-12: Splitting a database only requires one click.

3. When ready, click **Split Database**. In the Create Back-end Database dialog box, name and browse to where you want to store the data portion of the split database (Access adds a "_be" to the file name to signify "backend"). Click **Split**. When finished, a message box informs you the action was successful.

4. Distribute copies of the original database file that was split (the front end) to any users. (Users will need to have network access to the location where you stored the "_be" file.)

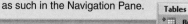
Use SQL Tables in Access

There are two main ways you can use Access as a front end to data stored in a SQL database. As described in other chapters in this book, you can link to a SQL table whereby you are working on a copy of the data that is connected to the SQL table, or you can import a table from a SQL database into an Access table (without a connection allowing real-time changes). In either case, the process starts using the ODBC Database tool in the External Data tab Import & Link group. After deciding whether to link or import a table, you initially need to create a DSN (Data Source Name) file, which sets the parameters for a connection between Access and SQL Server. To create a DSN that allows linking or importing SQL tables:

1. After making your linking or importing selection in the Get External Data – ODBC Database dialog box and clicking **OK**, in the Select Data Source dialog box, click **New**.
2. In the Create New Data Source dialog box, select **SQL Server** and click **Next**. In the following dialog box, name and browse to a location for the DSN file, click **Next**, and then click **Finish**. The Create A New Data Source To SQL Server Wizard starts, as shown in Figure 10-13.
3. In the subsequent wizard dialog boxes:
   - Provide a description for the data, and select the SQL Server on your network that you want.
   - Select a login ID authentication method, and create a logon ID and password, as necessary.

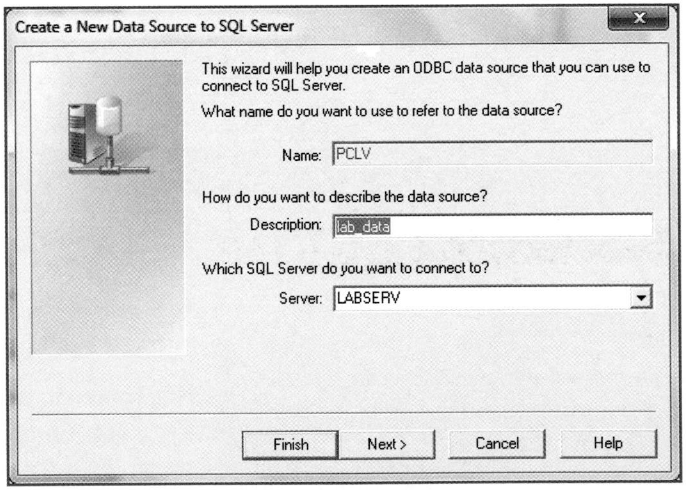

***Figure 10-13:* A wizard walks you through the creation of the DSN.**

NOTE

ODBC, or Open Database Connectivity, defines a connection that contains database parameters and accesses drivers to allow computers to communicate.

TIP

Connecting to a SQL database, especially in a corporate environment, typically requires the interaction of an IT professional to provide the needed logon data, DSN file location, and possibly other security access. Contact your IT department before you begin in order to make the process go much smoother.

QUICKFACTS

UNDERSTANDING SQL IN ACCESS

SQL, or Structured Query Language, is a powerful tool designed to interact with data. SQL, in its native form, is used in standalone products such as Microsoft SQL Server, in the most robust of data-intensive applications. To use SQL in this environment requires that you essentially learn a programming language to fully exercise its capabilities—not for everyone. Access, on the other hand, offers a bit of the best-of-all-worlds as it uses SQL behind the scenes, for example, whenever a query is run to filter or data is displayed in a form; it allows you to use SQL commands and statements, but shields you from them if you choose not to use them; and it acts as a user-friendly portal to access the data in, or move data to, SQL databases. While a full discussion of SQL is beyond the scope of this book, there are a few ways you can work with data located in SQL databases that are discussed in this section.

SQL command and syntax

Property Sheet
Selection type: Report

Report ▼

| Format | Data | Event | Other | All |

Record Source SELECT [Books].[Author], [Books]

● Select the database you want to connect to, create log files, and then review and test the data setup. Click **OK**, and then if all goes well, you'll be notified of the success. Click **OK**.

4. You are returned to the Select Data Source dialog box (see step 1), with your new DSN selected. Click **OK** and then log on to the SQL Server.

5. Select the table(s) you want, and select the primary key, as required. Depending on your earlier selections, the data from the SQL tables are now available in your Navigation Pane as linked tables or in a standard Access table as imported data.

Imported SQL table   *Linked SQL table*

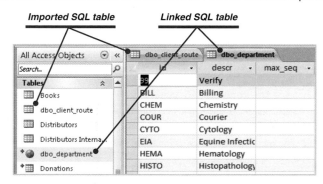

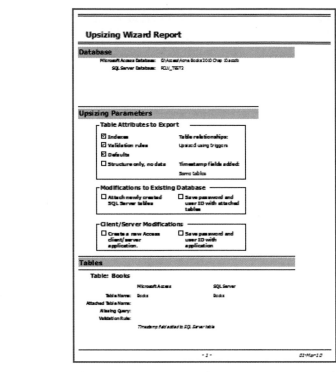

Figure 10-14: *Access provides a printable record of the upsizing results.*

Move Access Data to a SQL Database

If you have data in Access that you want to move into a SQL Server database, you can do so by adding it to an existing SQL database, or creating and populating a new database (the following steps assume an existing database is available and is used).

1. Open the database in Access whose data you want to move to a SQL Server database.

2. In the Database Tools tab Move Data group, click **SQL Server**. The Upsizing Wizard starts, where you can select to move to an existing or new database. Click **Use Existing Database**, and click **Next**.

3. In the Select Data Source dialog box, browse to the DSN for the SQL Server database you want, click **OK**, and then log on to the SQL Server.

4. Select the tables in your Access database that you want to export to the SQL Server, and click **Next**.

5. Select the table attributes you want to include in the upsizing, such as indexes and validation rules, and click **Next**.

6. Select whether to modify the existing application/database by creating an .adp application (see Note), linking the tables, or making no changes. Click **Next** and then click **Finish**. Access returns an Upsizing Report (see Figure 10-14) in Print Preview to inform you of the specifics of the upsizing. Figure 10-15 shows the structure of an Access table moved into an existing SQL Server database within the Microsoft SQL Server Management Studio (a feature of Microsoft SQL Server).

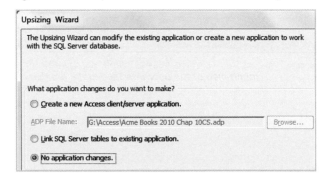

NOTE

An Access Data Project (ADP) is an Access database file format that contains database objects such as forms and reports, but data and other database parameters are stored on the server. This configuration provides front-end efficiencies over using conventional linked tables.

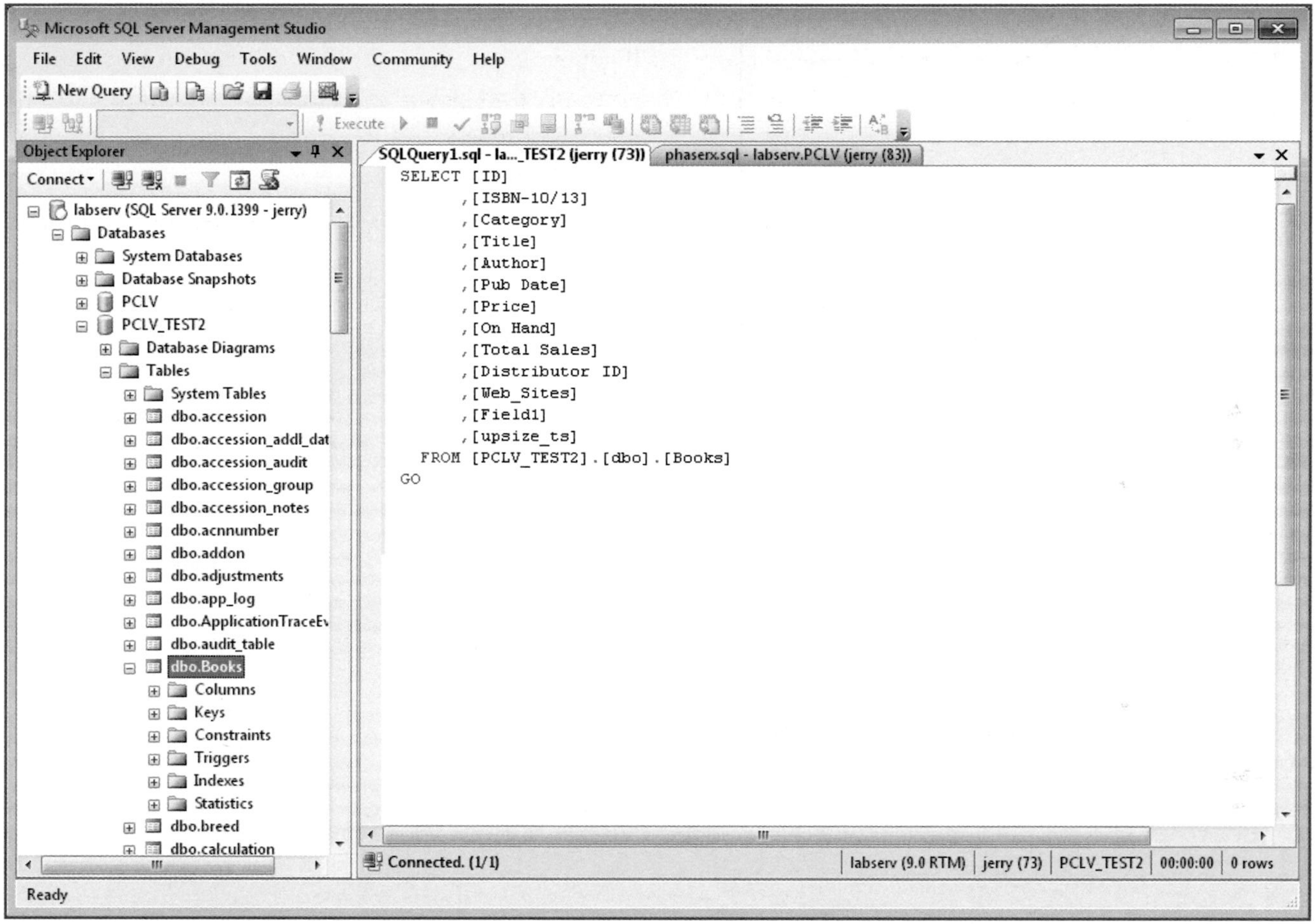

Figure 10-15: *An Access database maintains the same field structure when moved into a SQL Server database, though not much else of the user interface looks familiar.*

C

input mask character, 72
Calculate Percent Of Total For Sums option, 164
calculated controls, 144, 148–149
Calculated data type, 43
calculations
  report fields, 174–175
  table fields, 94
Caption Field property, 75
Cascade option, 26
Cascade Delete Related Records option, 57
Cascade Update Related Fields option, 57
Center tool, 169
certificate authorities, 204
certificates, 204–206
Change Font Size tool, 28
changing
  data types, 65–67
  primary keys, 51
  table properties, 63–65
characters
  copying and moving, 90
  input mask, 70–72
  uppercase, 68–69
Chart Wizard, 186–188
charts
  Chart Wizard, 186–188
  description, 145
  Excel features, 185–186
  inserting, 184–185
  PivotCharts, 229–230
Check box controls, 145
Choose Builder dialog box, 234
Choose Theme Or Themed Document
  dialog box, 194
clearing filters, 120
Clipboard, 90–91
closing
  Access, 23
  databases, 29, 40

  objects, 23
  queries, 127
  tables, 44–45
collapsing
  groups, 14
  Navigation Pane, 13–14
Collect Data Through E-mail Messages
  Wizard, 101–104
Collect Without Showing Office Clipboard
  option, 91
color
  conditional formatting, 184
  forms, 142
  gridlines, 108
  labels, 177–178
  reports, 169
  tables, 107
  text, 107–108
  themes, 191–192
Colors dialog box, 192
Column Width dialog box, 105
columns, 32–33
  deleting, 91–92
  vs. fields, 86
  hiding and unhiding, 106–107
  locking and unlocking, 108
  moving, 106
  PivotTables, 229
  positioning, 106
  printing, 198
  reports, 169–170
  selecting, 93
  sorting, 110
  width, 105
Combo Box Wizard, 147
combo boxes
  adding, 146–148
  description, 145
Command Button Wizard, 150–152
command buttons, 150–152

commands, ribbon, 20
Compact And Repair Database utility, 218–221
Compare To Other Records option, 183
compatibility of files, 15–16
complex sorts, 111
conditional formatting, 168, 181–184
Conditional Formatting Rules Manager
  dialog box, 181–184
Connection options, 27
Control Wizards tool, 142
controls, 144
  adding, 139–140
  aligning and spacing, 157
  arranging, 156
  bound, 146–150
  common, 145
  copying, 153
  deleting, 153
  layouts, 157
  moving and resizing, 155–156
  reports, 167
  selecting, 153–155
  unbound, 150–152
Conversion Errors table, 16
converting databases, 15–17
copies, printing, 199
copying
  characters, 90
  controls, 153
  data, 88
  fields, 91
  records, 91
  tables, 62–63
Create Back-end Database dialog box, 237
Create Digital Certificate dialog box, 204
Create Microsoft Office Access Signed Package
  dialog box, 205
Create New Data Source dialog box, 238
Create New Template From This Database
  dialog box, 215

DOWN ARROW key, 88–89
drop zones
 PivotCharts, 229
 PivotTables, 227–230
DSN (Data Source Name) file, 238
duplicate data, 231–233
duplicating tables, 62–63

E

e-mail, collecting data from, 101–104
Edit (Insert) Hyperlink dialog box, 214
Edit Relationships dialog box, 56
editing
 keyboard for, 88–89
 lookup lists, 82
effects, 108
embedded images, 180
empty cells, filtering by, 115
Enable Content option, 8
Enable Data Integrity option, 81
encryption, 207–208
END key, 88–89
ending Access sessions, 29
Enforce Referential Integrity option, 56–57
Enhanced Metafile (.emf) images, 180
ENTER key, 88
Enter Table Properties dialog box, 65
Enter Validation Message window, 74
entering data, 87
equal signs (=) in criteria, 118
equal to operator, 118
errors in reports, 176
ESC key, 89
Excel
 charts, 184–185
 spreadsheets, 99
exclamation points (!)
 criteria, 119

format symbol, 69
 input mask character, 70, 72
exclusion, filtering by, 116
existing fields for primary keys, 50
existing tables, entering data in, 87
exiting Access, 29
expanding
 groups, 14
 Navigation Pane, 13–14
Export All Customizations option, 20
Export dialog box, 211
exporting data, 210–211
Expression Builder, 72, 119, 126, 128–130, 172
expressions
 criteria, 119
 groups, 172
 queries, 126, 128–130
 validation rules, 72–73
Extend mode, 87
Extract Database To dialog box, 206

F

Favorites option, 8
Field List pane, 138
Field lists, 140–141
fields, 32–33, 59–60
 adding, 139–140
 calculations in, 94, 174–175
 caption, 75
 charts, 186
 vs. columns, 86
 copying and moving, 91
 data types, 42–43, 65–67
 Datasheet View, 41–44
 default values, 71
 deleting, 170–171
 displaying, 67–69
 filtering by, 115

hyperlink, 214
indexing, 75–77
input masks, 70–72, 190
inserting, 42–44
lookup, 78–83, 208–209
multivalued, 82
number formatting, 169
PivotCharts, 229–230
PivotTables, 226–230
primary keys, 49–51
renaming, 44
reports, 162–163, 166–171
selecting, 92–93, 169–170
size, 105, 169
smart tags, 77–78
tables, 47–48
text formatting, 168–169
validating, 72–74
zero-length strings, 74–75
File menu, 3–4
File New Database dialog box, 34, 39
File view, 5–7
files
 compatibility, 15–16
 default formats, 17
 printing to, 199
Filter By Group option, 14
filters
 advanced, 119–122
 clearing, 120
 Crosstab queries, 231–232
 by form, 116–117
 help searches, 28
 inputs, 115–116
 object display, 14
 operators, 118
 PivotTables, 230
 reapplying, 120
 records, 112

removing, 119
report fields, 170
by selecting, 113–115
wildcards, 119
Financial Symbol smart tag, 77
Find And Replace dialog box, 92–94, 119
finding
databases, 17
text, 92–93
first record, moving to, 88
folders
databases, 38
for security, 202–204
Font tool, 169
Font Color tool, 169
Font dialog box, 173
Font Size tool, 169
fonts, 106–107
conditional formatting, 184
forms, 142
labels, 177–178
reports, 168–169, 173
themes, 193
titles, 175
footers in reports, 166, 175–176
foreign keys, 49
Form tool, 132
Form view, 132
Form Wizard, 136–138
Format Painter tool, 169
formatting
conditional, 181–184
fields, 67–69
guidelines, 190
memo fields, 108
numbers, 169
text, 168–169, 194–195
forms, 32–33, 131–132
Blank Form tool, 138–139
buttons, 235

controls. *See* controls
date and time on, 143–144
description, 13
design changes, 140–142
Design View, 139–142
filtering data by, 116–117
Form tool, 132
Form Wizard, 136–138
linking to subforms, 149–150
multiple records, 135–136
multiple-table, 137
navigating, 153–154, 233–236
presentation. *See* presentation
sections, 144–145
securing, 209
selecting, 144–145
sorting records for, 112
split, 132–135, 197
titles, 142–143
forward-compatible files, 15
freezing columns, 108

gridlines, 108
Group By setting, 126
Group Footer section, 166
Group Header section, 166
Group, Sort, And Total pane, 171–174
Grouping Intervals dialog box, 164
groups
controls, 154
creating, 15, 19–20
deleting, 176
headers and footers, 175–176
Navigation Pane, 14
rearranging, 18–19
reports, 163–164, 170–173
ribbon, 5
in security, 210–211
totals, 174–175

H

handles for controls, 154
headers in reports, 166, 175–176
heading fonts, 193
height of rows, 108
help, 27–28
Hide Key Column option, 80
Hide Table of Contents option, 28
hiding
columns, 106–107
objects, 208–209
tools, 22
highlighting values, 113
HOME key, 88–89
HTML (HyperText Markup Language), 194
Hyperlink controls, 145
Hyperlink data type, 43, 67
hyperlinks, 209, 214, 217–218
HyperText Markup Language (HTML), 194